Identities on the Move

Studies on Culture and Society

Identities on the Move

*Transnational Processes in
North America and the Caribbean Basin*

Edited by
Liliana R. Goldin

Studies on Culture and Society
Volume 7

Institute for Mesoamerican Studies
Unversity at Albany
Albany, New York

Distributed by
University of Texas Press

For submission of manuscripts address the publisher:
Institute for Mesoamerican Studies
University at Albany
State University of New York
Albany, New York 12222

For copies address the distributor:
University of Texas Press
Post Office Box 7819
Austin, Texas 78713-7819

Library of Congress Cataloging-in-Publication Data

Identities on the move : transnational processes in North America and the Caribbean Basin / edited by Liliana R. Goldin.
    p. cm. -- (Studies on culture and society v. 7)
Based on a conference held at the University at Albany, State University of New York, 1996.
Includes bibliographical references and index.
ISBN 0-942041-18-6 (paperback)
    1. Immigrants--Psychology. 2. Identity (Psychology)--Social aspects--North America. 3. Identity (Psychology)--Social aspects--Caribbean Area. 4. Emigration and immigration--Psychological aspects--North American. 5. Emigration and immigration--Psychological aspects--Caribbean Area. I. Goldin, Liliana R. II. Series.

JV6109 .I34 1999
305.868'073--dc21   99-049467

Contents

Foreword

Since 1970, some one hundred million people around the world have come to reside permanently or temporarily in countries in which they were not born. In the United States, the number of such individuals is greater than at any time since 1920. Greater Los Angeles is second only to Mexico City in the numbers of urban inhabitants who claim a Mexican identity. The United States ranks approximately sixth in the world among Spanish-speaking nations. As of 1998, one in ten U.S. citizens is Latino. Transnational processes and identities will be among the major social, political, and economic phenomena of the twenty-first century.

Originating with a conference sponsored by the University at Albany in 1994, this superb collection of essays explores many dimensions of "identities on the move" in North America and the Caribbean Basin, including Mexico and Central America. The collection is truly interdisciplinary, with contributions from nationally and internationally known anthropologists, sociologists, literary critics, writers, psychologists, and economists—at least half of whom are, themselves, bearers of transnational identities. Methodologies and analytic styles range from ethnographic descriptions to autobiography, from statistical and documentary analysis to literary interpretation, from the testimony of U.S. Latino poetry to the extraordinary content of Mexican popular border art.

Identities on the Move is divided into two major sections. The first presents theoretical and conceptual foundations for approaching these new social and political spaces, which involve, often simultaneously, forces of both homogenization and differentiation. The second offers specific case studies of displacement, incorporation, and re-formulation of self and community in various transnational settings. The epilogue is a moving autobiographical portrait of a Mexican Jew who is also a United States Latino.

The most important contribution of this book lies in the delineation of new directions for social and literary analysis as the impact of the economic globalization and transnational processes is felt and incorporated into the national ideas of both sending and receiving nations. These essays document brilliantly that, just as the nation state and the concept of culture seem to be weakening in our time, so, too, new expressions of essentialism and xenophobia seem to lie on the horizon. This book provides a glimpse of what the next century will look like.

GARY H. GOSSEN
Distinguished Professor of Anthropology and Latin American Studies
University at Albany

Acknowledgments

This volume is based on a conference entitled Transnational Migration and the Construction of Identities in the Americas, which was held at the University at Albany, State University of New York in March of 1996. The conference was sponsored by the departments of Latin American and Caribbean Studies and Anthropology, the Center for Latin America, Latinos, and the Caribbean (CELAC), the Institute for Mesoamerican Studies (IMS), and a grant from the Office for Research, University at Albany, State University of New York. Edna Acosta-Belén and Judith Place assisted me in the planning and organization of the conference. Several graduate students in the department of Latin American and Caribbean Studies assisted with their time before and during the conference. I thank them all. I also thank Robert Carmack and John Watanabe for their valuable comments on the volume. I have included many of their insights in Chapter 1. I also included in that chapter the perspectives that emerged from the conference discussions, particularly the comments of discussants Gary Gossen and Edna Acosta-Belén. I thank the authors for the prompt and careful revisions of their contributions and Lisa Montiel for the excellent copy-editing of the volume. I also would like to thank Miguel Aguilera for his time and expertise as he discussed with me ideas for the cover.

1

Transnational Identities

The Search for Analytic Tools

Liliana R. Goldin

During the past ten years, the concept of transnationalism has received increasing attention from social scientists, both as a phenomenon and as a process. No one disputes the fact that the past decade has been characterized by tremendous technological changes on a global scale. It is also evident that these changes have altered the very nature of global economies, global politics, and communication and contact between disparate cultures. It is within such a context that the study and analysis of transnational processes are evolving. Transnational processes arise, in part, from the globalization of the world economy, the internationalization of production, and the consequent construction of intricate webs of new social relations. As capital moves around the world in search of "adequate" sources of labor, so does labor move around the world in search of better working conditions and new sources of potentially more profitable endeavors. In conjunction with these developments, nations create integrative networks which reinforce existing trends. For example, trade agreements throughout the Americas (such as NAFTA, MERCOSUR and the Caribbean Basin Initiative) come to support images of transnational spaces.[1] All of these developments are characterized by complex political, social, and psychological features, as individuals reevaluate their positions from within and consider their place in the new and extended social networks. In the definition of identities, individuals experience displacement, relocation, and redefinition of self and community as they confront the necessity of classifying the world around them. In the past, analyses of such phenomena focused on immigrants as they moved from one geographical location to another. However, the technological changes and globalization of the world economy are breaking down such a geographical emphasis. Processes of displacement, exile, and settlement occur at psychological, cultural and social levels and these can operate at "home" as well as "abroad." It is around these complex processes that this book is organized.

Following Szanton Blanc et al. (1995), I have adopted the notion of transnational *processes* for the title of this book to remind us of the fluidity and unfinished nature of identities in the making in a cross-national context. Scholars have urged us to move beyond definitions of transnationalism toward a better understanding of the impact of the phenomenon on people's lives (Basch et al. 1994). This was the objective of a conference which was held at the University at Albany, State University of New York in March of 1996. Scholars were invited to focus on the processes of identity formation in transnational contexts, to provide ethnographic, theoretical, and personal insights into these processes, and to contribute to the understanding of these complex issues. When planning the conference, I knew I was not focusing on entirely new developments. For generations, social identities changed as people explored economic opportunities and political openings. These have been studied primarily in the context of migration and adaptation to new environments. But there are clearly new perspectives on these issues, especially as we move away from simple descriptions of "push and pull" factors and how these affect two geographic regions. The effort in this book, which evolved from the conference at the University at Albany, is to concentrate on the processes of identity formation and the many cultural, social, political, and economic factors that participate in those processes. These new perspectives have developed out of current trends in social theory that offer critiques of modernist binary perspectives following unilineal forms of reasoning and understanding. In the past, emphasis has been on simple distinctions between the here and there, the center and the periphery, black and white, or tracking developmental transitions from one state to another. Such analyses are being supplemented by a whole set of new, unbounded concepts (Basch et al. 1994) that help us make sense of both traditional and emerging transnational processes. These concepts include multiplicity (Kearney 1996), border crossing (Rosaldo 1989), disjunction and ethnoscapes (Appadurai 1991), cultural hybridization (García Canclini 1990), porousness (Burns, this volume), webs (Lins Ribeiro 1997), and transnational communities (Glick Schiller 1992; Rouse 1991). The communities of analysis have been described as "imagined" (Anderson 1983, Chavez 1994, Duany 1996), binational (Baca and Bryan 1980), transnational families (Chavez 1992), and in terms of circular migration (Santiago-Rivera and Santiago, chap. 12). It is in these porous, web-like ethnoscapes characterized by "transition," "disjunction," and "reorganization" that new selves are being constructed. In my opinion, it is time to move beyond the terms and methodological tools that have served us so well in the past so as to forge the production of new ethnographies and ethnologies of the transnational landscape. This is a difficult task because it forces us to abandon some of the linearity with which our texts have been written and demands the pursuit of endeavors that may be beyond our limited training. As social scientists are becoming more specialized, our subjects (and ourselves) are becoming more interconnected, linked to peoples, places, and structures of power we often cannot easily place or even recognize. The field language we spent years trying to master and the methods and techniques we carefully developed may not be sufficient to describe and make sense out of the new transnational context. A focus on transnational processes may unbind us as social scientists, as we attempt to understand them. The present volume reflects these challenges. One of the ways that this is most evident is the multi-disciplinary character of the volume. Anthropologists, sociologists, literary critics, psychologists, and economists have contributed chapters that examine transnational processes using the tools of their disciplines. As they address some of the same issues from various approaches, the volume offers multi-methodological perspectives including ethnographic analysis in combination with observations, statistical analysis, and reflections on the literary production of the actors in a transnational context. The multiple perspectives highlight the underlying complexities and the need to contemplate the use of multiple methods and perspectives to understand intricate issues.

As with transnational domains, the papers in this volume do not fit neatly within any one section, but rather cut across domains. Some of the papers rely more heavily on ethnographic methods and others are based on documentary and statistical sources. Some are more theoretical in nature. They all rely on solid research. The diverse background and writing styles of the authors reflect the nature of the topic at hand. The placement of articles in the book is based on a distinction between those papers that tend to provide theoretical frameworks for understanding transnational processes, included in section I, and those that through ethnographic and statistical methods provide a close up of those processes: What do "processes of identity formation" look like? What are the actual dynamics that provide a stage for what we conceptualize as transnational identities? Language use, alternative discourse of definitions of self, perspectives on communities of belonging, the physical layout of borderland homes, or the actual survival strategies of people on the move, as they work out the mechanics of fitting in (being or acting legal), are some of the issues presented in section II.

THE NATURE OF TRANSNATIONAL PROCESSES

Transnational processes are characterized by cultural and social fields in which actors "take actions, make decisions and develop subjectivities and identities embedded in networks of relationships that connect them simultaneously to two or more nation-states" (Basch et al. 1994:7). The Maya worker in the Korean factory in Guatemala making blouses to be sold in Macy's (Goldin, chap. 8) has much in common with the Guatemalan Ladino[2] who works "as a Mexican" in a mariachi band in Florida (Burns, chap. 7). But beyond the irony suggested by such unexpected images characterizing the global economy, there are issues of power, domination, and resistance as well (Szanton Blanc et al. 1995). There are questions about the role of nation-states in the construction of transnational identities and the pervasive role of ethnic and racial categories of analysis in the determination of personal and community-based sociological spaces and identification. There are issues concerning how the renegotiation of identities in transnational spaces affects individuals and groups simultaneously in several locations (Montejo, chap. 10).

As an Argentinean living in the United States, and despite having been told time and again "you don't look like a Latina" (what do Latinos look like?), I am constantly confronted with the question "where are you from" as soon as I utter a word. I ultimately became a United States citizen because after almost twenty years in the United States, I wanted the right to say "we" instead of "you." When, a few years ago, I returned to Argentina with a United States passport, I felt at fault. Would I be "caught" by Argentinean customs agents? Would they recognize me as one of them with foreign papers? Would I have to discuss my newly acquired citizenship among my friends and family? Would they understand? I still recall vividly the moment when the customs agent in Buenos Aires said accusingly while pointing at the passport page where it shows place of birth, "You cannot use this passport, you are Argentinean!" Although legal requirements have recently changed, I still feel at fault. Like Ilan Stavans (chap. 13), who struggled since childhood with issues of race, ethnicity and nation—a red-haired Jewish boy growing up in Mexico, a Chicano in the United States—all of us who are actors in transnational landscapes, are at times proud, at others weary and disturbed by the labels we have to live with, our dual sense of citizenship, and our ambivalent attachments (cf. Duany 1996; Flores, chap. 6; Oboler, chap. 3).

It is my belief that transnational identities are best studied from a process perspective that emphasizes the fluid nature of ideologies, events, people, and locations. The processes that are of central interest to the construction of transnational identities are designated within the broad concepts of homogenization and differentiation, or the mechanisms of becoming someone similar to the rest (a version of internal or external assimilation) or one of distinction, both generated by the actors and by the larger society. Within those encompassing processes of homogenization and differentiation there are more subtle on-going aspects of individual and group identity construction that have to do with the elaboration of displacement, exile and (re) settlement and the use, acceptance or manipulation of the labels we live by. Processes of homogenization and differentiation are important because they emerge in the context of diverse contacts, including but not exclusively ethnic, national, racial, and/or cultural contacts. Through these processes, groups and individuals draw the lines of commonality and differences. Within these processes, institutions and the state contribute by setting guidelines and "giving order" to locate individuals and groups within pre-established categories. Some of the key scenarios within which individuals and groups become homogenized or differentiated are the nation-state, the establishment of citizenship status, the relations of domination and subordination between states as in the case of colonialism, and the shaping of identities along racial and ethnic lines.

Section I, *Theory on the Move: Processes of Homogenization and Differentiation* includes papers that articulate these issues and provide conceptual guidelines to frame the issues of identity formation. They provide an overarching theoretical perspective. In section II, entitled *Cases of Identity Formation*, I include papers that provide ethnographic and literary examples of how identities are constructed in local and transnational contexts. Processes of displacement, exile and settlement are critical because they reflect the traumatic context in which individuals and communities question their allegiances, produce a framework for understanding different forms of exile and separation, construct and confirm their new social and economic networks, and define the borders of their new existence as they also formulate their political and social claims. All of these processes are intertwined and, in some sense, it is not possible to study one in isolation from the other. They often happen not only in connection with one another but also simultaneously, as the transnational subject examines her/his position in the new space, forms alliances with others somehow like him or her, and at once experiences the feelings of loss, anguish and displacement.

In section I, Nina Glick Schiller views the process of becoming an American as simultaneously one of racialization and transnationalism. In order to find an identity as an American in the new world, European immigrants, according to Glick Schiller, focused on emphasizing their ties to their native land. By identifying with nation states in Europe, migrants identified themselves with a "civilized," white project, in opposition to people of color whose histories were not recognized by hegemonic forces. Identity with an ancestral land, Glick Schiller notes, was seen as a tool to lend allegiance to an American citizenry. Conceptions of nation and native lands informed the transnationalized nation-state through the language of race. Glick Schiller explicitly places a dialectic of homogenization and differentiation in a transnational context. The racialization of difference is also noted by Burns in his analysis of Mayan efforts to distinguish themselves from others.

Oboler also calls attention to issues of racism, sexism, and classism which express a crisis of community. In her paper, she examines the distortions that result from the labels we use. The stigmatizing and homogenizing effects of labels are contrasted to the ways in which they shape people's identities. By proposing an alternative to essentialism, Oboler urges us to re-examine the crisis of community and to pursue a transnational approach to these issues. In a similar frame, Michael Kearney suggests the need for reconceptualizing sectors of society, such as the peasantry, whose analysis was until now bounded by rigid dual categories. Kearney's critique of modern academic discourse forces us to evaluate our thinking about the presence of complex, multi-faceted subjects that consistently manage to elude our current theories and methods. He proposes a post-peasant social science located now in zones that, once marginal, will become central. The decentering of research should reflect the new research questions, moving away from an ideology of development, or a traditional-versus-modern continuum, and opening spaces to all expressions of identity.

Edna Acosta-Belén urges us to include the many expressions of U. S. Latino identity that contribute to a pan-ethnic sense of latinismo. Through examples from several Latino writers, she suggests that the new collectivity is based on opposition and subaltern positions, but she sees these as providing "cultural agency to...resist, contest, and transform dominant or colonized representations of self" (Acosta-Belén, chap. 5) Flores offers a somewhat different view as he reviews positions on the ethnic Latino landscape of the "New Nueva York" and, in particular, the identification of Puerto Ricans as part of a Latino or Hispanic group. He concludes that there is no alternative to a multiple-identities position. Due to the absence of good historical and comparative studies of each of the groups of Latinos that form the "Hispanic population" of the city, and subject to the "exception" syndrome, Puerto Ricans are often clustered as a group only to show their lower performance in several domains. Flores describes this situation as resulting from their ambivalent colonial status and the dubious privilege of citizenship.

In section II, Allan Burns examines Mayan identity in the diaspora through several examples from Indiantown, Florida. He explores the juxtaposition of essential and situational identities. Focusing on individuals, but treating them as reflections of identities constructed as groups, and through careful ethnographic accounts, Burns shows the ease with which people consciously enact their transnational identities.

In my own paper (Goldin, chap. 8), I explore transnational processes of identity formation in the international factories located in Guatemala. Mayas and non-Mayas, working side by side in the production of export goods, reformulate their conceptions of self and other, ethnicity, gender, and nation. In the new fields of action, with schedules and norms that transcend previously known practices, new identities are created in the context of complex economic backdrops. Here also, workers' discourse fluctuates between the newly found sameness in the factory and a world of ethnic and socioeconomic differences.

Duncan Earle's analysis of Texas's *colonias* (low income settlements for Mexican migrants) provides a picture of the dramas of transition and the ironies of public and national policies where illegality becomes part of the system. Earle suggests that because of the ambiguities of the border, residents live in a "third space" of post-national nature. It is in this increasingly transnational context that he foresees a blurring of the contrast between margins and the interior.

Montejo contributes an ethnography of exile as he unravels the forms that place and displacement take from the perspective of his own Jakaltek and Q'anjob'al cultural traditions. In this account, the *Elilal*, a massive and violent dislocation of entire communities, is contrasted with individual decisions to abandon the community, such as decisions related to economic needs. The source of all exile is explained in the context of the community's system of understanding and classification. Transnationalism is viewed in this form as a painful departure from the land with lasting consequences for the community of origin.

In a content analysis of Mexican migrants' *retablos* (votive paintings left at religious shrines in Mexico), Durand and Massey describe the migrant experience in the unfiltered words of migrants. In this sense, the retablos speak for them and express the anxieties, fears and joys of the often traumatic experience. The retablos show how intrinsic the migration experience is to Mexicans in general, as hundreds of thousands of families have relatives in the United States.

To illustrate mechanisms that result in different levels of commitment to settlement, Santiago-Rivera and Santiago examine the relationship between language proficiency and length of stay of Puerto Ricans in the continental United States. They observe that rather than economic forces, language proficiency and education seem to explain the type of circulatory migration we observe today, with language proficiency compensating for lack of education. As an icon for identity and a sense of belonging, language proficiency is viewed as predictor of settlement.

As an epilogue, *In First Person*, I include an autobiographical piece by Ilan Stavans who provides a first person account of an example of how the transnational experience is lived. Stavans reflects on exile and the construction of identity and artfully expresses what many of us, transnationals in the making, feel. He discusses being Mexican, Mexican American and Latino Jew, "in search of the ultimate clue to the mysteries of a divided identity" (Stavans, chap. 13) And he finds doubt. From Jew in Mexico to White Hispanic in the United States, Stavans reminds us of the ironies of transnationalism.

FUTURE DIRECTIONS

The emerging picture from this volume points to theoretical and methodological issues of importance in the study of transnational identities. Conceptually, the authors describe an atmosphere where actors make use of specific tools of identification to define their positions in social and political spaces. In addition, they access cultural means of presentation that allow them to express their frustrations (as in the use of art) and to participate in the new fields (as in "other" language acquisition). The tools of identification range from claims and adjudications of citizenship through various labels, enhanced allegiance to the "other" nation-state, and a revision of concepts of race and group. Labeling and manipulation of citizenship involve processes of homogenization and differentiation that run parallel to politics of domination, subordination, and exception. Methodologically, the authors highlight the tentative nature of the study of transnational identities and the need to analyze them from multiple perspectives. This includes historical studies of ethnic claims, the multiple and often contradictory discourses of race throughout the Americas, sociological and demographic reporting on the movements of labor and capital across territories, and detailed ethnographic accounts that provide close-ups on transnational developments.

The chapters in this volume explore the nation-state in the context of global and transnational processes of identity formation and point to the importance of reformulating traditional views of "nation." As one example, several authors suggest that the influx of migrants to the United States has evoked strong reactions from conservative sectors of society who question the spaces migrants have constructed for themselves and those that the nation has seemingly conceded. A xenophobic environment has developed parallel to one that presents multicultural affirmations at the national level. As the nation becomes redefined with the influx of new voices and the reactions from sectors of the old, one begins to wonder how pervasive, useful and whole the "nation" remains in the new context. Similar questions can be posed about countries of origin, such as Mexico, countries in Central America, and the Caribbean. How do these nations experience the impact of the transnational processes and consequent issues of identity? How do these nations deal with concepts of nationhood and citizenship as people multiply their affiliations? Is the idea of nation as defined by eighteenth-century mores, shared history, memory, ethnic identity and language, in the process of dying? Can the same be said of the concepts of culture and ethnicity, both of which seem somewhat fragile and equivocal in the context of the issues raised in this volume.

Although our traditional conceptions of nation may be becoming outdated, the papers in this volume also portray a repressive, colonial apparatus in hegemonic countries such as the United States; one that through labels and other classifications based on politics of exception produce subaltern sectors of society. As Oboler pointed out at the conference, national guards, passports, and militarized borders are commentaries on the force and perseverance of the nation-state. From this perspective, not all nation-states experience the same fragile role. As in other more familiar contexts, relations of power and domination also affect the construction of transnational identities, which are not exempt from the forces of a porous but "essentializing presence of United States definitions of citizenship and physical distinctions" (John Watanabe, personal communication). This is amply demonstrated throughout this book.

Based on his discussion of the "porous" characteristics of the diaspora identity, Burns (chap. 7) suggests that we need to take on three important tasks in the future: (1) to study the identities of people on the move; (2) to reconcile their essential and situational identities; and (3) to incorporate these concepts into our applied endeavors. Other scholars (see Jonas 1996) suggest that we think in terms of "trinational regions or spaces" in the case of the United States-Mexico- Central America connections. It is clear from this volume that we must, at a minimum, broaden the units of analysis to be more inclusive and most of all realistic, and to contemplate new types of intra-national mobility and a new positioning in the social, economic and political landscapes. This must be done in conjunction with historical research that documents the history of ethnicities in the context of the global economy and culture of which we are part (Carmack, conference communication). Transnational contacts represent some of the major forces shaping the Americas in the twenty-first century, and these forces need to be documented. Finally, we need more in-depth, detailed anthropological work that can register the many voices of transnational actors.

The papers in this volume suggest that the transnational processes that we study are not arbitrary and random but that they follow discernible patterns: The processes yield essentialized views; they play themselves out within prefabricated labels and categories along racial and national lines; they produce new versions of patriotic zeal from abroad; and they are expressed through various cultural forms such as art, and language use. An awareness and analysis of the processes of homogenization and differentiation is essential to untangle the complex sociological textile. Group identities based on negative markers, as in being "non-black," show that race is very much a part of the language of transnationalism. Nina Glick Schiller, for example, noted at the conference that nation-state building is not a completed project, but rather represents an ongoing hegemonic process where the rules of the game are always changing. While there have always been immigration laws, racial categories in the hegemonic nations have changed and identity construction takes place within the constraints of those changing factors. The present volume underscores just how contemporary and prevailing the issues of race and racism are.

In my opinion, we do not need to invent new terms to describe what is before us, only new forms of presentation, methods of analysis, and the use of approaches that do justice to what we all can see but sometimes find difficult to recount. In this book, through multi-disciplinary perspectives and diverse methodological strategies, the writers hope to portray an approximation of some of the fundamental processes involved in transnational analysis.

NOTES

1. NAFTA, North America Free Trade Agreement, is a trade agreement among Canada, Mexico and the United States. MERCOSUR, Mercado Común del Sur (Common Market of the South) is a trade agreement among Argentina, Brazil, Paraguay and Uruguay.

2. Throughout the volume, the authors use the terms Latino and Hispanic to refer to the same population. The choice of terms may have political implications, reflect the U. S. Census use, or simply the various authors' and subject's preferences. See chapter 5 for further clarification on these terms. In addition, authors writing about Central America use the term Ladino. It refers to non-Maya people, often of mixed background.

REFERENCES CITED

Anderson, Benedict
    1983   *Imagined Communities: Reflections on the Origin and Spread of Nationalism.* Verso, London.
Appadurai, Arjun
    1991   Global Ethnoscapes: Notes and Queries for a Transnational Anthropology. In *Recapturing Anthropology: Working in the Present*, edited by Richard G. Fox, pp.191-210. School for American Research, Santa Fe.
Baca, Reynaldo, and Dexter Bryan
    1980   *Citizenship Aspirations and Residency Rights Preference: The Mexican Undocumented Work in the Binational Community.* SEPA-OPTION, Compton, California.
Basch, Linda, Nina Glick Schiller, and Cristina Szanton Blanc (editors)
    1994   *Nations Unbound: Transnational Projects, Postcolonial Predicaments, and Deterritorialized Nation-states.* Gordon and Breach, New York.
Chavez, Leo
    1992   *Shadowed Lives: Undocumented Immigrants in American Society.* Harcourt, Brace and Jovanovich College, Fort Worth.

1994 The Power of the Imagined Community: The Settlement of Undocumented Mexicans and Central Americans in the United States. *American Anthropologist* 96:52-73.

Duany, Jorge
1996 Imagining the Puerto Rican Nation: Recent Works on Cultural Identity. *Latin American Research Review* 31:248-268.

García Canclini, Néstor
1990 *Culturas híbridas: estrategias para entrar y salir de la modernidad.* Grijalbo, Mexico City.

Glick Schiller, Nina, Linda Basch, and Cristina Szanton Blanc, (editors)
1992 *Towards a Transnational Perspective on Migration: Race, Class, Ethnicity, and Nationalism Reconsidered.* New York Academy of Sciences, New York.

Jonas, Susanne
1996 Transnational Realities and Anti-Immigrant State Policies: Issues Raised by the Experiences of Central American Immigrants and Refugees in a Trinational Region. In *Latin America in the World-Economy*, edited by Roberto P. Korzeniewicz, and William C. Smith, pp. 117-132. Prager, Westport, Connecticut.

Lins Ribeiro, Gustavo
1997 In Search of the Virtual-Imagined Transnational Community. *American Anthropology Newsletter*, May, p. 80.

Rosaldo, Renato
1989 *Culture and Truth: The Remaking of Social Analysis.* Beacon, Boston.

Rouse, Roger
1991 Mexican Migration and the Social Space of Postmodernism. *Diaspora* 1(1): 8-23

Szanton Blanc, Cristina, Linda Basch, and Nina Glick Schiller
1995 Transnationalism, Nation-States and Culture. *Current Anthropology* 36: 683-686.

Whiteford, Linda
1979 The Borderland as an Extended Community. In *Migration Across Frontiers: Mexico and the United States,* edited by Fernando Cámara, and Robert Van Kemper, pp. 127-140. Contributions of the Latin American Anthropology Group, Vol. 3. Institute for Mesoamerican Studies, State University of New York, Albany.

I

Theory on the Move

Processes of Homogenization and Differentiation

2

Who Are These Guys?

A Transnational Reading of the U. S. Immigrant Experience

Nina Glick Schiller

Who are these guys? The year was 1970 and I kept asking myself this question when, as a graduate student in anthropology, I found myself surrounded by people who identified themselves as Georgians, Ukrainians, and Serbs at the Office of the All Americans Council of the Democratic Party campaign headquarters in New York City. I was actually studying the adaptation of Haitian immigrants to U. S. society by working with Haitian immigrant organizations. However, when the Haitian American Citizens Society was invited to participate in the Goldberg-Patterson gubernatorial campaign in New York, I volunteered to assist with the campaign and found that the Haitians had been placed in the All Americans Council of the Democratic Party together with the Irish, Poles, Serbs, Croatians, Georgians, Slavs, and Czechs. The whole situation puzzled me. First of all, I could see that something more than a sentimental search for roots was at stake and that the word "nationalities" had a different connotation than "ethnic group." Yet many of the individuals claimed to be representatives of nations that I thought had disappeared decades ago, before some of these people were born. Second of all, I did not understand why the Haitians, as black immigrants, were put together with the Europeans and not with African Americans. All I knew was that what I was confronting did not fit into the literature on Americanization that I had studied assiduously before doing my research.

Now the year is 1989. Edner, a fifty-nine-year-old house painter, who has been unemployed for eleven years, stands in his yard in a poor, but not squalid, neighborhood of Port-au-Prince. The household (*lakou*) includes several generations and three of Edner's children, two of whom are leaving this week to join their mother and brother in New York. The entire household lives primarily on remittances sent by Edner's wife. To the accompaniment of the crowing of roosters, remnants of a more rural past and small bulwarks against the hunger that is a part of life in this neighborhood, Edner explains his understanding of Haitian identity. "A person is still a Haitian if he becomes a citizen of another country. His blood is still Haitian blood. It is only the person's title and name that is changed. The person's skin is still Haitian and besides that the person was born in Haiti and even if that person doesn't consider himself Haitian the whites in the country where he's living still consider him Haitian. Therefore I don't think a person should reject his country."

Underlying these two vignettes is, I believe, an unheralded transnational narrative about Americanization, a narrative that is simultaneously about the formation of nation, race, and class. In this paper I shall argue that Americanization has actually been, and continues to be simultaneously a process of racialization and transnationalization. As part of this process, immigrants have identified with both the United States and their nation-state of origin in ways not signaled by the classic theory of the nation-state (Gellner 1983; Hobsbawm 1990). To explicate the transnational context of Americanization and its relationship to "racial formation" (Omi and Winant 1986), I first examine the engagement of past generations of immigrants of European origin in transnational nation-state building and briefly contrast that experience with the history of U. S. immigrants who came from other regions of the world. I then explore the transnational politics of identification of contemporary immigrants from locations in the Caribbean, Latin America, and Asia, using the experience of Haitian immigrants as a case in point.

For the purpose of this paper, I use the word "state" to indicate a sovereign system of government within a particular bounded territory (see Fouron and Glick Schiller 1997). In contrast, the word "nation" evokes the sense of peoplehood that a particular population uses to distinguish itself from other national groups. If the state binds "us" together, the nation distinguishes "us" from "them."[1] Nation-state building is therefore identified as "a set of historical and affective processes that link disparate and heterogeneous populations together and forge their loyalty to and identity with a central government apparatus and institutional structure" (Fouron and Glick Schiller 1997). In the course of such a process, the class forces or coalitions that dominate the state strive to create the conditions in which culturally diverse and class stratified populations will identify themselves as a single people. To speak of a nation-state is to imply that populations that reside within a territory of a government also share a common identity as a nation (Gellner 1983). In the past, a coalition of class forces in the United States made up of the politicians, clergy, businessmen, social workers, journalists, and intellectuals constructed Americanization projects that tried to instill in immigrants a commitment to a shared national destiny. Public education, popular culture, national holidays, and the regulation of daily life developed and enforced common cultural norms and practices (Suskind 1992). Today different sectors of the U. S. population are engaged in competing Americanization projects that range from the English Only movement to multiculturalism. Those forces who promote multiculturalism as a nation-state building project develop discourses, practices, forums, and institutions that acknowledge the cultural contributions of populations racialized as different from that of the U. S. mainstream, yet instill a sense of shared commitment to the United States among such "culturally diverse" persons.

AMERICANIZATION AS A TRANSNATIONAL PROCESS: THE PAST REVISITED

First, let us examine the processes of U. S. nation-state building that have historically convinced a significant sector of immigrants to identify with the destiny of the United States and to see it as their own. In a curious historical dialectic, the modern sense of individualized personhood emerged among earlier generations of immigrants as persons of disparate class backgrounds, associational ties, and cultural histories learned to identify with the collectivity of the United States. In recent years, a growing number of scholars have demonstrated that that the process of learning to identify with a nation-state has meant that an individual must understand not only who he is, but also who he is not (Gilroy 1991). In the United States, the dialectics of homogenization and differentiation link together the concepts of race and nation so that Americanization has been a form of "racial formation" (Omi and Winant 1986; See also Lopez 1996; Roediger 1991; Takaki 1979; Winant 1994). We are coming to the realization that immigrants from Europe came to be American by striving not to be black. What scholars have yet to do, and what I hope to begin to do here, is to investigate how past generations of immigrants confirmed that they were not black by establishing that they were part of the communities of their ancestral lands. They were not black because they were people with a nation-state. The task before us is to put this dialectic of homogenization and differentiation that is so basic to nationalist projects within a transnational perspective.

Beginning with the founding fathers, U. S. political leaders, writers, jurists and others who have shaped political discourse have built a sense of an

American identity by differentiating between what Ben Franklin called "the lovely white" and all others; between civilized and barbarian; between free man and slave (Takaki 1979). These lines of distinction were embedded in the republican ideology which could unite artisans, plantation owners, and small farmers into a common identity of free white men who were beholden to no master. These equations were not directly unsettled in the early mills of New England because factory hands were women's hands and the status of wage work was linked to the subordinate status of unmarried Yankee daughters (Lamphere 1987). However, by the middle of the nineteenth century the unity of the republic was threatened by the efforts of the nascent capitalist class to recruit, discipline and domesticate an industrial workforce of immigrants, many of whom were male.

Roediger (1991) argues that, in the United States of the nineteenth century, artisans and immigrants came to accept the discipline of industrial labor by defining themselves as white and therefore different from and superior to blacks, who were portrayed as carefree, lazy, and not members of the working class. After the annexation of Mexican territory, immigrants from Europe who settled in the Southwest and on the West Coast sought to define their whiteness in opposition to persons of Mexican, Chinese, and Japanese descent. They strengthened their own claims to an American identity by defining these other populations as biologically incapable of culture and civilization (Lopez 1996; Winant 1994). Qualities that the dominant culture linked with blackness— savagery, lust, moral inferiority, and childishness—came to be associated with being Chinese (Takaki 1979). In 1854, the California Supreme Court found that "Black" was a generic term encompassing all nonwhites and thus included Chinese people. A similar finding was made by the Mississippi Supreme Court in 1925 (Lopez 1996:51-52).[2]

I am suggesting that this struggle to become white, which was waged by European immigrants, actually had two parts and that the second part has yet to be addressed by scholars of Americanization. In order for immigrants from Europe to imagine themselves as white, they had to imagine themselves as belonging to a nation-state in Europe. Having a European homeland differentiated these immigrants from racialized populations whose cultural histories were negated by U. S. hegemonic forces. Consequently, European immigrants actually became white and "American" through two related processes. Working class immigrants in the United States and their descendants identified with nationalist projects in Europe that glorified the accomplishments of their "ancestral" cultures because such projects bolstered their claim to civilization and civility. They then used their claims to a distinctive national identity in Europe to raise their social prestige within the United States. That is to say, European immigrants from the Irish to the Serbs became engaged in transnational, nation-state building politics in the United States as a way of not being black. In the process of struggle for their homeland, European immigrants had all become

White Americans by the 1940s or 1950s. It should be noted that the progression of European immigrants into whiteness was not an inevitable product of time, a form of gradual "race-relations cycle" (Park 1974a:149-151 [1925]). This racial transformation took place in the context of consistent struggles against populations that continued to be defined as nonwhite. The transformation was assisted both by the expansion of the U. S. economy during and after World War II.

This second aspect of the process of Americanization requires a revision of how we read immigration history. Previous studies of Americanization, as well as recent studies of contemporary transnational migration, share a myth about the nature of European migration. European peasants were portrayed as living mired for centuries in unchanging tradition until they suddenly packed up, left village life behind them forever, and moved to America (Handlin 1973; see Schneider 1994). None of these images are historically accurate. European migrations in the nineteenth and the beginning of the twentieth century were part of a history of labor migration that was several centuries old. As a result of the capitalization of the countryside, Europe experienced cycles of population growth and contraction accompanied by patterns of seasonal and return migration (Krickus 1976; Moch 1992).

A more recent reading of U. S. immigrant history reveals a wealth of home ties among numerous European immigrant populations (Hareven 1982; Thistlewaite 1964; Vecoli and Sinke 1991; Wyman 1993; Yans-McLaughlin 1982). Although earlier waves of immigrants maintained personal and political connections to home, the age of immigrant transnational commuting between home and host societies began in the 1880s. Observers at the end of the nineteenth century saw steamships as a technological break through that brought the globe into rapid contact. Tickets were relatively cheap, the trip took under two weeks, and many people crossed the Atlantic for seasonal labor migration (Cinel 1991; Wyman 1993). Dense transnational interconnections were reported for diverse populations (Kula et al. 1986; Thomas and Znanieki 1958 [1918]; Wyman 1993).

I want to be clear that the connections that were being maintained were not sentimental attachment to the homeland or to some dream of eventual return but ongoing exchanges of populations between home and host societies. To not just dream about but to organize a return migration necessitated the careful cultivation of relationships back home. Planning to return home, these past generations of migrants remained committed to the norms, values, and aspirations of the home societies. The core of most immigrants' transnational relations were familial, although the ties of family were economic as well as emotional. Employment in the U. S. was an integral aspect of supporting families and perhaps realizing aspirations for social mobility back home. Many Southern and Eastern Europeans migrated to be able to purchase land that was coming on the market as the result of the capitalization of the countryside (Tolopko 1988:37).

Because of these ongoing transnational relationships, one of the most significant early immigrant businesses in most U. S. immigrant populations involved banking and the transmission of remittances. Certain locations in Eastern and Southern Europe became remittance economies in much the way that many regions and countries in the Third World today are sustained by immigrant remittances.[3]

In addition to family relationships, immigrants arriving in the United States maintained ties to their home towns. They organized hometown associations, gaining status back home by improving local churches, cemeteries, schools, and public works. These associations sometimes served as burial and benefit societies to help people face hardships in their new life while maintaining immigrants ties to the old. These ties to old locations were indicators of the very localized identities of the majority of these immigrants. The state was something they tried to avoid rather than something with which they identified. Moreover, in some regions from which European immigrants migrated, the state, and even the language under which they lived and by which they were governed changed, more than once within an individual's lifetime (Krickus 1976; Soskin 1976).

Although these European immigrants may have lived their lives across borders, this process of border crossing did not remove them from the politics of identification generated by dominant classes within nation-states. On the contrary, it was through the process of immigration and settlement in the United States that many immigrants discovered their identity with their native land. This contradictory outcome of migration has been noted by generations of scholars who have observed that the national identities of European immigrants were made in America. (Fuchs 1990; Novack 1972). Robert Park in 1925 put it this way:

> Now, the first effect of city life is to destroy the provincialism of the immigrant, and to intensify his sense of racial and national solidarity. It is interesting fact that as a first step in Americanization the immigrant does not become in the least American. He simply ceases to be a provincial foreigner. Wurtemburgers and Westphalians become in America first of all Germans; Sicilians and Neapolitans become Italians and Jews become Zionists.[4](Park 1974b:157 [1925])

In 1954, in almost the same language, Nathan Glazer reported the following:

> The newer immigrants...became nations in America. The first newspaper in the Lithuanians' language was published in this country, not Lithuania...and the nation of Czechoslovakia was launched at a meeting in Pittsburgh...other immigrants were to discover in coming to America that they had left nations behind, actions in which

they had had no part at home. Thus the American relative of Southern Italians...became Italian patriots in America, supporting here
the war to which they had been indifferent at home. (Glazer
1954:167)

The connection between home ties to family and locality and the growth of
political identifications and active participation in nationalist activities oriented
toward supporting the motherland was not spontaneous. These new identities
were the result of complex nation-state building projects led by coalitions of
political leaders, clergy, and businessmen in the home country together with
people of similar social positioning among immigrants. Hungarian leaders based
in Hungary toured the United States to organize Hungarian immigrants in the
United States (Vassady 1982). Slovak leaders toured the U. S. organizing protests against the Hungarian government's suppression of Slovak nationalism
(Alexander 1987:127-129).

For aspiring political leaders, there were significant rewards in convincing
their disparate emigrants that they shared a common history, culture, and identity and should participate in building a nation-state back home. These leaders
may well have been committed to the struggle to build their nation; at the same
time, their possibilities of obtaining political position, career, fame, and fortune
depended on the success of their nationalist project. But what of the laboring
people, the men and women whose relationships to home societies were one of
kin and locality? Many of them had fled bitter experiences of class exploitation
back home that had led them to distrust the middle and upper class leaders who
now claimed them as their own.

Once in the United States, however, immigrant workers (both men and
women) faced the intensification of capitalist relations that marked the development of U. S. society. In their daily workplace experiences, workers found
they were treated as faceless, expendable labor. In the larger society they found
that newspapers, novels, and politicians branded them as racially inferior. In
contrast, in their neighborhoods workers found that aspiring nationalist leaders
offered fellowship and pride in an ancestral culture. It was in the local neighborhood setting of U. S. factory and mining towns that immigrant workers
began to commit their energies to their native land and became participants in
transnational nation-state building.[5]

For example, between 1892 and 1913 more than 17 percent of the population of Galicia left their native land, the majority emigrating to the United
States. In Galicia they experienced serfdom, a peasant rebellion in 1848, and
stark "exploitation by landlords and priests" (Lamphere 1987:79). In
places such as Central Falls, Rhode Island, they became the unskilled labor in
textile mills and other factories. Sick benefits, and life and accident insurance
were provided neither by the workplace or the state but by Polish nationalist

organizations such as the Pulaski Mutual Aid Society and the Society of Polish Knights, a part of the Polish National Alliance. These organizations were established in immigrant neighborhoods by Polish priests and middle class immigrants. Working class immigrants found in these organizations social solidarity and social standing that answered the aspirations for social mobility which had motivated their migration from Galicia and which they had not be able to obtain through industrial employment. So although Galician migrants left and returned home, and more than half returned to a Galicia that was part of the Austrian-Hungarian empire, they came to accept a definition of themselves as Polish. In a history of the Polish organizations of Central Falls, the writers describe their transformation from peasants to American citizens by evoking memories of the Polish Falcons, a paramilitary organization founded in 1908. They recounted that the organization "renewed the life of local Polonia through exercises, singing, marches, celebrations, balls, meetings, lectures, frequent travel contests, frequent theatrical performances, and collection of funds for armed struggle. Thus this organization contributed greatly to the well-being of the Fatherland" (Jubilee Book of the Pulaski Society cited in Lamphere 1987:113).

Over time, a local Galician identity, itself not institutionalized beyond hometown connections, gave way to a new national pride in the "Fatherland" of Poland. Treated as racially different and inferior in the mainstream U. S. culture, Galician peasants found a spiritual and cultural home in the Polish national project. Hegemonic forces in the United States that at first had subordinated these European immigrants workers by excluding them racially as despised laborers soon found that they had in their midst a body of militant Polish nationalists.

The task of incorporating these immigrants into the U. S. body politic became more pressing with the advent of World War I when U. S. political leaders called on the U. S. populace to fight and die for their country. The call to arms raised in new ways the issue of the loyalties of European immigrants, many of whom returned to Europe to fight for the independence of their native lands. Immigrants from Central Falls for example went to France to fight for Polish freedom (Lamphere 1987:113).

Scholars of U. S. immigration frequently have noted the flourishing of national identities among immigrants before World War I but assumed that these identities were abandoned as a result of the massive Americanization campaigns of the post-War period. I think the situation is more complex for several reasons that can help us understand the way in which Americanization was often a transnational project. It is true that the dual political loyalties that up until World War I had been taken for granted by millions of U. S. immigrants were specifically contested during and after the war. The issue became not the connection to home or the abandonment of identity with an ancestral land but the question of political allegiance and the loyalty of the American citizenry. For example, the National Society of the Daughters of the American Revolution published a *Manual of the United States: For the Information of Immigrants and Foreigners* in English and 17 other languages and distributed 2 million copies that stated, "America does not ask you to forget your old home. But in taking the oath of allegiance to the United States new citizens must promise to give up allegiance to your former country. ...You cannot have two countries" (Fuchs 1990:64).

The historical record also provides evidence that political leaders within immigrant populations and the political leadership of the United States up to and including U. S. presidents continued to reinforce immigrants' transnational political ties when these ties were defined in the U. S. national interest. This is the persistent but forgotten aspect of the continuation of identity politics among immigrants from Europe, Asia, and Latin America. The direction of this policy was set by the U. S. Congress after World War I when they accepted back into the fold those who had sworn allegiance and fought in foreign armies, as long as they had been fighting enemies of the United States. At the same time they engaged immigrants in institutions and practices that secured their political allegiance to the United States. The Pledge of Allegiance became an institutionalized practice and its wording was changed so that the flag saluted was specified as that "of the United States of America."

Nationality groups were and are useful if they articulate U. S. foreign policy interests. With the advent of the Soviet Union, exiles organized oppositional nationality groups within the United States. Leaders of these groups maintained relationships with both members of Congress and U. S. government officials. After World War I, when the flow of immigrants from Eastern Europe was cut off, many of these anticommunist nationality groups continued their efforts to organize immigrant transnational politics. They were strengthened after World War II, and after the Hungarian and Czech uprisings, by a flood of refugees, who were allowed into the country under special immigration waivers for refugees from communism.

U. S. political parties played an important role in fostering immigrant transnational political activities and identities. However, the implications of this role rarely have been mentioned in the scholarly literature on migration history because the relationship between U. S. nationalities and political parties has been discussed under the rubric of the ethnic vote rather than as immigrant transnational relationships. What comes to mind is the campaigning politician posing here with a pizza, there with a souvlaki, next with a knish. In point of fact, "ethnic" votes were wooed and obtained in part by recognizing the continuing ties of immigrants to their homeland and by designating these groups as "nationalities." After World War II both the Democratic and Republican parties developed aggressive "nationalities" divisions. These divisions assumed and built on relationships between immigrant populations and their states of origin. The

Republican organization, entitled the National Republican Heritage Groups, took shape in Nixon's 1968 campaign division and was described at the time as the largest and most aggressive undertaking by any national party in American history (Weed 1973:166). Republican candidates routinely not only marched in ethnic parades but promoted national identities among U. S. immigrant populations that were linked to nationalities in the Soviet Union. The interaction between Ralph Smith, the 1970 senatorial candidate in Illinois, and ethnic organizations was typical of the Cold War period. Smith told a meeting of Hungarian-Americans that "I hope your nation behind the wall of Communism will again see the light of freedom we all love so dearly" (Weed 1973: 162). The Republican National Committee, through its Slovak advisor, played an active role in helping organize activities such as the Slovak World Congress that met in Toronto in 1971 (Weed 1973:166).

A Nationalities Division of the national Democratic Party was created in 1936 under Franklin Roosevelt's presidency but until Harry Truman's 1948 campaign it remained fairly dormant between presidential elections (Sendelbach 1967: 19-20). In that campaign, the Nationalities Division was credited by the Party Chairman as playing a key role in Truman's surprise presidential victory. The transnational nature of the politics emerge clearly in his memoirs.

> Although loyal to the United States, many Americans of foreign descent were nevertheless also deeply concerned with the future of the country of their forefathers. Many of them had close relatives still in the old country and they had friends there with who they corresponded regularly...Before the campaign began, concrete evidence of the President's interest in the problems of the countries menaced and conquered by Communism had been given over and over...For voters of foreign origin the issues were clearly with the Democratic Party. What remained for us was to carry out an aggressive program of driving those issues home. (Redding 1958: 205, 223)

After that election, the Nationalities Division continued to expanded to become a working arm of the Democratic National Committee, both during and after elections. It was housed within the offices of the Democratic National Committee beginning in 1963 (Sendelbach 1967:23), and, although its name was changed to the "All Americans Council," the transnational politics of immigrants continued to be a concern of Council meetings and activities. For example, in 1967 Nobert Dengler, chairman of the German Division of the All Americans Council, indicated that "the German-Americans, or any ethnic group for that matter, could become a bridge of communication in our foreign policy. These second and third generation ethnic could meet with dignitaries and officials from the countries of their national origin as representatives of the nationality here in America. Likewise they could visit these countries and help create bonds of friendship between the two nations" (from Sendelbach 1967, based upon her interview with Nobert Dengler, May 5, 1967).

In the 1970s, the Democrats had active ties with a multitude of immigrant populations, each with its own "Nationality Division Chairmen" from Georgians to the Irish. Two years after the Czech uprising, the head of the All Americans Council was Czech. It was among these "oppressed" nationalities that the leaders of the Democratic Party placed the Haitian immigrants of bourgeois backgrounds that they had recruited into the party in the late 1960s. A dynamic of race and transnational politics was again being activated, but in a changing historical conjuncture. I return to this theme below when I contrast the differences between past and contemporary Americanization projects.

Here it is important to reflect upon the continuing use of transnational ties of immigrants, including European immigrants, by U. S. foreign policy makers. As Waters (1990) and Alba (1990) indicate in their work, sectors of those whose parents or grandparents became white increasingly fail to maintain home ties and are relatively unconcerned about their ancestry or choose forms of "symbolic ethnicity"(Gans 1979); yet, a transnational organizational core with an institutional base persists. They serve as a political base that can put leaders in place in Europe who have ties, loyalty, and even citizenship in the United States. After the dissolution of the Soviet Union and of Yugoslavia, citizens of the United States of eastern and southern European ancestry returned to positions of power in a number of countries, including Serbia, Bosnia, and the Czech republic. Greek-Americans have been a part of a transnational movement to deny the name Macedonia to one of the states of the former Yugoslavia (Karakasidou 1994).

In this particular paper, the history I have presented focuses on the transnational ties that non-Anglo-Saxon Protestants of European descent built as part of the process through which they became White Americans. It is important to remember that as immigrants from Europe came to be seen as European and white, immigrants from everywhere else became defined as nonwhite. However, racialization is a constantly contested process. The dynamic of resisting a social location of blackness through the politicization of personal transnational connections has been practiced by immigrants to the United States from throughout the world. Even as they were being defined as nonwhite in counter-distinction to an emerging European whiteness, immigrants from the Caribbean, Latin America, and Asia engaged in their own politics of identification in which they strove through their home ties to differentiate themselves from U. S. blackness (Basch et al. 1994; Bodnar 1985; Charles 1990; Richardson 1983; Wong 1982). As in the case of immigrants from Europe, political leaders from Latin America, the Caribbean, and Asia, and aspiring middle class immigrants from within immigrant communities, have been key players in the process of transnational nation-state building, linking immigrants in the United States to the political processes of their home countries.

Within the transnational and racializing processes by which European immigrants became American, even as they became linked in their identities to European homelands, it is possible to identify the differential benefits achieved by different class fractions of the immigrant population. Immigrant populations have never been uniform in terms of their class composition. If the building of national identity has been a part of the organization of capitalism, it is also part of class formation. I have sketched the way in which white workers came to see themselves as white rather than as workers. In both the past and present, patriotic projects have allowed for the legitimization of structures of exploitation that provide some benefit for aspiring immigrant leaders but maintain the political and economic subordination of the vast majority of immigrants. Historians such as Miller have made clear the way in which class formation and Irish national identity were shaped transnationally. An alliance of middle class immigrants and Irish clergy who came to lead the Catholic church in the United States taught acceptance of poverty and bourgeois family values, and a patriotism that conjoined loyalty to Ireland and loyalty to the United States. By being good Irish Catholics, Irish workers were told they were becoming "good Americans" with the habits of self-control and domestic purity that made good citizens (Miller 1990:114). In this process middle class Irish immigrants emerged as ethnic leaders in the United States and national leaders in Ireland. And in most cases intellectuals have played an important part in constructing and popularizing these hegemonic projects.

Although the expansion of U. S. based capitalism allowed the majority of past generations óf immigrants from Europe to achieve some success with this strategy, the costs have been high both to all people defined as nonwhite and to the past and future efforts to challenge the power of capital. Aspiring immigrant leaders achieved wealth and political power, while workers rose from the social and economic bottom of the society that continued to be reserved for people of color, particularly African Americans. At the same time, the working class that was formed was strongly divided by lines of class and race. The identity of White American that arose was, and continues to be, a deeply corrosive form of identification. It is a negative identity in which the unity of whiteness relies on assertions of the inferiority of blackness (Page 1997a, 1997b).

PRESENT DIASPORAS AND CURRENT DAY NATION BUILDING PROCESSES

What about the identities and political loyalties of contemporary immigrants? As in the past, contemporary migrants are viewed as nonwhite and as coming from cultures and histories that differ dramatically from that of the United States. As in the past, contemporary immigrants have been racialized, defined not in terms of their individual national origins but as Hispanic, Asian, and Black. And certainly, and perhaps to even a greater degree than in the past, contemporary immigrants are engaged both in transnational social relations and in transnational political projects.

However, there are important differences between the global context of contemporary migrations and past migrations to the United States. While some authors point to technological change, which has facilitated transnational travel and communication, as a central difference between past and present migrations (Wakeman 1988), it is more likely that the fundamental difference between past and present transnational migrations is the changing nature of global capitalism (Basch et al. 1994; Glick Schiller et al. 1992; 1995; 1994). While capitalism developed as a global system of exploiting labor and extracting resources, within the past few decades, those who hold the largest amounts of capital have developed new forms of articulating relationships between production and accumulation. From the time of the early Dutch and British trading companies, the lines of profitability stretched across state boundaries. However, with the growth and expansion of capitalism came the rise of national economies. Profit structures were maintained by state structures that provided for uniform standards and regulations to promote the efficiency of production, institutions of banking and insurance to safeguard profits, and taxation for public investments in education, transportation, communication, and public health. Today we are facing a reconstitution of the structure of accumulation so that the profits accumulate globally and the structures through which that economy is organized are global rather than national (Sassen 1996). In a world dominated by transnational corporations, the organization of production, financial transactions, and the control of capital increasingly takes place on a global terrain. Competing capitalist conglomerates are still based in nation-states, and, yet, they have organized a massive restructuring of the forms of profit-making, a restructuring sometimes summarized by the term "globalization" (Mittleman 1997).

This restructuring is described in Europe and the United States as "deindustrialization" and "down-sizing"; in Latin America, the Caribbean, and Africa as "structural adjustment"; in Asia and Eastern Europe as "privatization"; and everywhere as the neo-liberalism of the free market. These processes rearrange the relationships among the processes of the exploitation of labor, the economic restraints imposed on commercial activity by the institutions and policies of various states, and the ways in which populations located within various states are socialized, disciplined, and constrained by competing national narratives. However, the connections between the restructuring of capital, the global inter-state system, and the heightened degree of nationalism around the globe constitute a vast and pressing subject that awaits exploration.[6]

Rather than take on the entire topic of globalization, in the final section of this paper, I offer some thoughts about the relationship between contemporary transnational migration and the Americanization process, understood to be an ongoing, if altered, aspect of U. S. nation-state building. I present as a case study the response of Haitian immigrants to the efforts to politically incorporate them into the United States. My particular interest is the ways in which sectors of Haitians of all classes, both in Haiti and in the United States, now define Haitian national identity in a way that differentiates it from legal citizenship and from the locus and format of political activity. An increasing number of Haitians believe that Haitian immigrants should become citizens of the United States, and they envision these immigrants as participants in U. S. political processes. Haitians in both Haiti and the United States include in their definition of political processes a range of activities such as demonstrating, lobbying, speaking publicly on radio and television, joining political organizations and voting. Many Haitian immigrants who remain linked to Haiti through either personal and/or organizational networks have begun to act on this belief that they should obtain U. S. citizenship.

However, the taking of U. S. legal citizenship or the engagement of Haitians in U. S.-based activities in which they see themselves as actors within the U. S. nation-state does not necessarily mean that these Haitian immigrants see themselves as no longer part of the Haitian body politic (Glick Schiller and Fouron 1998). Many believe that by becoming American citizens, and fulfilling the responsibility of American citizens through voting, participation in civic life, and obedience of the law, they are able to assist Haiti. Loyalty to the United States becomes an act of patriotism towards Haiti. Elsewhere, I have argued that this changing understanding of nationalism is making it possible to institute a new form of colonial regime in Haiti (Fouron and Glick Schiller 1997; Glick Schiller 1995). Here I wish to examine briefly the ways in which the dialectic between racialization and transnational political processes contributes to the emergence of a new theory of the nation-state, that of the transnational nation-state.

As I have already indicated, transnational politics on the part of immigrants is not new. However, until recently political leaders engaged in transnational nation-state building generally defined their political project as focused within the territorial borders of their state. They called on their diasporas to return and build the country. Those emigrants who insisted on settling permanently abroad were sometimes defined as traitors to the motherland (Feldman-Bianco 1992, 1995). This was certainly true in Haiti until 1991. The Duvaliers labeled the Haitian immigrants as *kamoken*, suspect and disloyal elements who were betrayers of their racial and national legacies (*apatrid*).

Between 1959 and 1993, 302,458 Haitian immigrants and 1,381,240 Haitians with nonimmigrant visas entered the United States. Haiti had about five million people living within its territorial boundaries in 1960. Consequently, within the past three decades, approximately a third of the Haitian population came to the United States to visit or to settle. As I indicated in the second vignette that introduced this paper, Haitian immigrants are among the growing number of immigrants in the United States who live transnational lives. They have settled permanently in the United States yet maintain strong ties to the country they still call "home." People of all class backgrounds in Haiti live their lives across national borders, connected to family, friends, business associates, and political movements located in Haiti. Remittances from Haitian immigrants sustain households throughout Haiti. As one unemployed man in Haiti put it, "When someone is in the U. S. he is the wealth of people here."

Although immigration from Haiti became significant in the 1950s, Haitian immigrants did not present themselves publicly as a community in the United States until the 1980s. Arriving from Haiti divided by class, color, and politics, Haitians have had difficulty organizing as a community and developing collective identities. Members of the light-skinned Haitian upper class identified themselves as French and kept themselves separate from their darker skinned and lower status compatriots. In the United States, however, Haitians were generally viewed as black.

Black immigrants such as Haitians soon learn that, in the United States, black is a social location against which all other persons, immigrant or nonimmigrant, measure their social status. To be black in the United States without an ethnic label is to be a person without history or country. Haitians and other black immigrants from the Caribbean struggle to define themselves publicly in terms other than blackness. Haitians speak of not wanting to be "black twice" (Charles 1990). To be black once is to be Haitian. Haitians have always defined their nation racially, portraying it as a black nation. Since the forging of Haiti in a successful slave rebellion in 1804, Haitian intellectuals and political leaders, whatever their color, have understood that, in the eyes of Europe and the United States, Haitians are defined as black. They responded by seeing Haiti as the representative of African peoples and the mission of the nation and its people is to prove the equality of all people (Nicholls 1996:5). But to be black twice is to accept the designation of black within the United States—that is, to take on the identity of African American, which is to say not fully American.

At the same time the Haitian identity has been a particularly ignominious identity in the United States. In the 1970s and 1980s, Haitians found themselves scapegoated by the U. S. media and politicians who stigmatized Haitians as impoverished, illiterate, and diseased. Although the U. S. Centers for Disease Control later rescinded the inaccurate specification of Haitians as a "risk group" for HIV, a designation based on a misinterpretation of the data, their action had long term effects on Haitian immigrants. Many people lost their jobs, had increased difficulty finding employment, or were attacked because of the inappropriate labeling. At first, many Haitian immigrants coped by hiding their Haitian identity, and individual Haitians may still employ this strategy. However, Haitian immigrant leaders began to stage public protests against the treatment of their refugees and the stigmatization of the population, and many immigrants began to take on a public identity as Haitians. In so doing, they reacted both to their understanding of the racialization process in the U. S. and to the stigmatization of Haitian immigrants by an increased sense of Haitian nationalism. The stirring of the grassroots movement in Haiti, and its success in overthrowing the Duvalier dictatorship in 1986, fanned Haitian national pride among Haitian immigrants. Haitians traveling the New York City subways wore buttons announcing their Haitian identity; Haitian taxi drivers declared their love of Haiti through bumper stickers.

By the end of the 1980s, Haitian immigrants in the United States also began referring to themselves as members of the Haitian "diaspora." When they used the word diaspora, Haitians were signaling their belief that they were a community of people who had been forced to leave Haiti because of the difficult political and economic conditions of their homeland but that, in some sense, Haiti was still their home. Given their experience that being Haitian is an ascribed status that gives a person of Haitian descent a Haitian identity, no matter their legal status, many Haitian immigrants and their children have learned to look to Haiti as a home base within a hostile world. As Immacula, a woman who arrived illegally in the United States by small boat but who finally won legal immigrant status told me, "No matter what your citizenship is, they always see you as Haitian."

This understanding of the continuity of Haitian identity is shared by impoverished Haitians who never left Haiti. It appears in the efforts of Edner, the unemployed painter in the opening vignette, to define Haitian identity. In the same research, another Haitian man—age sixty-six, also unemployed and dependent on remittances—explained that Haitian identity transcends legal citizenship: "Haitians could go abroad and see there are opportunities and in order to get those opportunities he should become a citizen [of the U. S.]. But that doesn't mean that he abandoned his country."

Almost as if reading from the same script, a third man, whose children send remittances from the United States, explained: "There are those who go there and naturalize themselves and become citizens of the country which they are living in but they never forget their country. ...[Even if he is an American citizen] he is always a Haitian; the blood remains Haitian."[7]

For Haitians, the current construction of the transnational nation-state revitalizes a deeply rooted ideology of race that was forged in the Haitian revolution when Haiti was defined as a black nation. However, the language of blood that defines an enduring Haitian identity is not a static cultural survival. It is an ideology of identity that emerges from the Haitian historical experience, and it is constantly being renewed by the conditions that Haitians face at home or abroad. It is within an Americanization process that continues to define immigrant labor in racialized terms that unemployed workers living on remittances in Haiti (such as Edner) and "boat people" who have been able to settle in the United States (like Immacula) welcome the current efforts of Haitian political leaders to reconstruct Haiti as a transnational nation-state.

However, it was not until the 1990s that these transnational connections were recognized, legitimated, and celebrated by Haitian political leaders. In 1991, Haitians in the United States were designated part of "The Tenth Department" of Haiti with the implication that the diaspora was now part of the Haitian state. The territory of the Haitian state is divided into nine geographic divisions called "departments." The designation of a "Tenth Department" gave public recognition to the participation of Haitian immigrants in political processes that affect Haiti, including lobbying, demonstrating, and organizing in the United States. Over the years, increasing numbers of Haitians have decided to become U. S. citizens, such that, in 1994, 40 percent of the Haitians with permanent resident visas who had completed the requisite period of time necessary for citizenship became naturalized U. S. citizens.

Haitian leaders are not alone in re-envisioning their country as a transnational nation-state. Faced with a situation in which significant sectors of their populations have migrated but established familial, economic, religious, and social relations with persons left behind, political leaders of labor-sending states such as Haiti have begun to look to their diasporas for economic and political support. The leaders of these labor-sending states find that although their states are formally equal to the core capitalist states within the interstate system, they actually are economically penetrated by international banking and financial interests and are politically dominated by the United States. These leaders respond by following a political strategy of activating their diasporas within the United States. To reach out and mobilize their diasporas, leaders employ an ideology of descent that links immigrants and their descendants to the state. The politics of identification, a form of cultural politics, is thought to be rooted in biology.

In a world in which the U. S. has emerged as the dominant political force in a new world order, political leaders of states that send or have sent significant populations to the United States see their transmigrants living in the U. S. as sources of political capital as well as of remittances. Consequently, nation-states that include the Dominican Republic, Portugal, Colombia, Mexico, Greece, the Philippines, and Haiti are developing both an ideology and the institutions of a transnational nation-state (Basch et al. 1994; Feldman-Bianco 1992, 1995; Grahm 1997; Guarnizo 1997, 1998; Guarnizo and Smith 1998; Sanchez 1997; Smith 1997, 1998).[8] Citizenship in these states becomes defined not in terms of culture or even by legal documents but in terms of ancestry. It is a form of citizenship of blood, capable of linking together people who live embedded in numerous other nation-states and tying them to the land of their ancestors. By transforming their definition of citizenship into one that is rooted in biology, these emigrant-sending countries are adopting a view of citizenship that is also being used by some European states. Germany has a history of citizenship laws based on blood, and France has adopted a principle of *jus sanguis* (the law of blood).[9]

THE U. S. RESPONSE

The United States is responding in a complex manner to the contemporary forms of immigrant transnationalism and the efforts of immigrant-sending countries to form deterritorialized nation-states. The economic realignment of the world forms the context of the refashioning of contemporary transnational migrants into U. S. citizens. Loyalty to the United States continues to be demanded but in a context in which immigrant transnational connections become instruments of economic as well as political penetration, which serve the interests of major multinational corporations that use the U. S. as a staging area. Policies that range from the restriction of immigration to multicultural education are moving to insure immigrant identification with the U. S., even as immigrants are enlisted in the extension of the interests of U. S.-based multinational capital into the state processes of other nation-states around the world.

The 1994, passage of the General Agreement on Trade and Tariffs (GATT), California's Proposition 187, and recent federal legislation that denies vital services to undocumented immigrants are a matched set of policy initiatives. GATT further dismantles the national economy by facilitating access of U. S. based firms to the cheap labor and unregulated working conditions of Mexico. It is another step in the globalization of production which in the past two decades has meant worsening economic conditions for 80 percent of the population in the United States. Low wage jobs without benefits have been accompanied by the reduction of real wages and the shifting of the tax burden from corporations and the wealthy to the middle and working classes. In the context of the rearrangement of conditions of employment and taxes to benefit the growth of multinational corporations, and simmering public anger, politicians and the media have projected a bunker mentality, convincing the majority of the population that there still is a national economy and that the worsening systems of health and education that they experience are caused by the burdens of excessive immigration. United States citizens, including people who are themselves immigrants, are being rallied to defend the national borders against the undocumented workers who are said to be the cause of the deterioration of the infrastructure and the lack of public services.

The strategy of U. S. hegemonic forces forming a national consensus by depicting immigrants as enemies of the nation is not new. What have been somewhat different are the political rhetoric and policies that do not halt immigration, but rather draw distinctions between legal residents and naturalized citizens. In the debate in California concerning Proposition 187—the law that denies crucial public services such as education and health care to the undocumented—legal residents were distinguished from the undocumented. The debate was as much about confining immigrant loyalties to the United States as it was about reducing the flow of immigration. Documented immigrants were drawn into the debate on the side of enforcement, validating their right to belong by differentiating themselves from other immigrants.

A dialectic between inclusion and exclusion is developing that disciplines and subjugates transnational migrants by focusing public attention on the degree to which they belong in the United States. Transnational connections themselves are not in question. Rather, the question is to which nation-state the immigrant, embedded in both home and host society, will be loyal. With which nation-state will the immigrant identify? Which national destiny will the immigrant see as his or her own? The attacks on illegal aliens prompted those who are documented to take a public stance of identifying themselves as law-abiding, tax-paying residents or citizens. They learned to accept the construction of the U. S. nation-state as a bounded structure of laws and institutions.

The stakes were raised, however, in 1995 and 1996 on both the state and federal levels with policy initiatives and laws that excluded legally documented residents as well as the undocumented from public services. Immigrants have responded by applying to become U. S. citizens in record numbers. As in the past, this side of Americanization provides a certain level of socialization, requiring immigrants to learn more about the U. S. Constitution and history than most high school graduates currently have mastered. Moreover, in the course of the naturalization ceremony, the new citizens are asked to abjure all foreign loyalties and to swear allegiance to the United States. Although this oath can no longer be enforced in a court of law, it is a dramatic symbolic statement of enrollment of the new citizen in the U. S. body politic.

Some versions of the present-day Americanization process are being coupled with the vision of an expanding cultural citizenship, so that the U. S. is projected as a multiracial/cultural society. Multiculturalism is an ideology that builds identification with the U. S. nation-state, even as it recognizes differentiations within the body politic and links those lines of difference to notions of race. But these colors are not only the fabric of America, they are the many colors of capitalism (Mitchell 1993:263).

U. S. multiculturalism is being accorded a role in the armory of weapons utilized by several different sectors of U. S.-based transnational capitalists in their efforts to compete globally. The situation in Florida is indicative of a larger trend. On the one hand, political leaders in Florida have been targeting illegal aliens, calling national attention to the issue by suing the federal government for 1.5 billion dollars to recover state expenses for providing services to the undocumented (Sun-Sentinel 1994:3S). At the very same time, immigrants are seen as providing new economic opportunities to Florida, exactly because they represent transnational connections to global markets. In the past decade, Miami has conducted 26 billion dollars worth of trade with Latin America, not counting tourism (Sun-Sentinel 1994:6S). According to Lt. Governor Buddy Macaw, "south Florida will increasingly benefit from its growing presence as the de facto capital of Latin America if it embraces its growing international makeup. Florida's future lies in looking south and outward, and not north and inward. We've got this huge opportunity and we've got to take steps...to capitalize on it" (Sun Sentinel 1994:9S).

That this economic strategy has a cultural agenda is made clear by this special section of the southern Florida newspaper, the *Sun Sentinel,* in which Macaw's comments were highlighted. Within this special section a story entitled "U. S. Strategy: End Illegal Tide, Tap New Potential" reports on a symposium of "legislators, academics and immigration officials" who were brought together by the newspaper to advance initiatives for "better managing immigration." The *Sun Sentinel* went on to say, "the children of immigrants, comfortable in both cultures and benefiting from an American education, will be the key to that opportunity, even if today's immigrants are less inclined than previous generations to blend into the homogenous American landscape" (1994:9S).

A similar discourse about culture and profitability is emerging in California and Hawaii. Asian American transnational ties are recognized and valued as long as it is clear that these ties are use for the interests of U. S.-based capital. Aihwa Ong has documented this phenomena in her interviews with corporate executives who had seen Chinese Americans and multiculturalism as part of their corporate strategy. She reports that "Corporate America views Asia as the source of specific economic and cultural capital that, embodied in Asian American, can be converted into forces against Asian-Pacific economic ascendancy" (Ong 1993:766).

The head of the Dole Corporation, a company with investment in more than 50 countries, provides us with an example of this current form of logic when he extolled the value of executives who can operate in China but are U. S. citizens. "This knowledge and ability can help Americans achieve political and business success in the region...Much of their insight and ability can help in opening doors for the U. S. to build a new structure for peace in the Pacific" (cited in Ong 1993:766). Note the way in which this executive conflates the interests of his transnational corporation with those of all "Americans," as well as the way in which he constructs persons of Chinese descent as both as Americans and racially/culturally different. Multicultural Americans become useful human capital in competition with Asian-based corporations. In other settings, transmigrants who are well incorporated in the U. S. are increasingly becoming major players in the ministries of various other nation-states. Often they have been educated in U. S. universities and, while living again in their home countries, own houses, maintain family networks, and participate in organizational structures in the United States. For example, many of the ministers of the Aristide government, and of the Preval government that replaced it, have been transmigrants embedded in either the United States or Canada as well as Haiti.

CONCLUSION

In this paper I have explored the unheralded relationship between the past transnational projects of immigrants and the processes of Americanization. I first argued that transnational political projects contributed to a drawing of racial lines that excluded all but European immigrants from an American identity. I then suggested that the transnational projects of contemporary immigrants of color are linked in important but unmarked ways to the efforts to construct a racially diverse but patriotic American work force under the rubric of multiculturalism.

This transnational identity-making is a complex form of U. S. nation-state building that exists in a realm outside of classic theories of the nation-state and of standard conceptualizations of the process of Americanization and racial and ethnic formation. The national identities of European immigrants are usually placed under the rubric of ethnicity. Their ties to homelands are viewed as lingering sentimentality among persons who are understood to be White American or U. S. ethnics. It is more historically accurate to see U. S. white ethnic identities as a product of transnational connection and racial differentiation. The myths of past migrations have influenced the ability of both scholars and immigrants to analyze the way in which transnational connections have been linked to past and contemporary processes of U. S. nation-state building processes. It was because my perceptions of the present were shaped by the Americanization narrative of the past that I could not make sense of the All Americans Council of the Democratic Party. Many of the men I met were generally not first generation immigrants. Yet they still had a sense of connection to homelands in Europe. Moreover, they did not just seem to be parading their ethnic heritage as a means of getting votes in U. S. elections. What I found unsettling, although I did not at the time delve further, was that I sensed connection to transnational political processes, not just sentimental imaginings of the native land. At the same time that the myth of the European immigrants who have abandoned their homeland and embraced their new nationality was being popularized, the old ties of nationality were being selectively fostered. Furthermore, Haitian immigrants were being encouraged by the Democratic Party in their project of not being black twice. They were encouraged to see themselves not as part of the embattled African American population but as a separate nationality with a different destiny.

The post-1965 U. S. immigrants, exemplified here by Haitian immigrants, are learning and adopting the strategy of separating themselves out from the social location of blackness by embracing a transnational connection to nationalist projects back home. However, they will not obtain the social mobility and incorporation into the mainstream that previous generations of immigrants realized through this strategy. The present moment is one of vast global economic restructuring of capitalism that is affecting the way in which all sectors of the population are incorporated into U. S. society. In this global context, there is less incentive to invest in entire national economies. It has become more profitable to base global operations in certain cities and regions that are emerging as centers of communication and organization (Sassen 1991). Capitalists have less interest than in the past in fostering investment in the infrastructure of nation-states, and hinterlands are increasingly stripped of infrastructures. Workers, managers, and professionals in all countries of the world find themselves competing in a global market place.

Yet it is also becoming clear that the increased intensity of global economic processes is not causing states to wither away since they remain repositories of varying degrees of armed might and still serve as base areas for competing transnational corporations (Panitch 1997). Moreover, although transnational corporations are global in the dynamics of their investment, communication, coordination, staffing, production, and distribution, they rely on the legitimacy and legal, fiscal, and policing structures of nation-states.[10] In addition, the task of creating capitalist subjects—that is, the task of governing populations who will work in and accept the world of vastly increased inequalities of wealth and power,—continues to reside primarily in different and unequal states into which the globe is divided. And it is here, especially when we examine the emerging ethnographies of transnational migration, that the nation-state and the dominant classes within these states make their appearance as veteran performers with revitalized class acts (Williams 1989).

Challenging us to reflect on the history of discourses of identity, Rouse (1995:362) has urged scholars to look at the ways in which class relations and the "politics of identification" are inextricably entwined. He notes that dominant classes engage in efforts to "frame the ways in which people understand what it is to be a person, the kinds of collectivities in which they are involved, the nature of the problems that they face, and the means by which these problems can be tackled" (Rouse 1995:356). Together with scholars such as Richard Handler and Katherine Verderey, Rouse reminds us that a preoccupation with personal and political identities is not a universal human experience but rather an aspect of a Foucauldian regime of truth of "a taxonomic state" (1995:362). However, if the politics of identification are not universal they are central to the nation-state building project that came to be known as Americanization. The challenge to contemporary scholars of Americanization is to acknowledge the transnational social and political relationships within which this form of cultural politics developed and continues to be shaped.

ACKNOWLEDGEMENTS

Earlier versions of this paper were delivered at the conferences "Americans Becoming, Becoming American," sponsored by the Social Science Research Council, January 1996; "Transnational Identities" at the University at Albany (SUNY), March 1996; and "Rethinking Americanization: Transnational Migration, Ethnicity and Citizenship in the Twenty-First Century," University of California at San Diego, May 1996. I would like to thank Josh DeWind, David Gutierrez, Stephen Reyna and Liliana Goldin for the encouragement to develop these ideas and Georges Fouron for his continuous intellectual support and generosity. The paper builds on an analytical framework for the study of migration that I jointly developed with Cristina Szanton Blanc and Linda Basch. My thanks to Patricia Pessar and Gaddis Smith and the Mellon Foundation for a fellowship year at the Global Migration Project of Yale University, which provided me with financial support and a compatible academic environment in which to finish this paper, and to Lucie Plourde for technical assistance.

NOTES

1.   Sometimes, as in the history of Haiti, populations that find it difficult to identify with the state (i.e., the political apparatus of the nation) because of its coercive and oppressive nature or its remoteness still may consider themselves part of the nation. However, even rural populations who resist an oppressive state may have a theory of the state and make demands against the state.

2.   Read in this context, the laws that excluded Asians, Native Americans, and Mexicans from U. S. citizenship and from intermarriage with Europeans were part of the process of the shaping and disciplining of the white working class.

3.   This was also true for many other regions of the world including Turkey and South China.

4.   It should also be noted that Park reported that these transnational connections stretched in all directions. He saw Mexican, Canadian, and Greek (whom he classified

as non-European) as well as European immigrants participating in transnational nation-state building once they had settled in the United States. Also significant is Park's reference to "racial and national solidarity." He wrote at a time when national identities were seen as racial (Glick Schiller and Fouron 1997).

5.   The extent to which home country nationalism was experienced differently by men and women needs further investigation. Patriotic activities directed to the home country did involve women, although men assumed the leadership roles in most organizations. Both men and women participated in transnational family relations; both experienced alienation from the process of production and racialization although the organization of the workplace and racism were gendered.

6.   See Sassen (1996) and Mittleman (1997) for some important steps beyond Harvey (1989).

7.   The rhetoric of common blood, it should be pointed out, has also been used by the majority of the population in their struggle against the elite who defined themselves as mulatto and hence superior to the darker skinned Haitian majority. One of the men living on remittances cited above explained: "If I cut myself and also they cut themselves the blood would be the same color. But because they are looking at the skin color they are saying there is mulatto and black. But in reality we are the same nation of the same color, black, and we are the same blood."

8.   This process is not confined to the United States, however. In the Greek Macedonian dispute, persons who originated from the area were used by political leaders in Greece and the former Yugoslavia to obtain legitimacy for political projects as well as capital for these projects (Danforth 1995; Karakasidou 1994).

9.   The Germans use their definition of citizenship both to exclude those of Turkish descent born in Germany and to legitimate the rights of so called "ethnic Germans" who were born in regions of the former Soviet Union. The adoption by the French of the principle of *jus sanguis* helps them to exclude the descendants of immigrants of color from citizenship.

10.   Appaduarai (1993) has made a similar point but does not include military and police functions.

REFERENCES CITED

Alba, Richard D.
   1990   *Ethnic Identity: The Transformation of White America.* Yale University Press, New Haven.
Alexander, June Granatir
   1987   *The Immigrant Church and Community: Pittsburgh's Slovak Catholics and Lutherans, 1880-1915.* University of Pittsburgh Press, Pittsburgh.
Basch, Linda, Nina Glick Schiller, and Cristina Szanton-Blanc (editors)
   1994   *Nations Unbound: Transnational Projects, Postcolonial Predicaments, and Deterritorialized Nation-States.* Gordon and Breach, New York.

Bodnar, John
   1985   *The Transplanted: A History of Immigrants in Urban America.* Indiana University Press, Bloomington.
Charles, Carolle
   1990a   *A Transnational Dialectic of Race, Class and Ethnicity: Patterns of Identity and Forms of Consciousness Among Haitian Migrants in New York City.* Ph.D. dissertation, Department of Sociology, State University of New York, Binghamton.
   1990b   Distinct Meanings of Blackness: Patterns of Identity among Haitian Migrants in New York City. *Cimarron* 2(3):129-138.
Cinel, Dino
   1991   *The National Integration of Italian Return Migration, 1870-1929.* Cambridge University Press, Cambridge.
Danforth, Loring
   1995   *The Macedonian Conflict: Ethnic Nationalism in a Transnational World.* Princeton University Press, Princeton.
Feldman-Bianco, Bela
   1992   Multiple Layers of Time and Space: The Construction of Class, Race, Ethnicity, and Nationalism Among Portuguese Immigrants. In *Towards a Transnational Perspective on Migration*, edited by Nina Glick Schiller, Linda Basch, and Cristina Szanton-Blanc, pp. 145-174. New York Academy of Sciences, New York.
   1995   The State, Saudade and the Dialectics of Deterritorialization and Reterritorialization. In *Oficina do CES*, Vol. 46, pp. 1-36. Centro de Estudos Sociais (Center for Social Studies), Universidade de Coimbra, Portugal.
Fouron, Georges, and Nina Glick Schiller
   1997   Haitian Identities at the Juncture Between Diaspora and Homeland. In *Caribbean Circuits*, edited by Patricia Pessar, pp. 127-159. Center for Migration Studies, Staten Island.
Fuchs, Lawrence
   1990   *The American Kaleidoscope: Race, Ethnicity, and the Civic Culture.* University Press of New England, Hanover.
Gans, Herbert
   1979   Symbolic Ethnicity: The Future of Ethnic Groups and Cultures in America. *Ethnic and Racial Studies* 2:1-20.
Gellner, Ernest
   1983   *Nation and Nationalism.* Blackwell, Oxford.
Gilroy, Paul
   1991   *There Ain't No Black in the Union Jack: The Cultural Politics of Race and Nation.* University of Chicago Press, Chicago.
Glazer, Nathan
   1954   Ethnic Groups in America: From National Culture to Ideology. In *Freedom and Control in Modern Society*, edited by Monroe Berger, Theodore Abel, and Charles H. Page, pp. 158-173. D. Van Nostrand Company, New York.
Glick Schiller, Nina
   1995   The Implications of Haitian Transnationalism for U. S.-Haiti Relations: Contradictions of the Deterritorialized Nation-State. *Journal of Haitian Studies* 1(1): 111-123.

Glick Schiller, Nina, Linda Basch, and Cristina Szanton-Blanc
   1992   Transnationalism: A New Analytic Framework for Understanding Migration. In *Towards a Transnational Perspective on Migration: Race, Class, Ethnicity and Nationalism Reconsidered*, edited by Nina Glick Schiller, Linda Basch, and Cristina Szanton-Blanc, pp. 1-24. New York Academy of Sciences, New York.
   1995   From Immigrant to Transmigrant: Theorizing Transnational Migration. *Anthropological Quarterly* 68:48-63.
Glick Schiller, Nina, and Georges Fouron
   1997   "Laços de sangue" Os Fundamentos Raciais do Estado-nação transnacional. *Revista Crítica Ciêcians Sociais* 48 (June):33-66.
   1998   Transnational Lives and National Identities: The Identity Politics of Haitian Immigrants. In *Transnationalism From Below*, edited by Michael Peter Smith, and Luis Eduardo Guarnizo, pp. 130-161. Transaction Publishers, New Brunswick, New Jersey.
Grahm, Pamela
   1996   Nationality and Political Participation in the Transnational Context of Dominican Migration. In *Caribbean Circuits: New Directions in the Study of Caribbean Migration*, edited by Patricia R. Pessar, pp. 91-125. Center for Migration Studies, New York.
Guarnizo, Luis Eduardo
   1997   The Emergence of a Transnational Social Formation and the Mirage of Return Migration Among Dominican Transmigrants. In Transnational Processes and Situated Identities, edited by Nina Glick Schiller, Special Issue of *Identities: Global Studies in Culture and Power* 4(2):281-327.
   1998   The Rise of Transnational Social Formations: Mexican and Dominican State Responses to Transnational Migration. *Political Power and Social Theory* 12:45-94.
Guarnizo, Luis Eduardo, and Michael Peter Smith
   1998   The Locations of Transnationalism. In *Transnationalism From Below*, edited by Michael Peter Smith, and Luis Eduardo Guarnizo, pp. 3-34. Transaction Publishers, New Brunswick, New Jersey.
Handlin, Oscar
   1973   *The Uprooted*. Second edition. Little, Brown and Company, Boston.
Hareven, Tamara K.
   1982   *Family Time and Industrial Time: The Relationship Between the Family and Work in a New England Industrial Community*. Cambridge University Press, Cambridge.
Harvey, David
   1989   *The Condition of Postmodernity: An Enquiry into the Origins of Cultural Change*. Blackwell, Cambridge.
Hobsbawm, Eric J.
   1990   *Nations and Nationalism Since 1780*. Cambridge University Press, Cambridge.
Karakasidou, Anastasia
   1994   Sacred Scholars, Profane Advocates: Intellectuals Molding National Consciousness in Greece. *Identities* 1(1): 35-61.

Krickus, Richard
1976   *Pursuing the American Dream.* Anchor Press/Doubleday, New York.
Kula, Witold, Nina Assorodobraj-Kula, and Marcin Kula
1986   *Writing Home: Immigrants in Brazil and the United States 1890-1891.* Edited and translated by Josephine Wtulich, East European Monographs No. 210, Boulder.
Lamphere, Louise
1987   *From Working Daughters to Working Mothers: Immigrant Women in a New England Industrial Community.* Cornell University Press, Ithaca, New York.
Lopez, Ian F. Haney
1996   *White By Law: The Legal Construction of Race.* New York University Press, New York.
Miller, Kirby
1990   Class, Culture, and Immigrant Group Identity in the United States: The Case of Irish-American Ethnicity. In *Immigration Reconsidered: History, Sociology, and Politics,* edited by Virginia Yans-McLaughlin, pp. 96-129. Oxford, New York.
Mitchell, Katharyne
1992   Multiculturalism, or the United Colors of Capitalism? *Antipode* 25:263-294.
Mittleman, James
1996   The Dynamics of Globalization. In *Globalization: Critical Reflections,* edited by James Mittleman, pp. 1-19. Lynne Reinner, Boulder.
Moch, Leslie Page
1992   *Moving Europeans.* Indiana University Press, Bloomington.
Nicholls, David
1996   *From Dessalines to Duvalier: Race, Colour, and National Independence in Haiti.* Revised edition. Rutgers, New Brunswick, New Jersey.
Novack, Michael
1972   *The Rise of the Unmeltable Ethnics.* McMillan, New York.
Omi, Michael, and Howard Winnant
1986   *Racial Formation in the United States.* Routledge, New York.
Ong, Aihwa
1993   On the Edge of Empires: Flexible Citizenship Among Chinese in Diaspora. *Positions* 1:745-778.
Page, Helan
1997a   White Public Space: Routine Practices of Racialized Social Production. Paper presented at the conference *POST-Boasian Studies in Blackness and Whiteness.* New York Academy of Sciences, New York.
1997b   "Black Images", African American Identities: Corporate Cultural Projection in the "Songs of My People".
Panitch, Leo
1997   Rethinking the Role of the State. In *Globalization: Critical Reflections,* edited by James Mittleman, pp. 83-113. Lynne Reinner, Boulder.
Park, Robert
1974a [1925]   Our Racial Frontier on the Pacific. In *The Collected Papers of Robert Ezra Park: Perspectives in Social Inquiry,* Vol. 1, edited by Everett Hughes,

Charles Johnson, Jitsuichi Masuola, Robert Redfield, and Louis Wirth, pp. 138-165. Perspectives in Social Inquiry. Reprint. Arno Press, New York.

1974b [1925]   The Immigrant Community and Immigrant Press. In *The Collected Papers of Robert Ezra Park: Society*, Vol. 3, edited by Everett Hughes, Charles Johnson, Jitsuichi Masuola, Robert Redfield, and Louis Wirth, pp. 152-164. Perspectives in Social Inquiry. Reprint. Arno Press, New York.

Redding, Jack
1958   *Inside the Democratic Party*. Bobbs-Merrill, Indianapolis.

Richardson, Bonham
1983   *Caribbean Migrants: Environment and Human Survival on St. Kitts and Nevis*. University of Tennessee Press, Knoxville.

Roediger, David R.
1991   *The Wages of Whiteness: Race and the Making of the American Working Class*. Verso, London.

Rouse, Roger
1995   Questions of Identity: Personhood and Collectivity in Transnational Migration to the United States. *Critique of Anthropology* 15(4):351-380.

Sanchez, Arturo Ignacio
1997   Transnational Political Agency and Identity Formation Among Colombian Immigrants. Paper presented at the conference *Transnational Communities and the Political Economy of New York*. New School for Social Research, New York.

Sassen, Saskia
1991   *The Global City: New York, London, Tokyo*. Princeton University Press, Princeton, New Jersey.

1996   *Losing Control? Sovereignty in an Age of Globalization*. Columbia University Press, New York.

Schneider, Jo Anne
1994   Fieval is an Engineer: Immigrant Ideology and the Absorption of Eastern European Refugees. *Identities* 1(2-3):227-248.

Sendelbach, Sara
1967   The All Americans Council: A Study of the Role of the Ethnic Group in Partisan Politics. Unpublished manuscript, Paper submitted for the Washington Semester of the School of Government and Public Administration, The American University, May 1967.

Smith, Robert
1997   Transnational Migration, Assimilation, and Political Community. In *The City and the World: New York City' Global Future*, edited by Margaret Crahan, and Alberto Vourvoulias, pp. 110-132. Council on Foreign Relations, New York.

1998   Transnational Localities: Community, Technology and the Politics of Membership within the Context of Mexico-U. S. Migrations. In *Transnationalism From Below*, edited by Michael Peter Smith, and Luis Eduardo Guarnizo, pp. 196-240. Transaction Publishers, New Brunswick, New Jersey.

Soskin, Rose
1976   The Hungry Child. In *Jewish Grandmothers*, edited by Sydelle Kramer, and Jenny Masur, pp.30-44. Beacon Press, Boston.

Sun-Sentinel
1997   The Price of Freedom: Immigration and Its Impact on South Florida.
        30 October:2S-14S. Miami, Florida.
Takaki, Ronald
1979   *Iron Cages: Race and Culture in 19th-Century America*. Oxford University
        Press, New York.
Thistlewaite, Frank
1964   Migration From Europe Overseas in the Nineteenth and Twentieth Centuries.
        In *Population Movements in Modern European History*, edited by Herbert Moller,
        pp. 73-92. McMillan, New York.
Thomas, William, and Florjan Znaniecki
1958 [1918]   *The Polish Peasant in Europe and America*, 2 volumes. Dover,
        New York.
Tolopko, Leon
1988   *Working Ukrainians in the USA: Book I (1890-1924)*. Ukrainian American
        League, New York.
Vassady, Bella
1982   "The Homeland Cause" as a Stimulant to Ethnic Unity: The Hungarian-
        American Response to Karolyi's 1914 Tour. *Journal of American Ethnic History*
        2(1):39-64.
Vecoli, Rudolph J., and Suzanne M. Sinke
1991   *A Century of European Migrations, 1830-1930*. University of Illinois Press,
        Urbana.
Wakeman, Fredric, Jr.
1988   Transnational and Comparative Research. *Items* 42(4):85-88.
Waters Mary
1990   *Ethnic Options: Choosing Identities in America*. University of California Press,
        Berkeley.
Weed, Perry
1973   *The White Ethnic Movement and Ethnic Politics*. Praeger, New York.
Williams, Brackette
1989   A Class Act: Anthropology and the Race to Nation across Ethnic Terrain.
        Annual Reviews in Anthropology 18:401-444.
Winant, Howard
1994   *Racial Conditions: Politics, Theory, Comparison*. University of Minnesota
        Press, Minneapolis.
Wong, Bernard
1982   *Chinatown: Economic Adaptations and Ethnic Identity of the Chinese*. Holt,
        Rinehart and Winston, New York.
Wyman, Mark
1993   *Round-Trip to America: The Immigrants Return to Europe, 1880-1930*.
        Cornell University Press, Ithaca, New York.
Yans-McLaughlin, Virginia
1982   *Family and Community: Italian Immigrants in Buffalo, 1880-1930*.
        Cornell University Press, Ithaca, New York.

3

Racializing Latinos in the United States

Toward a New Research Paradigm

Suzanne Oboler

"Personally, I prefer 'Latino'."
"Well, I personally prefer 'Hispanic'."

—From a dialogue between two "Latino" college students, Spring 1995

> Certainly there are very real differences between us of race, age, and sex. But it is not those differences between us that are separating us. It is rather our refusal to recognize those differences, and to examine the distortions which result from our misnaming them and [from] their effects on human behavior and expectation.

—Audre Lorde (1988:353)

Are we Hispanics or Latinos in the United States? "I prefer Latino [or, 'I prefer Hispanic']. But I don't really know which term I should use." I have heard this question many times since I first began to study the meaning and social value of ethnic labels and the social and political issues they raise in the United States. Generally speaking, there is no ready answer to it. After all, the ethnic label Hispanic only began to be widely disseminated by state agencies after 1977, when it was officially created by Directive 15 of the Office of Budget and Management (Forbes 1992; Hayes Bautista and Chapa 1987). The alternative term, Latino, was adopted by grassroots social movements in the mid-1980s and is used today by certain, but by no means all, sectors of the population of Latin American descent in some regions of the United States. The main difference between the labels is that, unlike the term Latino, the ethnic designator Hispanic *officially* identifies people of Latin American and Spanish descent living in the United States today.[1] Before the 1970s, people of Latin American descent were not officially homogenized into one ethnic group, nor were they identified as such by the state. This official categorization has had serious implications for "Latinos" born after 1970. Unlike earlier generations, and regardless of either the historical period or manner in which their respective national origin groups were incorporated into U. S. society, people born and/or raised in this country after 1970 are the first genera- tion to be specifically designated by mainstream institutions as "Hispanics" in the United States. The same is true, of course, for the other population groups who, in the 1970s, were also aggregated under officially created ethnic labels such as Asian American, Native American, African American or White European.

In other words, as Michael Omi and Howard Winant's (1986) "racial for- mation" framework suggests, the historical conjuncture in which the question "What are we?" is asked changes the meaning and value of the label, whether "Hispanic" or "Latino." Moreover, people's decisions to adopt and use particu- lar names and ethnic labels are also shaped by the ways that social, gender and racial issues are articulated in the particular region where they live.

Still, regardless of historical and regional particularities, as Audre Lorde suggests above, there is no doubt that ethnic labels do create distortions and that labeling as a social process affects both human behavior and expecta- tions. Using the term Hispanic as a case study, the purpose of this paper is to examine the consequences of ethnic labels in shaping the identities, behaviors and expectations of "Latinos" and "non-Latinos" in the United States. My aim is to suggest that the current understanding of diversity in U. S. society has been shaped through an emphasis on ethnic labels that homogenize identities, instead of through an emphasis on citizenship rights which, by their very na- ture, designate and affirm difference. In the following pages, I will first provide a brief background on the construction of the contemporary meanings and val- ues of ethnic labels. This will serve as context for my later discussion of some of the difficult issues raised and obscured by the use of labels. In the conclu- sion, I suggest new avenues for exploring what I argue here is the continuing fundamental issue that structures the arena of identity politics in the United States: the persistent problem of racism in U. S. social dynamics (Gregory and Sanjek 1994; Winant 1994).

WHY ASK THE QUESTION AT ALL?

What is the relevance of the question, "Are we 'Hispanic' or 'Latino'?" It is not self-evident that these umbrella designations are even valid given the diversity of the populations of Latin American descent in the United States, and the structural and sociopolitical differences within the "Latino" community. As a census group or a statistical aggregate, for example, "Hispanics" do not share a common experience of a long history in the United States: some have been here for over a century; others only began to arrive in large numbers during the 1980s. "Hispanics" include descendants of conquest, like sectors of the Mexican American populations in the Southwest who have been U. S. citizens since 1848 (Acuña 1988; McWilliams 1990). It also includes colonized people in the United States, such as Puerto Ricans who had U. S. citizenship imposed on them in 1917 (Meléndez and Meléndez 1993), although the population on the island still do not have the right to vote in national elections. But the labels Hispanic and Latino also combine these native-born U. S. citizens with immigrants from, for example, Mexico, Panama, Costa Rica, the Dominican Republic, and various South American countries—immigrants who may have crossed the border twenty years ago, last year, or even yesterday in search of jobs or a better standard of living.

These labels bring together recent political refugees, like the Guatemalans and Salvadorans, with older political exiles, such as the first wave of Cubans who began to arrive in the early 1960s. In addition, there are political exiles who have now become economic immigrants, for example, sectors of the Nicaraguan population who settled in Miami and California during the 1980s. Moreover, for many people in this country, Brazilians are considered to be "Hispanics," even though Brazilians do not necessarily consider themselves as such, since they neither speak Spanish nor share the Spanish colonial heritage of Latin America. We also have to consider that when we use the terms Hispanic and Latino, we may be overlooking the many different linguistic, ethnic and racial categories in each Latin American country: the various indigenous people, the descendants of enslaved African populations, and the waves of immigrants to Latin America from every country in Europe, Asia, Africa, and the Middle East. Representatives of all of these Latin American groups are coming to the United States. As soon as they cross the border into this country, they become "instant Hispanics" in the eyes of the dominant society, but not necessarily in their own, given the often negative connotations attributed to the term.

My point is *not* that "Latinos" have absolutely nothing in common when they come to the United States. They are, after all, rooted in Latin American history and traditions and, in spite of their distinct national experiences, their nations do share a history of hemispheric political and economic relations between Latin America and the United States that dates back to the Monroe

Doctrine of 1823. Many "Latinos" believe that beyond language and culture, this historical relationship between Latin America and the United States is one of the main factors influencing the construction and affirmation of their cultural identity in this country. It is a relationship which goes beyond individual national histories of conquest, economic exploitation, colonization and political dictatorships (Hayes Bautista and Chapa 1987).

I certainly believe that there are general political, cultural and linguistic commonalties that differentiate people with ties to Latin America from other population groups in U. S. society. On the other hand, I am also aware that people in Latin America also share an equally long history of power relations that organize deeply hierarchical societies and traditions within Latin America. These relations account for profound historical differentiations among various sectors and groups *within* their nations, and are specific to them. Along with their national specificities, each group also brings social, gender, racial, ethnic, linguistic and religious traditions and values from its respective country. These differences have also been a serious obstacle to unifying Latin America since the first republics were forged in the early 1800s (Oddone 1987).

It could be argued that both at home and abroad, Latin Americans' identities have always been characterized by a creative and often conflict-ridden tension between their commonalties and differences. Thus, I suggest, on the one hand, that the search for an all-encompassing self-identity in the United States context is certainly a legitimate and desirable one, given the present political dynamics of U. S. society. But, on the other hand, it seems to me that in the legitimate effort to find such an umbrella term, "Latinos" and "non-Latinos" alike run the risk of neglecting to think about that creative tension between commonalties and differences.

Therefore, I think we have to take a step back and look at the meanings and social values of ethnic labels today, so that we can assess how they are actually shaped and by whom. These questions are prerequisite to discussions of what term, if any, should be adopted and what it means to be "Latino" or "Hispanic" in the United States today. Moreover, addressing these questions may also point to new research directions for scholars and students interested in the fields of Latino Studies and Latin American Studies—in short, in the construction of the study of the Americas as a field of inquiry.

Given the diversity within Latin America, and the almost 200 year search for an identity begun by Simón Bolívar, followed by others such as José Martí, my point of departure for understanding this homogeneous "Hispanic" identity is that *it is a product of the United States*: the label Hispanic has indeed been "Made in the U.S.A." In view of the complex history of Latin America, and in spite of some identifiable language and cultural commonalties that perhaps transcend national boundaries, neither "Latino" nor "Hispanic" is an identity ready-made that can be brought to the United States. Therefore, we cannot look for the meaning or social value of the ethnic labels Hispanic or Latino either in contemporary Latin American history and society, or in the colonial legacy of Spain in the Americas. Instead, we have to look for its origins, its meaning and social value, in the racial and ethnic history of the United States and in the debates on terminology as these have been constructed and publicly articulated in the history and context of this country.

WHO IS CONSTRUCTING THE "HISPANICS"?

Two parallel processes of identity construction and affirmation have long been at work in this country. The first is the process of cultural and linguistic affirmation among "Latinos" in the U. S. context, which, of course, is not new. The second is the construction of the "Hispanic" group by the state and social institutions of the United States. Turning first to the process of cultural and linguistic affirmation, it is certainly true that people of Latin American descent have lived in what is now the Southwest, California, Florida and other parts of the country for centuries. Like many "Latinos" today, they also forged their own real *and* "imagined" communities in the United States, with clear recognition of their ties to specific Latin American regions and countries. Writers such as Bernardo Vega (1984), for example, have chronicled the mutual support of sectors of the Cuban and Puerto Rican populations who lived in the United States during the nineteenth century and collaborated in the struggle for the independence of their respective islands from Spain (Sánchez Korrol 1983). Similarly, researchers have documented the multiple community organizations of Mexicans, Mexican Americans, and others of Latin American descent throughout the Southwest and California. These self-help organizations ensured the maintenance of the language and cultures "Latinos" inherited from the Spanish empire in the Americas. They also helped Mexican Americans and Puerto Ricans in their struggle against discrimination and against their persistent exclusion from access to full and equal rights in this society (Acuña 1988; Barrera 1988; Deutsch 1988; McWilliams 1990).

What has changed in the past two decades, then, is *not* "Latinos'" sense of themselves as communities bound by language, by cultural heritage, by an acknowledgment of their Latin American heritage, by the common goal of expanding and protecting the rights of "Latinos," or by the aim of improving their lives and communities' standards of living. Rather, what is at issue is the second process of constructing "Latino" identity I mentioned above: the construction of the "Hispanic population" as a homogenous group by the history, society and social institutions of this country.

The history of homogenizing "Hispanics" goes back to the mid-nineteenth century. During the California gold rush, for example, "whether from California, Chile, Peru, or Mexico, whether residents of twenty years' standing or immigrants of one week, all the Spanish-speaking were lumped together as interlopers and greasers" (Pitt 1966:59). From the early nineteenth century to the present day, then, Latin Americans have been unceremoniously and indiscriminately brought together regardless of class, race, or nationality, and homogenized whether under the encompassing label of "Mexicans," "Greasers" or, later, "Spics" (Acuña 1998:119). The difference today is that there is a renewed and different emphasis in U. S. politics on ethnic categories and their changing attributions. The real change since the 1960s is in the nature of the state's allocation and withdrawal of resources, according to the shifts in the social and therefore strategic meaning of ethnic categorization. Hence, it is important not to underestimate the implications of the origins of the ethnic label Hispanic as a *state-created* artifact imposed by state administrative agencies on the population of Latin American descent in the United States.

The term Hispanic actually began to be heard during a period in which Mexican Americans and Puerto Ricans were affirming their presence and identity *at a national level* for the first time in U. S. history; and they were doing so, not in pan-ethnic "Hispanic" or "Latino" terms, but largely in specific cultural, nationalist terms. More specifically, the emergence of the label Hispanic coincided with developments in the Civil Rights era of the 1960s, when racial minority groups fought to affirm their presence as U. S. citizens and to redefine the boundaries of political inclusion in the national community. In one way or another, those participating in the Civil Rights movements expressed their determination to name, to voice, to recognize and to acknowledge both their individual experiences and the collective historical and social trajectories of their communities. This included a double affirmation of the moral and political imperative of participation primarily to themselves, to one another, to their group and, ultimately, to the society as a whole. This affirmation was thus a way of establishing an identity in the public sphere and, consequently, in the struggle to redefine the way the United States was "imagined" as a nation.

In the case of both the Puerto Rican and Mexican American populations, what Richard King (1992) in a different context refers to as the *experience of exclusion* has long been a significant factor in shaping both the histories of the diverse communities and the individual lives of movement participants. Both Mexican Americans and Puerto Ricans joined other minorities in the struggle to reverse their historical invisibility and exclusion from the national public sphere.[2] In the process of demanding its rights, each national origin group rooted itself in cultural nationalism, acknowledged its racial and ethnic heritage, rejected being categorized in the census as "White," and reaffirmed the specific national, cultural and linguistic traditions, values, symbols, and myths that for decades had ensured their respective communities' survival (Klor de Alva 1991; G. Padilla 1991).[3]

In other words, the emphasis on cultural nationalism was important in that, through this strategy, Puerto Ricans and Mexican Americans alike countered stigmatizing stereotypes encapsulated in derogatory and homogenizing terms like "Spic." The strategies that their traditional organizations adopted were articulated with newer forms of mobilization that both emphasized collective values and cultures and responded to the specific local and regional needs of their communities. These strategies helped the participants of these grassroots movements to establish their respective identities in ethnic-national terms, even as they adopted a wide range of liberal, reformist, radical, and separatist strategies in their struggle for citizenship rights.

Sectors of the Puerto Rican community in New York City, for example, participated in Civil Rights hearings (Thomas 1971). Others took part in various community projects, joined political organizations such as the Young Lords Party, and/or participated in various debates and actions aimed at achieving the island's independence (Abramson and Young Lords Party 1971; Rodríguez-Morazzani 1991). Many began to refer to the island by its original *Taino* name, *Borinquen*, and to themselves as *Boricuas*. In short, their emphasis on cultural nationalism focused the national society's attention for the first time on Puerto Ricans *as Puerto Ricans,* on the specificity of their historical experience and, particularly, on the impact of the island's ongoing neocolonial relation to the United States.

A similar case can be made concerning cultural nationalism among the various sectors of Mexican Americans, who were also mobilizing in distinct ways. Rooted in the legacy of the conquest of Mexico's lands, the historical experiences of Mexican Americans have been shaped in both urban and rural contexts, which, consequently, diversified both their movements' constituencies and the respective strategies and aims of their leaders (Hammerback et al. 1985; Muñoz 1989). The pervasive poverty and caste-like status of Mexican Americans in rural areas, for example, led César Chávez and Dolores Huerta to organize the United Farm Workers movement in an effort to end the discriminatory policies against migrant laborers (Chávez 1976; Matthiessen 1969). The Alianza movement, organized by Reies López Tijerina, focused on reappropriating lands stolen from Mexican individuals and small farming communities in the aftermath of the 1846-1848 Mexican-American War (Gardner 1970).

While Chávez and López Tijerina organized in the rural areas, Mexican American students and working class youth, many of whom began to refer to themselves as "Chicanos," organized two different forms of political mobilization to address the urban realities of socioeconomic deprivation and persistent racism that continued to exclude generations of Chicanos from first-class citizenship and equal rights and protection under the law: La Raza Unida Party founded in Texas by José A. Gutiérrez, and the Chicano Power movement led by Rodolfo Corky Gonzales (Muñoz 1989; Rosaldo 1973).

In one way or another, the leaders of these four Mexican American/ Chicano mobilizations incorporated and ultimately redefined the meaning of the cultural values and traditions in their communities—albeit some more overtly and self-consciously than others. By addressing the diversity of Mexican Americans' historical experiences in the United States, it is apparent that their distinct movements each contributed toward establishing the identity and presence of Mexican Americans as a group, that is, as more than a statistical entity in the "national community."

It is important to note that both Puerto Rican women and Chicanas played an active role in organizing the movements of their own distinctive national origin groups. Emphasizing the specificity of women's experience and their role in ensuring the historical survival of their communities and cultural traditions, Chicanas and Puerto Rican women in particular hailed diversity within their communities as a strength, and increasingly challenged the lack of recognition of gender differences within their respective movements. Some actively called for the need to confront the potential divisiveness of difference in forging the growth of their political mobilizations and alliances as a whole (Abramson 1971; A. García 1989). Indeed as some scholars suggest, the inability to acknowledge and negotiate the diversity of gender and racial experiences, along with differences in tactics and political infighting ultimately contributed to the fracturing of both the Puerto Rican and the Chicano movements (Gutiérrez 1993; Marable 1991).

In short, while the distinct demands of Puerto Ricans and Mexican Americans were rooted in particular historical, sociocultural and political contexts, they had a common strategic reliance on cultural nationalist symbols which forged a broader communal spirit that more clearly defined and strengthened the demands of their particular mobilizations. Ultimately, then, the adoption of cultural nationalism was an important strategy for achieving the acknowledgment of the long and distinct presence of Puerto Ricans and Mexican Americans in the history and society of the United States. In doing so, both Puerto Ricans and Mexican Americans achieved visibility in the public sphere, and thus, gained national attention as citizens with what Hannah Arendt, in a different context, called "the right to have rights" (Arendt 1979:296)—one of which is the right to citizenship *in spite of* particular differences from the mainstream society.

By the mid 1970s, then, there was no doubt that Puerto Ricans like Mexican Americans had established their identities in both ethnic-national terms and as citizens of the United States. As Edna Acosta-Belén (1988:99) suggests, their presence was at least acknowledged in the "national community." Yet it was precisely at this point that the term Hispanic began to be heard. The racial, class, and gender heterogeneity and the very real strategic and ideological differences that women in particular had raised within their respective communities began to be de-emphasized. At the same time, the dissemination of the label gradually obscured the specific roots of each group's particular experiences in the United States. Both Puerto Ricans and Mexican Americans were once again thrown into social invisibility, but this time, their homogenization came in the form of an umbrella term ostensibly aimed at strengthening awareness of "ethnic diversity" within the "national community."

What are the effects on the lives of Mexican Americans and Puerto Ricans almost twenty years after the label Hispanic was coined? There is little doubt about the political solidity or grounding that officially designated categories like "Hispanic" have come to acquire, or of the benefits of affirming "Latinismo" (F. Padilla 1985) in specific political contexts. At the same time, this political reality should not be allowed to obscure, negate, or undermine the acknowledgment of diversity linked to historical specificities of the community. No doubt the emergence of the term Hispanic in the post 1970s period contributed significantly to the increased social visibility of "Latinos" in the public sphere (after all, there is power in numbers!). Nevertheless, the overall effects on the lives of Mexican Americans and Puerto Ricans are perhaps more ambiguous and controversial.

The 1960s' struggles of Puerto Ricans to create national awareness of their second-class "citizenship" status and the situation of Puerto Ricans on the island as well as in New York have been all but forgotten by the national community. To this day, Puerto Ricans continually have to remind the greater U. S. society that, at least juridically, they *are* U. S. citizens and have been since 1917, and that they are decidedly *not* an immigrant population. This is a point which I think cannot be overemphasized.

It is interesting, for example, to take a closer look at the impact that the homogenization and racialization of people of Latin American descent has had on the relationship between Puerto Ricans and other "Latinos." Consider the following two points: on the one hand, the ties between Puerto Rico and the United States are unique within the "Hispanic" community (indeed they are an anomaly in the broader context of the global history of colonialism); on the other hand, the label Hispanic racializes and homogenizes the diverse histories and experiences of all the "Latino" population. Together these two points mean that the ongoing neocolonialism that structures Puerto Rican identity is today shaped *both* in relation to and counter to the label Hispanic coined in the 1970s, *and* in relation to the invented traditions and attributes that have become associated with the term since then. In short, the emergence of the label Hispanic has served to obscure two important and related factors: first, that the specific situation of Puerto Ricans throughout the twentieth century in U. S. political history has structured and shaped the context of the "Latino"

experience in this country, and second, that *Puerto Ricans today are both a part of "Latinos" and "Latinos' Other"*.
The case of Mexican Americans, in this sense, parallels that of the Puerto Ricans. As the oldest and largest national origin group, the historical perception and treatment of Mexican Americans (Acuña 1988) have also significantly shaped the experience of all people of Latin American descent in the United States. Regardless of their time of arrival to the United States or their political status (whether as U. S. citizens, residents, legal immigrants or undocumented workers), as a population group they share both a Mexican national heritage and a concentration on territory that once belonged to Mexico and was annexed by the United States through war. This is not to deny the obvious political, regional, social, generational, religious, racial and gender differences that shape individuals' daily experiences and political positions toward contemporary issues such as undocumented immigration, bilingual education, racism and affirmative action, that directly affect all "Latinos" in the United States.

Still, unlike other "Latinos", as various writers and scholars have noted, the historical memory of conquest means that regardless of citizenship status, all people of Mexican descent in the United States can tie their ethnic identity to territorial belonging (Anzaldúa 1987; Castañeda 1995; Fuentes 1996; Gómez-Peña 1988). Minimally, this raises questions about the contemporary implications of the historical and territorially related ethnic reality that grounds the variety of ways that distinct sectors of Mexican descent coexist, interact, and define their belonging in the broader U. S. society.

What is to be gained, or lost, from the broader society's lack of knowledge about the history of the U. S-Mexican border, or about the varied roles of people of Mexican descent in the development of the nation's economy? To what extent, for example, does this reality justify the recent hunger strikes by Chicano students to create Chicano Studies departments, programs and courses as a means of ending the exclusion of Mexican Americans' history and experience from higher education curricula in the United States? How does the lack of public awareness of the historical and territorially grounded ethnicity of Mexican Americans impact on the possibility of real citizenship—that is, of a national community of social equals in the United States? In fact, the broader society has consistently shown little if any concern over the demeaning treatment and the violation of rights of their fellow U. S. citizens of Mexican descent, who regularly are looked upon and treated as "foreign" presumably because they do not conform to the "White European" image of U. S. citizens. And yet, together with Native American populations, Mexican Americans are the only ethnic group in the United States mainland and among the "Latinos" that has a direct link between ethnic identity and territorial belonging. Again, in view of this specificity, and no less than Puerto Ricans, *Mexican Americans are also both a part of the "Latino" group and "Latinos' Other"*.

In part, the homogenization of "Hispanics" and the embracing of a putative "Hispanic heritage" is the result of the deliberate absence of information about Mexican Americans' historical experience and about the ongoing neocolonial relations between Puerto Rico and the United States. This homogenization is reinforced by the disregard of the implications of the diverse citizenship status of "Latino" groups, and of the impact of racial, social, ethnic, national and linguistic differences among the populations of Latin American descent. As a result, this unexamined "Hispanic Heritage" contributes toward minimizing the distinct social and political experiences of Mexican Americans and Puerto Ricans, makes them interchangeable, and simultaneously equates their distinct experiences with those of more recently arrived Latin American populations (e.g., Argentineans, Paraguayans, Salvadoreans, Bolivians, or any of the other nationality groups currently in the United States). In this context, President Nixon's decision to designate an "Hispanic Heritage Week" in 1969—like the attitudes of Mexican American elites toward the label (Gómez 1992)—is revealing. Nixon's action coincided precisely with the period when Mexican Americans and Puerto Ricans' political and cultural mobilizations affirmed their presence in U. S. society *as two distinct groups,* with two distinct colonial and cultural histories, two distinct socioracial populations, and two distinct historical and political relations to the United States. While further research is needed to fully address this subject, my point here is that the implications and repercussions of this designation were as significant and complex then as they are today (Forbes 1992; Giménez 1989).[4]

For example, one of the most significant aspects of the 1970s Chicano and Puerto Rican student movements was their emphasis on indigenous and Third World legacies. Yet as Jack Forbes (1992) has argued, the proclamation of "Hispanic Heritage Week" neither mentions nor even attempts to acknowledge the primarily mestizo, indigenous and black populations that make up the majority of the Central American nations whose independence Nixon's original proclamation celebrated. Similarly, the Spanish European legacy of "Hispanics" in the New World is emphasized to the detriment of the indigenous and mestizo cultural roots that both the Chicano and Puerto Rican students had stressed in their movements. From the perspective of cultural representations, "Hispanic Heritage Week" has paved the way for what Forbes (1992:67) calls "a conscious effort...to build a *historically European Spanish-based and Spanish dominated group rather than a regional 'Latin' group or a regional 'American' group"*—known today as Hispanics in the United States.

WHAT ARE THE IMPLICATIONS OF THE TERMS?

What are the implications for today of amalgamating 24.5 million people under an official homogenizing label? Does it matter? I would say, yes, it does. There are both positive and negative consequences to the story of ethnic labels. Feeling oneself a member of a group which is 24.5 million strong can be very reassuring and empowering. As Murgia (1991) among others has suggested, this group membership has certainly provided most "Latinos" with a strong sense of who they are in this country and a recognition of commonalties across and beyond specific Latin American nationalities. Indeed, in spite of any problematic meanings and values which the label Hispanic might connote, it has helped to create intergroup alliances as well as to affirm the presence and social significance of "Latinos" both to themselves as individuals and to the society at large.

But what about the stigmatizing side of ethnic labeling? The comments of one individual I interviewed, a black Honduran, illuminate some of the problematic issues within the "Latino" community that the term serves to obscure:

> My language is Garifuna,[5] it's similar to English, and some of the words we use are identical to English words. I speak perfect Spanish because I wasn't brought up with my race. ...Now, I don't get offended when they call me Hispanic, even though I'm not Hispanic. What bothers me is when they call me black, because I don't offend anyone and I don't like it when anyone offends me.

Not only does this "Afro-Honduran" (to use the contemporary U. S. system of ethnic classification) point out that there are different languages within the Hispanic category, his comment also suggests that there are different meanings attributed to the term. He notes for example, that as a Garifuna, he perceives Spanish speakers, regardless of race, as the Other, whether in Honduras or in the United States. And, just as importantly, he reveals the existence of offensive racial distinctions and discrimination within the "Hispanic" community.

Given the diversity among peoples of Latin American descent, it could easily be argued that there is no "generic Hispanic," just as there is no celebrated "average American." Hence, it is perhaps not surprising that the people who debate these racial and ethnic categories in mainstream institutions are constantly confronted by the problem of how to clarify the definition of the Hispanic category.[6] As a result, politicians and policymakers, researchers, statisticians, interest groups, the media, business concerns, and the advertising industry, all attribute different weights to the various constitutive elements (e.g., language, race, class, parents' citizenship and surname) of the label. On the other hand, "Latinos" are also struggling to avoid an inflexible, prejudiced and monolithic classification that directly and, I believe, often negatively, affects their daily lives precisely because it is monolithic.

The problem with the notion of a "Hispanic" ethnic group is that since no one is absolutely certain who or what a "Hispanic" is, the term invariably has strategic and conflicting political, economic and social meanings and values. From the perspective of the dominant society, for example, "'Hispanic ethnicity" is stereotyped as a welfare-ridden, AIDS-ridden, drug-ridden, drop-out ridden, and teenage pregnancy ridden, socioracial category. No wonder some arriving Latin American immigrants shy away from the term and its bearers. From the perspective of business entrepreneurs, "Hispanic ethnicity" identifies a lucrative market segment, a good box office. For politicians, it suggests a significant voting block. (It is important to note that a similar phenomenon occurs in relation to other groups: Asian Americans, African Americans, Native Americans, Jewish Americans, etc.)

So, while the term Hispanic may be empowering, and has certainly made the presence of "Hispanics" visible in the United States, it is also important to ask: What kind of presence and what kind of social visibility does the label Hispanic in fact affirm? What does it obscure? And for what purposes?

Findings from a census report (Goldberg 1997:1, 16) recently documented the decline in income and educational levels of "Hispanics," showing that they have now surpassed African Americans to become the poorest group in U. S. society.[7] This cannot be attributed to the recent large increase in immigration from Latin America for, according to the 1997 National Council of La Raza report, Puerto Ricans are the poorest group within the "Latino" population. What does this imply about the need to look at the specificity of their neocolonial status? As for the educational achievement of "Hispanics," only 9.1% are college graduates and only 60% of "Hispanic" students finish high school compared to nearly 90% of white and black students (Goldberg 1997:16). The drop out rate among Hispanic youths is persistently high at 30% compared to 8% among whites and 13% among blacks (New York Times Online 1998). Moreover, data suggests that third generation Mexican Americans have a significantly higher drop out rate and lower self-esteem than their parents (Romo and Falbo 1996).

These new data come at a time when, as Herbert Gans has recently pointed out, there is an ideology of undeservingness that is increasingly tied to difference—particularly, different values and behavior. His critical summary of the findings in the current literature on poverty in the United States suggests the extent to which nineteenth-century perceptions of "the poor" in England, or turn of the century beliefs about the poor in this country, continue to prevail in the broader society:

If poor people do not behave according to the rules set by mainstream America, they must be undeserving. They are undeserving
because they believe in and therefore practice bad values, suggesting that they do not want to be part of mainstream America culturally
or socially. As a result of bad values and practices, undeservingness
has become a major cause of contemporary poverty. If poor people
gave up these values, their poverty would decline automatically,
and mainstream Americans would be ready to help them, as they
help other "deserving" poor people. (Gans 1995:6)

One interesting point the above data raises is the contradictory role that
"Hispanic" plays to reaffirm this ideology of stigmatization in the U. S. context. On the one hand, it is precisely due to the existence of a Hispanic category
that the overall decline in the social and economic status of people of Latin
American descent in this country can be tracked. On the other, the association
between the "ideology of undeservingness" and the "bad values" of the poor
pointed out by Gans, has decidedly negative consequences for "Latinos."
After all, as I have argued elsewhere (Oboler 1995), the politics of the United
States in this hemisphere has historically ensured that regardless of time or way
of arrival, citizenship status, or length of residence, "Latinos" in the United
States are perceived as foreigners. Hence, the fact that "Hispanics" are socioeconomically on the lowest rung of the ladder suggests that they are "poor and
undeserving" because they have values that are foreign to the hegemonic image
of American values and attitudes. In other words, since it is now strategically
equated to "Hispanics", the ideology of "undeservingness" appears to have
become a self-fulfilling prophecy.

Far from being merely a bureaucratic method of social categorization, then,
labels are also a means of social stigmatization—that is, they are *stigmatizing
labels* that ultimately negate and undermine the diversity within the "Latino"
population. For two decades, the term Hispanic has served to throw the specific
history and experience of long time Mexican American and Puerto Rican citizens back into obscurity, and therefore the label appears to have ultimately served
to racialize these groups and hence to deny them their right to difference.
As such, the specificities of the historical exclusion of Puerto Ricans and
Mexican Americans, as well as of the diverse experiences of other populations
of Latin American descent in this country, show that to discuss the U. S. "Latino"
experience today involves both including and specifying the extent to which
their differences and commonalties are affected by their respective group's
historical ties to the United States, to U. S. territory, to their sense of national
belonging and hence to their experience of citizenship. Moreover, it suggests
that the emergence of a U. S. "Latino identity", as distinct from the officially
imposed "Hispanic ethnic group" identity, transcends intra- and intergroup

distinctions. As such, the creation of a U. S. "Latino identity" would involve confronting the dynamics between, on the one hand, the hegemonic homogenization of people of Latin American descent (i.e., their racialization as "Hispanics") and, on the other, the intergroup social histories and struggles against exclusion, class divisions, racial prejudices, etc.

In this respect, generational differences are also important to consider. For along with and beyond the instrumental role the term Hispanic has played in providing the new generation with a sense of empowerment and affirmation, it has also served to focus the main dilemma that young "Latinos" born and raised in the United States confront with respect to both personal and political identities as citizens, and to the meaning that cultural ethnicity acquires in this country. The emphasis at the official level is not on citizenship and rights, as these are officially defined and supposedly guaranteed by birth in this country, but primarily on what is perceived to be one's cultural-qua-racial affiliation to a specific ethnic group. Needless to say, this ultimately undermines the notion of equality and justice under the law. "Latinos" in U. S. society remain "Hispanics" first and foremost—and United States citizens second. In other words, as is the case with all minority groups, "Latinos", generally speaking, continue to be marginalized and perceived as second-class citizens. Indeed, my own observations and discussions with students in various academic settings suggest that "Latinos" of the post-1970s generations can only wonder about their status as U. S. citizens while simultaneously searching for a sense of national belonging and, in some cases, citizenship in other countries (more specifically, in their parents' Latin American nations).

One negative consequence of the emphasis on ethnic labels and identities today seems to be that young "Latinos" cannot root their identity in a nation that, despite their legal citizenship status, denies their right to difference, which homogenizes and lumps them indiscriminately together as "Hispanics," which treats them as "foreign others" and tells them that they are not "really" Americans.[8] Another, of course, is the absence of adequate information about their respective groups' histories and national backgrounds. This knowledge could help them and the society as a whole to better understand the history of this country, and hence to ground the debates on multiculturalism in the nation's historical context, rather than in ideological abstractions that stem largely from the nation's inherited racial and social beliefs. It also could help young "Latinos" to better understand the implications of the historical, cultural and national specificities involved in the struggle for recognition of their rights as U. S. citizens.

The absence of information seems to have resulted in a tendency among the young to set up a "synthetic" Latino ethical norm, the slightest deviation from which becomes problematic. The practical effect of this tendency is that there is little, if any, recognition that identities are always multiple and in flux. Under democratic conditions, personal and/or political, they are always in a process of being and of becoming—rather than just the end product of some external fixed notion of "ethnic authenticity." Ultimately then, what we are currently witnessing on college campuses is a conjunction of history, politics, stereotyping and counter-stereotyping. Along with the development of more Latino Studies programs and courses that introduce students to the scholarship and historical trajectories of "Latinos" in the United States, it is essential that we create greater awareness of the critical role of the school system (greatly responsible to this day for concealing the political status of Puerto Ricans, and for silencing knowledge about the sociohistorical specificity of Mexican Americans and of other populations of Latin American descent in the United States). It is also important to create the political and cultural space for "Latino" students to be able to say "I don't know," when questioned about the histories and cultures of their own or any other group since they were not taught them in schools.

At the same time, beyond providing information on each group, scholars studying U. S. "Latinos" also have to think seriously about alternative approaches to "essentialism" and "authenticity," and to create new research paradigms that shift the direction of the debates on multiculturalism and identity politics. In short, we need to construct a new way of thinking about the problems and values of difference to include considerations about individual groups' identities, their history of struggle for rights, as well as about the affirmation of values of social solidarity beyond ethnicity, gender, and sociocultural differences, as being the values of real citizenship.

WHERE DO WE GO FROM HERE?

For the foreseeable future, ethnic labels such as Hispanic, like Black/African American, Native American, Arab American, Jewish American, Asian American and White European, are here to stay—whether or not they are eventually scrapped as U. S. Census categories or rejected as a means of implementing affirmative action policies. Yet, as I have tried to suggest above, ethnic labels, particularly stigmatizing ethnic labels, not only have increasingly essentialized people's individual identities, but also have functioned to maintain the practice of prejudicial "relativity" with respect to the reality of citizenship. I strongly believe that this "unnatural" relativity, which allows for the persistent second-class status of racial minorities, is ultimately responsible for the ongoing struggle over labels. It seems then appropriate to ask ourselves: Is there no other way of thinking about the question of rights and difference? Are there other ways to approach the question of the right to have equal rights *in spite of* difference?

The acknowledgment of difference as an essential aspect for achieving full citizenship requires thinking about difference in a larger context. In this sense, I suggest that underlying the spiraling weight attributed to difference today is another equally significant crisis—a crisis in the very understanding of national communities, of human collectivities, themselves. In other words, what is increasingly at stake today is *not only* the issue of difference itself, but also the whole question of what binds people together into a collectivity. The unprecedented weight currently attributed to difference only makes sense in the context of questioning what does, what should, or actually what could bind people together today. In short, the very prevalence of the notion of difference itself can also be understood as a symptom of the crisis of community and, actually, as a contributing factor to it.

Certainly the contemporary struggle over multiculturalism and cultural diversity can be defined as a concerted effort to confront the crisis of community. In fact, I suggest that it is precisely because these struggles have been taking place primarily in the cultural rather than in the political arena that difference has been privileged over and above the political question of collectivity and citizenship. But, as we have seen, focusing on difference alone is invariably reduced to the individual uniqueness of each *officially designated* ethnic group. It does not take into account either the implications of people's *right* to difference (i.e., to belong in spite of difference within their group) or the inter-relatedness of these groups. Hence, it does away with the very notion of a collectivity and, by extension, of citizenship itself. After all, the very category of citizenship is an acknowledgment of the existence of a community in which the fundamental principles of communal living have been established— in the case of a democratic community, negotiated and agreed upon—ideally, for the benefit of all. From this perspective, it is important to focus more attention on addressing the obstacles to an individual group's access to citizenship rights in the broader terms of the underlying issues (such as racism, sexism, classism, homophobia) that affect social relations in the nation as a whole.

There is no doubt that the homogenizing of "Latinos" and their historical exclusion from full citizenship is indicative of the pervasive racism in the social relations of the United States. From this point of view, the struggle to affirm the presence of "Latinos" in U. S. society, to insist on their right to difference, and to establish their identity as citizens of this nation is key to the struggle against racism. After all, the visibility of human experience, however diverse, *is* a basic condition for affirming belonging, and hence community, whether in a family, a neighborhood or a nation.

Yet, as Howard Winant (1994:2) has cogently argued, "race remains the fundamental organizing principle, a way of knowing and interpreting the social world...in those *milieux* where, historically, race has been foundational—that is in most if not all human societies—its centrality continues, even after the original reasons for invoking it have disappeared." Thus, given the historical meanings still attributed to racial difference in this country, and the ambiguous repercussions of the nation's current census categories on personal identities, it is important to focus on the ways that racial ideologies act as obstacles to the acknowledgment of the existence of community—and in this sense do away with the very notion of citizenship—whether we are referring to "Latinos" or to any other group.

Insofar as racism is a social phenomenon, racial perceptions and practices are inextricably bound to gender, class and social status. As such, "race" is and has always been an eminently political issue that continues to manifest itself in distinct ways in different countries. At the same time, in view of the growing presence and circular migration of people of Latin American descent to and from the United States, it seems increasingly pertinent to ask: To what extent are Latin American racial ideologies penetrating this country through immigration? And if they are, to what extent are they changing the nature of race relations in this country? For example, there seems to be a growing acceptance of the notion of racial mixture, *mestizaje*, in the United States, visible in the recent debate on making "multiracialism" a census category in the year 2000 (Marriot 1996; L. Wright 1994).

Yet, as various authors have noted, *mestizaje* has long perpetuated class-based, caste-like socioracial hierarchies in the national societies of Latin America (Hale 1996; Minority Rights Group 1995; W. Wright 1995). Tied to what Peter Wade (1985) called a "racial continuum," *mestizaje* has been the key to the Latin American nations' insistence on nationality (i.e., "We are all Colombians" or "We are all Peruvians") as a unifying force, at the expense of social and political equality. While poverty, illiteracy, and other class-related issues are understood in social terms that should be addressed by the society as a whole, racial and ethnic prejudice and discrimination is relegated to the private sphere, and its solution is understood in individual terms: "marry white," "improve the race," and thus contribute to forge and consolidate the nation. This is the way "to pull yourself up by your bootstraps" (Oboler 1996). In other words, the same "ideology of undeservingness" that today is being attributed to nonwhite and poorer populations in the United States, has long characterized the experience of dark-skinned populations in Latin American societies.

In conclusion, insofar as the experience of Latin Americans has shown that "multiracialism" is no guarantee of citizenship in the United States, I would suggest instead that we develop a transnational, hemispheric approach to the articulated issues raised by race, class, gender and generation. This approach could provide one avenue for getting around the "identity politics" conundrum created by the official and social use in this society of ethnic labels such as Hispanic, White European, African American, Asian American, Native American, etc. It would also allow a fuller assessment of the articulating nature of ideologies of racism, and of their impact both on the experience of different groups in the United States and, more generally, on the contemporary relationship between citizenship and national belonging. Whether our field of specialization is Latino Studies, Latin American Studies, or American Studies, this involves acknowledging the effects of transnationalism, globalization, and the immigration of people of Latin American descent to both the United States and throughout the hemisphere (Fernandez Kelly and Portes 1992; Jonas 1996; Rouse 1991; Sassen 1996). More specifically, it entails exploring how these contemporary phenomena are ensuring that the varied and distinct racial ideologies of the societies of the Americas are currently being reconfigured to (re)shape the sociopolitical and daily life of the United States.

NOTES

1.   In shunning the government-imposed designator Hispanic and replacing it with the term Latino, progressive sectors sought to signify both their rejection of the Eurocentric connotations of the label Hispanic and their acknowledgment of the cultural and linguistic commonalties rooted in their Latin American heritage. But as various "Latino" writers have noted in poems, novels, essays, satires, and debates, the term Latino also does not reverse the homogenizing principle of ethnic labels. Moreover, like the term Hispanic, Latino also obscures the indigenous and African influences in Latin American societies, since it does not override the European roots of the continent's languages. In this paper, I use "Hispanic" and "Latino" interchangeably, and use quotation marks when they are not preceded by the words "term" or "label," in order to emphasize that they are socially constructed categories.
2.   On the Mexican American experience in the post-war period see Gómez Quiñones (1991). Two excellent biographical narratives that span much of the current century and discuss the post-war Mexican American struggle for inclusion are Lucas and Buss (1993) and M. García (1994). To my knowledge, there are still no comparable full-length studies of the experience and participation of the Puerto Ricans during the Civil Rights period. For the experience of one sector of this community see Abramson and the Young Lords Party (1971). Some of the issues the Puerto Rican community confronted in New York are raised in Thomas (1971).
3.   Ultimately, of course, as Ramón Gutiérrez (1993) among others has discussed, there were very real limitations to the emphasis on cultural nationalism.
4.   While the actual decision to designate a "Hispanic Heritage Week" is itself a subject in need of research, some researchers (Gómez 1992; Melville 1988) have begun to make inroads to increase our knowledge about the presence of and role of the Mexican American and Puerto Rican political elites and representatives in Congress at that time.
5.   Garifunas are Black Caribs who settled along the Central American coast. According to González (1987:150), "Although generally indistinguishable from other

Afro-Americans, they are unusual in that they speak a South American Indian language and share about one-quarter of their genetic makeup with native Americans."

6.   As J. H. M. Choldin says: "Was it [the "Hispanic" population] to be defined as those persons who had ancestors from Mexico; if so how many ancestors? Was it those persons who spoke Spanish? Or was it those who called themselves Mexican-Americans or some other 'Hispanic' name? What if someone had parents from Mexico but did not consider himself or herself to be Hispanic?" (cited in Giménez 1989:568)

7.   The statistics presented in this recent study are indeed alarming:

> Census data show that for the first time the poverty rate among Hispanic residents of the United States has surpassed that of blacks. Hispanic residents now constitute twenty-three percent of the country's poor, up eight percentage points since 1985. Of all Hispanic residents, thirty percent were considered poor in 1995, meaning they earned less than $15,569 for a family of four. That is almost three times the percentage of non-Hispanic whites in poverty. Of the poorest of the poor, those with incomes of $7,500 or less for a family of four, twenty-four percent were Hispanic. ...Over all, income for Hispanic households has dropped fourteen percent since 1989 to under $22,900, from about $26,000, while rising slightly for black ones. (Goldberg 1997:1,16).

8.   On the political and policy implications of the term Hispanic see Giménez et al. (1992).

REFERENCES CITED

Abramson, Michael, and The Young Lords Party
    1971   *Palante: The Young Lords Party.* McGraw Hill, New York.
Acosta-Belén, Edna
    1988   From Settlers to Newcomers: The Hispanic Legacy in the United States. In *The Hispanic Experience in the United States*, edited by Edna Acosta-Belén, and Barbara Sjostrom, pp. 81-106. Praeger, New York.
Acuña, Rodolfo
    1988   *Occupied America. A History of Chicanos.* Third edition. Harper & Row, New York.
Anzaldúa, Gloria
    1987   *Borderlands/La Frontera: The New Mestiza.* Spinsters/Aunt Lute, San Francisco.
Arendt, Hannah
    1979   *The Age of Totalitarianism.* Penguin Books, New York.
Barrera, Mario
    1988   *Beyond Aztlan: Ethnic Autonomy in Comparative Perspective.* University of Notre Dame Press, Notre Dame, Indiana.
Castañeda, Jorge
    1996   *The Mexican Shock: Its Meaning for U. S.* New Press, New York.

Chávez, César
1976   The California Farm Workers' Struggle. *The Black Scholar* 7(9):16-19.
Deutsch, Sarah
1987   *No Separate Refuge: Culture, Class, and Gender on an Anglo Hispanic Frontier in the American Southwest 1880-1940*. Oxford University Press, New York.
Fernandez Kelly, Patricia M., and Alejandro Portes
1992   Continent on the Move: Immigrants and Refugees in the Americas. In *Americas: New Interpretive Essays*. edited by Alfred Stepan, pp. 248-74. Oxford University Press, New York.
Forbes, Jack
1992   The Hispanic Spin: Party Politics and Governmental Manipulation of Ethnic Identity. *Latin American Perspectives* 19:59-78.
Fuentes, Carlos
1996   *La frontera de cristal: Una novela en nueve cuentos*. Alfaguara, Mexico City.
Gans, Herbert
1995   *The War Against the Poor: The Underclass and Antipoverty Policy*. Basic Books, New York.
García, Alma M.
1989   The Development of Chicana Feminist Discourse 1970-1980. *Gender and Society* 3:217-138.
García, Mario T.
1994   *Memories of Chicano History: The Life and Narrative of Bert Corona*. University of California Press, Berkeley.
Gardner, Richard
1970   *Grito! Reies Tijerina and the New Mexico Land Grant War of 1967*. Bobbs-Merrill, New York.
Giménez, Martha E.
1989   'Latino'/'Hispanic' Who Needs A Name? The Case Against A Standardized Terminology. *International Journal of Health Services* 19:557-571.
Giménez, Martha, Fred A. Lopez III, and Carlos Muñoz (editors)
1992   *The Politics of Ethnic Construction: Hispanic, Chicano, Latino. Special Issue of Latin American Perspectives* 19(4).
Goldberg, Carey
1997   Hispanic Households Struggle Amid Broad Decline in Income. *New York Times* 30 January:1, 16.
Gómez, Laura
1992   The Birth of the "Hispanic" Generation: Attitudes of Mexican-American Political Elites Toward the Hispanic Label. *Latin American Perspectives* 19(4):45-58.
Gómez-Peña, Guillermo
1988   Documented/Undocumented. In *The Graywolf Annual Five: Multi-Cultural Literacy*, edited by Rick Simonson, and Scott Walker, pp. 127-134. Graywolf Press, St. Paul, Minnesota.
González, Nancie
1987   Garifuna Settlement in New York: A New Frontier. In *Caribbean Life in New York City: Sociocultural Dimensions*, edited by Constance R. Sutton, and Elsa M. Chaney, pp.150-159. Center for Migration Studies, Staten Island.

Gregory, Steven, and Roger Sanjek (editors)
1994   *Race*. Rutgers University Press, New Brunswick, New Jersey.
Gutiérrez, Ramón
1993   Community, Patriarchy and Individualism: The Politics of Chicano History and the Dream of Equality. *American Quarterly* 45:44-72.
Hale, Charles R.
1996   Introduction. *Journal of Latin American Anthropology* 2(1):2-3.
Hammerback, John, Richard Jensen, and José Angel Gutiérrez
1985   *A War of Words*. Greenwood Press, Westport, Connecticut.
Hayes Bautista, David, and Jorge Chapa
1987   Latino Terminology: Conceptual Basis for Standardized Terminology. *American Journal of Public Health* 77:61-68.
Jonas, Susanne
1996   Rethinking Immigration Policy and Citizenship in the Americas. *Social Justice* 23(3):69-70.
King, Richard
1992   *Civil Rights and the Idea of Freedom*. Oxford University Press, New York
Klor de Alva, Jorge J.
1991   Aztlán, Borinquen and Hispanic Nationalism in the United States. *Aztlán: Essays on the Chicano Homeland*, edited by Rudolfo Anaya, and Francisco Lomeli, pp. 135-171. University of New Mexico Press, Albuquerque.
Lorde, Audre
1988   Age, Race, Class and Sex: Women Redefining Difference. In *Racism and Sexism*, edited by Paula Rothenberg, pp. 352-358. St. Martin's Press, New York.
Lucas, María Elena, and Fran Leeper Buss (editors)
1993   *Forged Under the Sun/Forjada Bajo el Sol: The Life of Maria Elena Lucas*. University of Michigan Press, Ann Arbor.
Marable, Manning
1991   *Race, Reform and Rebellion: The Second Reconstruction in Black America, 1945-1990*. University Press of Mississippi, Jackson.
Marriot, Michael
1996   Multiracial Americans Ready to Claim Their Own Identity *New York Times*. 20 July:A1, 7.
Matthiessen, Peter
1969   *Sal Si Puedes*. Random House, New York.
McWilliams, Carey
1990   *North From Mexico: The Spanish Speaking People of the United States*. Praeger, New York.
Meléndez, Edwin, and Edgardo Meléndez (editors)
1993   *Colonial Dilemma*. Southend Press, Boston.
Melville, Margarita
1988   Hispanics: Race, Class, or Ethnicity? *Journal of Ethnic Studies* 16:67-83.
Minority Rights Group (editor)
1995   *No Longer Invisible: Afro-Latin Americans Today*. Sage Publications, London.
Muñoz, Carlos
1989   *Youth, Identity, Power: The Chicano Movement*. Verso, London.

Murgia, Edward
1991 On Latino/Hispanic Ethnic Identity. *Latino Studies Journal* 2:8-18.
The New York Times Online
1998 Hispanic Group Pushes Education Fix. http://www.nytimes.com, 21 July.
Oboler, Suzanne
1995 *Ethnic Labels, Latino Lives: Identity and the Politics of (Re)Presentation in the United States.* University of Minnesota Press, Minneapolis.
1996 *The Foreignness of Racism: Pride and Prejudice in Contemporary Lima.* Mimeo, Providence, Rhode Island.
Oddone, Juan A.
1987 Regionalismo y nacionalismo. In *America Latina en sus ideas,* edited by Leopoldo Zea, pp. 201-238. Siglo XXI Editores/UNESCO, Mexico City.
Omi, Michael, and Howard Winant
1986 *Racial Formation in the United States: From the 1960s to the 1980s.* Routledge and Kegan Paul, New York.
Padilla, Félix
1985 *Latino Ethnic Consciousness: The Case of Mexican Americans and Puerto Ricans in Chicago.* University of Notre Dame Press, Notre Dame, Indiana.
Padilla, Genaro
1991 Myth and Comparative Cultural Nationalism: The Ideological Uses of Aztlan. In *Aztlán: Essays on the Chicano Homeland,* edited by Rudolfo Anaya, and Francisco Lomeli, pp. 111-134. University of New Mexico Press, Albuquerque.
Pitt, Leonard
1966 *The Decline of the Californios: A Social History of the Spanish-Speaking Californians, 1846-1890.* University of California Press, Berkeley.
Rodríguez-Morazzani, Roberto
1991 Puerto Rican Political Generations in New York: Pioneros, Young Turks, and Radicals. *Centro Bulletin* 4:102-107.
Romo, Harriet D., and Toni Falbo
1996 *Latino High School Graduation: Defying the Odds.* University of Texas Press, Austin.
Rouse, Roger
1991 Mexican Migration and the Social Space of Postmodernism. *Diaspora* (I)1:8-23.
Rout, Leslie
1976 *The African Experience in Spanish America 1500 to the Present.* Cambridge University Press, New York and Cambridge.
Sánchez Korrol, Virginia
1983 *From Colonia to Community: History of Puerto Ricans in New York City, 1917-1948.* Greenwood Press, Westport, Connecticut.
Sassen, Saskia
1996 *Losing Control? Sovereignty in an Age of Globalization.* Columbia University Press, New York.
Thomas, Piri
1971 Puerto Ricans in The Promised Land. *Civil Rights Digest* 2:7-38.
Vega, Bernardo
1984 *Memoirs of Bernardo Vega: A Contribution to the History of the Puerto Rican*

Community in New York. Edited by César Andreu Iglesias. Translated by Juan Flores. Monthly Review Press, New York.

Wade, Peter
1985   Race and Class: The Case of South American Blacks. *Ethnic and Racial Studies* 8:233-249.

Winant, Howard
1994   *Racial Conditions: Politics, Theory, Comparisons.* University of Minnesota Press, Minneapolis.

Wright, Lawrence
1994   One Drop of Blood. *The New Yorker.* 25 July:46-55.

Wright, Winthrop R.
1995   *Cafe Con Leche: Race, Class, and National Image in Venezuela.* University of Texas Press, Austin.

4

Neither Modern nor Traditional

Personal Identities in Global Perspective

Michael Kearney

The way in which social identities are defined, and indeed often constructed, by social scientists is always due to an interplay between such identities and the state of the social science in question. Of utmost importance in shaping any specific social science tradition is its relationship to the modern nation-state in which it develops. For example, the history of British Social Anthropology is inextricably interwoven with the history of the British Empire within which it for the most part developed, just as the history of American sociology is only understandable within the context of industrialization, urbanization, and city life in the United States in the twentieth century. Thus the thesis that is suggested by such relationships is that as the shape of any particular nation-state within the global context changes, so do such changes condition the character of the social sciences that are embedded within them.

In a recent book, I have taken anthropology as a case in point to illustrate its changing history in relationship to its subjects within the changing national and global contexts in which both are embedded (Kearney 1996). Within this social history of anthropology seen as deeply conditioned by its position within the changing state of the nation-state, I take one specific identity, that of "the peasant," as a case in point. The pages that follow examine the genealogy of the peasant concept in anthropology from its appearance to its present ongoing passing from the anthropological scene and from the social sciences in general; a process that this essay aims to hasten. Throughout this exercise it is thus necessary to maintain a focus on two subjects: one of which is peoples identified as peasants, and the other of which is the anthropology and sister disciplines that so identify them.

THE PEASANT CONCEPT

Within anthropology, peasant and development studies in general, "The peasant" was constructed from residual images of preindustrial European and colonial rural society. Informed by romantic sensibilities and modern nationalist imaginations, these images are anachronisms, but nevertheless robust anachronisms even at the end of the twentieth century. As such, they are appropriate targets for a house-cleaning that clears space for alternative theoretical views.

Evaluation of the peasant concept—its inception, growth, and demise—is inseparable from an evaluation of the broader transnational intellectual context of social anthropology in which it emerged (Kearney 1995a). I will therefore discuss the concept in this context and return to the more narrow issue of development in the conclusion. Although a comprehensive assessment of social anthropology is impossible in this format, I would like to suggest some general features of different phases of the discipline's history, each of which predisposed anthropology to construct its objects of study in characteristic ways. Moreover, this outline of social anthropology's history extends anthropology's holistic purview to encompass the discipline itself. Whereas most intellectual histories establish ideas within the context of their own genealogies and the intellectual pedigrees of their authors, this historical sketch seeks to extend the framing context to recent global history. What is called for in a fully anthropological history of anthropology is not just a situating of ideas within the context of the discipline but also a situating of the discipline within the global context.

In brief then, the thesis is that, as the world changes, rather distinct periods can be discerned, each of which conditions anthropology to construct itself and its subjects in ways distinctive of each such moment. This being so, a fully anthropological assessment of an anthropological category such as the peasant requires reference to this broader historical context. The working assumption underlying this paper is that the present shape of the global context is predisposing social scientists to such a comprehensive reflexivity.

In my estimation the single most incisive statement of the political economy and ideology of "peasants" is Eric Wolf's (1966) book of that title, which provides an important benchmark for subsequent reference. Thus, if we take

Wolf's book as a state of the art in 1966, we can assess what developments have occurred in the intervening thirty some years along the road to the dissolution of the category. I make these comments on Wolf's (1966) *Peasants* having the benefit of more than a quarter of a century distance in time from its appearance, and although I call for a discarding of the idea of the social category it set out to explain, I do embrace the broad outlines of Wolfian historical-structural theory and method.

In *Peasant Wars of the Twentieth Century*, Wolf (1969:xiv) portrays peasants as populations that are existentially involved in and making autonomous decisions about cultivation. The initial formulation of this definition is his landmark "Types of Latin American Peasantry," which establishes three basic criteria of peasants as a social type: (1) primary involvement in agricultural production, (2) effective control of land, and (3) a primary orientation toward subsistence, rather than reinvestment (Wolf 1955:453-454). Invoking these and other criteria, numerous social scientists reify a social category which more often than not has no singular objective ethnographic or class basis. For in reality, the great majority of the world's so-called peasants reproduce themselves within complex economic and social relationships of which autonomous cultivation of a nonfarmer type is relatively unimportant— and increasingly so. Indeed, a glance at rural peoples reveals a plethora of forms not only in the material constitution of their relationships, but also in their self-perceived identities and consciousness. Such manifold identities are most evident in "peasant migrant workers," or "land-owning proletarians" and other such contradictory categories which call into question any theory that reifies the peasantry.

In short, before one attempts to deal with presumed social types such as "the peasant," "the proletarian," or for that matter any such unidimensional identity, one needs to elaborate a critique of social science representations itself. In such a critique, I regard ethnography as literature while simultaneously elaborating an alternative form of representation of the other. As a case in point, I shall apply such a critique to ways in which "the peasant" is constantly reinvented. For such a critique to be anthropologically reflexive it must situate the production and consumption of representations of the peasantry within the relationships that join the anthropological self to "the peasant" other that it presumes to represent. In other words, it is not sufficient to situate only "the peasantry" within a global setting; the conventions, the texts, whereby it is represented must also be so contextualized.

Only with such anthropological reflexivity can we ask and answer such question as why peasant studies within conventional anthropology continue to dwell on questions of peasant rationality, decision-making, personality, and economic differentiation. To note, for example, that theoretically these studies are situated within developmentalist visions of the "peasant community" and that such research is consistent with the methodological individualism that informs it only elaborates variations on the original question.

I hope to develop a more comprehensive, incisive critique that opens the way for alternative views. Likewise, a similar critique must also be mounted of radical peasantology. Classic Marxist studies of the peasantry, as compared to neoclassical and cultural anthropological approaches, have attended to the social issues of class and history, but class defined categorically such that until recently Marxist social scientists had to adopt either a peasant (e.g., Maoist) or proletarian (e.g., Leninist) line of one kind or another. This peasant-proletarian debate has now been largely superseded, but there is still much need of intellectual housecleaning to prepare for postpeasant studies.

At its inception anthropology was distinct from the other Western social sciences in that it was predicated on the difference between the Western anthropological self and the alien ethnographic other epitomized by "the primitive." This difference was constructed on several bases, one of which was the geographic separation between self and other such that the self was in "the West" and the other was located in "non-Western" areas. The other bases of difference were sociocultural and temporal: "Primitive" others were different kinds of peoples because they had technologies and ways of life that were comparable to previous phases in the social evolutionary past of Western society which had "advanced" beyond these "simpler" forms to become modern. Implicit in the definition of the modern is this contrast with the primitive that it has transcended. Just as the modern represents a structural opposition to the primitive, so is it also a historical antithesis that exits at the end point of history, far removed from the distant past of human beginnings.

This oppositional difference between modern and primitive was the axis upon which anthropology was initially constructed and practiced. No wonder, then, that the disappearance of the primitive implied a crisis for anthropology insofar as it was a kind of natural history of "primitive peoples" based on field research. But the crisis was averted in the period following the Second World War by the discovery of another type—"the peasant"—and also by the concomitant emergence in the social sciences of a deep concern with "development" in large areas of the globe that came to be defined as the Third World. Indeed, the peasant was deemed to be the primary inhabitant of the Third World, as attention in anthropology, economics, political science, agronomy, and other disciplines focused on the cultural transformation of these extensive peasant communities to modern societies. The peasant has been a problematic type for anthropology and, to a lesser extent, the other social sciences ever since; problematic not only in a theoretical sense but also with respect to the constitution of anthropology itself.

The initial anthropological construction of oppositional and evolutionary difference between modern and primitive was itself the practice of a distinctly modern sensibility and world view. This style of thought tends to make the continuous discrete and to cast difference into binary oppositions. In this sense such thought is manifest in digital programming and logical positivism, which are both thus structurally consistent with empiricist epistemology, based as it is on a categorical distinction between self and other. Furthermore, such binary, categorical thinking is associated with notions of absolute, bounded space, consistent with the spatial consciousness that informs the formation of modern nation-states (Hastrup and Olwig 1997:4-5). The more general argument here is that this style of binary, but nondialectical, thought is predicated upon and leads to social practices that perpetuate social differentiation, both locally and globally.

The thesis, then, is that "the peasant" is associated with a major development in the history of anthropology—a crisis of sorts—of which the peasant is both symptom and cause. The argument is that the basic structure of classic anthropology is put into place in the late nineteenth and early twentieth centuries. This structure is a dualist world view comparable to that of classic world views, hence its name. But it differs from them in that it is reconstructed within the context of young nation-states, colonialism and imperialism, and assumes forms, such as social evolutionism and positivism, that explain and justify devaluation of non-Western others. A preceding Formative phase culminates in Frazerian anthropology, whereas classic anthropology is associated with the Malinowskian revolution. The Formative period, typified by Frazer's encyclopedic *The Golden Bough*, eclectically assembled bits of ethnographic data from around the world in efforts to reconstruct the broad outline of human social evolution, while Malinowski pioneered the study of entire "primitive" communities in which cultural traits could be examined in their living social context.

Subsequent world events associated with World War II and its aftermath coincide with the end of the Classic period and emergence of modern anthropology, which is distinguishable from classic anthropology by a more pronounced decay of its dualist structure and also by the appearance of the peasant as the new prototypic ethnographic other, which was subsequently essentialized in ways comparable to the way in which the primitive was previously constructed out of its difference with the modern. But the peasant brought with it into anthropology implications for the structure of the discipline that were not implied by "the primitive." For unlike the categorical absoluteness of the primitive, which is the primary conceptual antipode of the modern, the peasant is located on the margin—geographic, historical, classificatory—between them. Because it is marginal it is conceptually ambiguous, and because of this ambiguity the peasant is the most problematic social type within the social typology of anthropology. Turning attention from primitives to peasants saved anthropology as a field-based discipline. But it was an imperfect solution to the degree that the peasant is, categorically, an imperfect social type for modern sensibilities, which think in terms of discontinuous, absolute categories such as subject and object, self and other. Because the peasant relocates anthropological practice and thought to the margins of the modern and the primitive, its appearance within anthropology contributes to the deconstruction of the primary opposi- tional metaphysical categories out of which anthropology invented not only its others, but also itself. Further intentional critical work, such as this essay and the book on which it is based, is but the conscious articulation of this general historic trend.

The peasant as an anthropological type is still robust, as is indicated by the still frequent reference to it in the literature. I would maintain however, that since its invention as an anthropological category, the term peasant has increasingly become out of alignment with "reality" and thus has become a disruptive category. Hence, the continued use of such terms as ethnic group, national minority, and peasant in the ethnographic literature on social identity are often, in Frederic Jameson's terms, "strategies of containment" (Jameson 1981; see Kearney 1996). In other words, anthropology, and other social sci- ences that have staked so much of their future on the peasant as an essentialized type, must continue to contain identities that are disposed to other forms of self representation to this type. Thus certain strategies of containment are mobilized by both right-wing and left-wing anthropologies, strategies that co- incided with the postwar foreign policies for the "containment of communism." Indeed, both the anthropological peasant and the strategies for its containment were invented during the Cold War, which was a historic moment that elevated the dualistic "us versus them" structure of the classic world view to levels of hysteria that appear within the context of the nation-state. It was within these specific cultural dynamics of the Cold War nation-state that anthropologi- cal essentialization of the peasant occurred, thus enabling its containment in time and space.

But containment is only necessary because counter forces are at work. Global tendencies have been promoting the dissolution of the temporal and spatial dualisms that underlie the essentialization of the peasant in the modern- ist mode. The preliminary conscious awareness of these trends, contrary to the modernizationist interpretation of history, has its own sociology and ideo- logical loadings, which can be summed up as romantic reactions (Kearney 1996:73-114). Although these intellectual currents also reified social types, they were, nevertheless, important phases in the reconceptualization of the peasantry.

INTERNAL AND EXTERNAL DIFFERENTIATION OF PEASANTS

I now turn from the categories of anthropology to the sociology and consciousness of ethnographic subjects: to those peoples designated as peasants. To carry forward the analysis of how anthropology has essentialized the peasant I turn here to a rethinking of that most debated and controversial issue in peasant studies—namely social differentiation by class—and recast it in terms of internal differentiation as compared with the more common notion of external differentiation whereby individuals are differentiated into classes and class fractions (Kearney 1996:136-150). The theory of internal differentiation is not offered as an alternative to external differentiation, as is the case with most postmodernist critics of Marxist theory and most analysts of new social movements, but as an addition to it.

Whereas external differentiation is concerned with how the individual, taken as the basic social and analytic unit, is positioned by class, the theory of internal differentiation takes account of how the seemingly unitary individual (e.g., "the peasant") actually occupies numerous distinct and often contradictory class and other social positions. The analytic and the political challenge then becomes one of finding, and indeed of inventing, dimensions of identity that meaningfully subsume such diverse and often contradictory identities within individuals. Ethnicity is one dimension of identity that is notably effective in coalescing internally differentiated individuals into collective action. Similarly, ecological issues have a potential to generate political projects that can coherently mobilize such complexly differentiated identities. This reconceptualization thus presents an analysis of class as more complexly structured than is the case with dualist models that posit unitary class strata and identities.

The standard view of differentiation, that is, external differentiation, should not be seen as wrong, for indeed in many nineteenth-century situations it was an adequate representation of class structure. Instead it should be seen as a first approximation of the relationship between relations of production and consciousness. Thus, rather than rejecting class analysis, it should be taken for what it is, the still most powerful theoretical perspective for understanding the differentiation of identities in complex societies.

The basic argument advanced here is that postpeasant theory and research must turn from obsessive concern with the external differentiation of types of peasants (which are but reified objects) to the internal differentiation of subjects. The shift from an anthropology of peasants as unitary objects to peasants as complex subjects marks a maturation of peasant studies whereby the very idea of peasant is transcended such that its continued invocation serves only to constrain the anthropology of communities formerly known as rural and peasant.

POSTPEASANT SOCIAL SCIENCE

Anthropologists and other social scientists constructed the peasant concept within a modernist, dualist world view that had distinctive assumptions about space and history. Peasants were seen as embodiments of "traditional" society and as residing in peripheral, rural areas that would be developed— modernized—out of existence by the spread of the technology and other influences of modernity radiating from the developed centers of the world (Kearney 1996:10, 51, 117, 120). Indeed, one of the major tasks of applied anthropology was to facilitate such modernization of peasant communities. But now, at the end of the twentieth century, it appears that history is not following this unilinear path in which modernity inexorably replaces "peripheral," "traditional," "rural" forms. Thus, just as the distinctions between rural and urban have broken down, so is the contrast between modern and traditional dissolving into cultural, social, and technological forms that are characteristic of this present global phase of history.

The permutation of peasants into internally differentiated subaltern forms that are neither modern nor traditional coincides with shifts in the discourse of developmentalism as it comes up against the ecological limits of modernization. Thus, the realization that vast masses of postpeasants will not become modernized in the conventional sense of attaining middle-class incomes and lifestyles has coincided with shifts in developmental theory and programs toward sustainable agriculture, sustainability, and fulfillment of basic needs, rather than an exclusive concern with the attainment of full modernization.[1] As for issues of identity, modernization was supposed to have developed "traditional" identities out of existence as they were incorporated into the modern nation-state, which was to have been the highest social, cultural, and political expression of modernity. But what we are now seeing is that the conditions of postpeasant society are consistent with the reassertion of seemingly "traditional" expressions of identity such as ethnicity and indigenous peoples.

Whereas the peasant was constructed within and consistent with the dualist structuring of the modern nation-state, now-emerging postpeasant subjects often have transnational identities. This transnationalism is most readily apparent in the high and growing rates of transnational migration of poor rural people, whereby they dissolve the spatial and occupational dualisms that structure images of the peasant and traditional society. But transnational migration, although a major one, is but one of many contemporary global processes eroding the power of the nation-state to inform identities.

Several of these transnational trends in consciousness and their corresponding social and political forms are emerging as vehicles for the reconceptualization of rural types formerly known as peasants. Briefly, whereas the peasant was essentialized as having a primordial connection with land, a condition that made the agrarian issue the fundamental peasant concern, postpeasant rural politics are increasingly elaborated in terms of human rights, ecopolitics, and ethnicity (Kearney 1996:171-186). Human rights conceived as universal, ecopolitics conceived as global, and ethnicity conceived as inherently transnational are thus consistent with the postpeasant, who has moved from periphery to center, from past to present, and from object to subject and who in doing so has largely dissolved the distinctions between these oppositions upon which the idea of the peasant was based. As the dissolution of these categories undermined the concept of the peasant, so also did it undermine the basic assumptions about society and history that were the foundation of theories of development.

Development was, and still to a great extent is, conceived as the progress of nation-states. Indeed, development has been largely defined as the incorporation of peasants, primitives, and racial and ethnic minorities into the social and cultural mainstreams of nation-states. But this definition of development is everywhere challenged by forms of persistent and emergent cultural difference that defy the cultural homogenizing power of the nation-state. At the same time, recent turns in development thinking—from assumptions that full modernization is not only desirable but possible, to the realization that all peoples of the world will not be brought up to middle-class living standards—are based on a recognition that development and modernization must be rethought, and so too must nation-states as the social, cultural, and political forms in which they take place.

Perhaps the greatest social and political achievement of modernity was the creation of the modern nation-state. But it has been a project with mixed blessings. For in addition to improvements in living standards and political institutions for many, its age has also brought modern total warfare, massive despotism, and the blight of underdevelopment, which is perhaps more appropriately referred to as "de-development." And it has also been accompanied by extensive environmental degradation.

Thus, in some cases a decline in the political and cultural hegemony of the nation-state seems to be opening up spaces for the advancement of democratic and economic projects of postpeasant subalterns. Such seems to be the case with the Zapatistas of southern Mexico who have gained major concessions from the Mexican state by projecting themselves into global attention, not as peasants, but as "indigenous peoples" (see Barry 1995; Ross 1995). Similarly, Mixtecs of Oaxaca, Mexico have been able to organize within a transnational context so as to better defend themselves both in Mexico and the United States (Kearney 1988, 1995). And other indigenous peoples of Latin America have gained concessions from nation-states that throughout the twentieth century were largely determined to assimilate them or otherwise eliminate them as distinct identities (Kearney and Varese 1995). Such examples of postpeasants advancing their political and cultural projects beyond the territorial and cultural hegemony of nation-states abound (see, for example, Basch et al. 1994). But lest we become overly sanguine about such declines in the cultural and political hegemony of the nation-state, it is important to keep in mind that its demise may also make possible unanticipated forms of violence and suffering. Cases in point are recent events in the former Yugoslavia, and in Rwanda, Zaire, and Afghanistan where central power has broken down.

Throughout the world the nation-state as a social, cultural, and political form seems to be under assault from the forces of transnationalism and globalization (Kearney 1996) as its powers bleed downward to regional levels, such as in the recent formation of a Scottish parliament, and upward, as in the case of the formation of the European Community, NAFTA, and other transnational arrangements. Concomitantly with these historic shifts in power there are occurring the reconfigurations in personal identity that, as kind of shorthand, I have referred to herein as postpeasant. Such postpeasants are arguably the prevalent social form of identity of the contemporary moment. And here I do not so much mean an identity in the sense of a bearer of a distinct class, ethnic, national, or racial label. Rather we are talking about a general form of identity that, in its complexity, is often resistant to the unidimensionality and binary logic of identity as defined by modern nation-states.[2]

The idea of the postpeasant is a thus a tentative contribution to better understanding of personal identities in the contemporary world. As such, it is a way of reading downward toward the local level of the personal. But such a reading is only understandable by situating postpeasant identities within national and global contexts. And to the degree that such social milieux are comprised of postpeasants, this concept of identity may be of some use in illuminating these larger social spaces.

NOTES

1. For related discussions of developmentalism see Escobar (1991) and Ferguson (1990).

2. The sociology of such complex identities is explored at greater length in Kearney (1996), which introduces the concept of "the polybian" to imagine their complexity and formation. Suffice it here to say that the polybian is characterized by a high degree of internal differentiation, as defined above.

REFERENCES CITED

Barry, Tom
1995   *Zapata's Revenge: Free Trade and the Farm Crisis in Mexico.* South End Press, Boston.
Basch, Linda, Nina Glick Schiller, and Cristina Szanton Blanc
1994   *Nations Unbound: Transnational Projects, Postcolonial Predicaments, and Deterritorialized Nation States.* Gordon and Breach, New York.
Escobar, Arturo
1991   Anthropology and the Development Encounter: The Making and Marketing of Development Anthropology. *American Ethnologist* 18:658-682.
Ferguson, James
1990   *The Anti-Politics Machine: "Development," Depoliticization, and Bureaucratic Power in Lesotho.* Cambridge University Press, Cambridge and New York.
Hastrup, Kirsten, and Karen Fog Olwig
1997   Introduction. In *Siting Culture: The Shifting Anthropological Object*, edited by Karen Fog Olwig, and Kirsten Hastrup, pp. 1-14. Routledge, London and New York.
Jameson, Frederic
1981   *The Political Unconscious: Narrative as a Socially Symbolic Act.* Cornell University Press, Ithaca.
Kearney, Michael
1988   Mixtec Political Consciousness: From Passive to Active Resistance. In *Rural Revolt in Mexico and U. S. Intervention*, edited by Daniel Nugent, pp. 113-124. Monograph Series No. 27. Center for U. S.-Mexican Studies, University of California, San Diego.
1995a   The Local and the Global: The Anthropology of Globalization and Transnationalism.
1995b   The Effects of Transnational Culture, Economy, and Migration on Mixtec Identity in Oaxacalifornia. In *The Bubbling Caldron: Race, Ethnicity, and the Urban Crisis*, edited by Michael Peter Smith, and Joe R. Feagin, pp. 226-243. University of Minnesota Press, Minneapolis.
1996   *Reconceptualizing the Peasantry: Anthropology in Global Perspective.* Westview Press, Boulder.
Kearney, Michael, and Stefano Varese
1995   Latin America's Indigenous Peoples Today: Changing Identities and Forms of Resistance in Global Context. In *Capital, Power and Inequality in Latin America*, edited by Richard Harris, and S. Halebsky, pp. 207-231. Westview Press, Boulder.
Ross, John
1995   *Rebellion from the Roots: Indian Uprising in Chiapas.* Common Courage Press, Monroe, Maine.
Wolf, Eric R.
1955   Types of Latin American Peasantry: A Preliminary Discussion. *American Anthropologist* 57:452-471.
1966   *Peasants.* Prentice Hall, Englewood Cliffs, New Jersey.
1969   *Peasant Wars of the Twentieth Century.* Harper & Row, New York.

5

Hemispheric Remappings

Revisiting the Concept of Nuestra América

Edna Acosta-Belén

As we approach the gate to the twenty-first century, we face a world of increasing interconnections, interdependence, and economic integration among nations and regions. Since the early 1980s, the global economic reorganization of the new capitalist world order also confronts us with cultural phenomena that can no longer be circumscribed by unified, autonomous, or purist notions of national cultures immune to the penetrating forces of the transnational market. Among these transnational forces are major migratory displacements of people who are impelled primarily by the gap between their socioeconomic aspirations and the conditions that prevail in their countries of origin to seek a different life in industrialized Western nations. The expanding presence of the Latino population in the United States and the transnational linkages that Latino (im)migrants[1] maintain with their Latin American and Caribbean countries of origin, immediately suggest new challenges and changes in our conventional interpretations of the history and culture of the Americas, both North and South.

This chapter is an expanded and revised version of the first Schomburg-Moreno Lecture, "Revisiting the Concept of *Nuestra América* in Latin American and Latino(a) Studies," presented at Mount Holyoke College, April 10, 1995. Parts of this essay also appeared in "Merging Borders: The Remapping of America" (with C.E. Santiago), *Latino Review of Books* 1.1 (Spring 1995): 2-12.

The global diffusion of the consumption patterns, ways of life, and perceived opportunities associated with industrialized Western societies accounts for most of present-day international migration flows (Portes and Rumbaut 1990). The fragmentation and plurality of our postmodern condition and the innumerable intersections between the local, national, and transnational spheres produce new forms of interaction and hybridization that influence the construction and reconfiguration of national cultures and identities (García Canclini 1989, 1995). These new identities perform different functions depending on the context in which they are inserted.

In this essay, I introduce some stimulating ways to look at these transnational linkages, and at cultural and racial diversity, and the formation of identities that is taking place in the Americas—both Anglo and Latin—two multicultural and multiracial spheres where we find diverse populations bound by a shared legacy of colonialism, racism, displacement, and dispersion.[2] My main objective is to support the need to transcend or redefine the conventional boundaries that have constrained our study and understanding of the peoples of Latin America and the Caribbean vis-á-vis their counterpart emigrant populations who live in the United States.

I begin my analysis by revisiting the nineteenth-century concept of *nuestra América* (our America), first used by several nineteenth-century Latin American intellectuals, but mostly associated with Cuban writer and patriot José Martí.[3] The concept originated from an intellectual attempt to articulate the emergence of a Latin American nationalist consciousness, marked by quests for continental solidarity and unification in the midst of anticolonial struggles, first against Spanish rule, and subsequently, against spreading U. S. imperialist incursions in the region. In my analysis I try to establish a link between past projects of constructing and defining a pan-national or continental Latin American identity and contemporary constructions of a U. S. Latino identity that have emerged as a response to the realities and imperatives faced by populations of Latin American and Caribbean origin in U. S. society.[4] Some of the fundamental issues I explore in this essay are how the two parts of the Americas are being bridged by (1) existing transnational interconnections between specific Latin American and Caribbean countries and their respective U. S. diasporas; (2) collective forms of cultural affirmation, resistance, and hybridization that are taking place among Latino groups in U. S. society and in their countries of origin; and (3) overlapping issues of race, gender, nationality, ethnicity, and class. My efforts at examining some of the interconnections among the cultures of the Americas across time and geographic divides aim to bring fresh insights into this cultural meeting ground to the same degree that they attempt to contribute to modifying the fragmented way in which we look both at the U. S. Latino experience and at the Latin American/Caribbean experience. I emphasize the need to both transgress and extend the cultural parameters of analysis beyond those already imposed by spurious geographic national frontiers or artificial boundaries. Rather than look at each population as a separate, cultural sphere of analysis unrelated to the other, I focus on the importance of reciprocal interactions and bi-directional exchanges between these populations. Finally, I use the work of selected U. S. Latino(a) writers to illustrate different ways in which new "border" cultures and hybrid identities are being constructed by these authors to articulate the experiences of their respective individual groups while, at the same time, they affirm a broader pan-ethnic sense of *latinismo* or Latinoness. Being, for example, Chicano(a), Nuyorican, or Boricua in the United States, but also part of a broader Latino(a) collectivity involves the construction of oppositional subjectivities, and provides cultural agency to subaltern groups to resist, contest, and transform dominant or colonized representations of self. A pan-ethnic Latino identity affirms a shared heritage of cultural and linguistic commonalties and a subaltern position based on a collective history of class, racial, and gender oppressions and counter-responses to these conditions. It also reaffirms transnational linkages with the individual countries of origin as well as with a broader Latin American/Caribbean cultural context.

Through my analysis, I hope to encourage Latin Americanists, Caribbeanists, U. S. Latino, and American Studies specialists to move away from the monolithic and homogenizing conceptualizations of Latino cultural identity— conceptualizations that frequently impair our understanding of the cultural interactions and bi-directional exchanges that U. S. Latino (im)migrants from diverse nationalities maintain with their respective countries of origin and which play a pivotal role in the molding of contemporary Latino identities.

THE CONCEPT OF NUESTRA AMÉRICA

For almost two centuries, Latin American and Caribbean intellectuals have attempted to develop continental visions of the Americas that take into consideration the common experiences that bind together the colonized peoples and cultures of the hemisphere, but also recognize the basic estrangement of large segments of the population brought about by local class, racial, and ethnic divisions. But the asymmetrical distribution of wealth and power found within these countries transcends any national or local conditions and are also evident in the prevailing socioeconomic differences between a developed North America and the undeveloped nations south of the border.

José Martí lived in New York City as a political émigré from 1881 to 1895 and wrote his celebrated essay "Nuestra América" in 1891. Yet, the vision of a continental Latin American imagined community that transcends national or ethnic differences and favors regional solidarity and unification did not originate with Martí. It is an idea that was already evident in the early nineteenth-century writings of some of the creole leaders of the Latin American independence movement.

Martí came to New York at the age of 28. Fourteen years later he returned to Cuba, where he was killed by Spanish troops shortly afterward in 1895. Thus the New York period represents a significant part of his adult life. While in New York, Martí organized the Cuban independence movement and published a good portion of his major writings. He was a frequent contributor to both Latin American and U. S. newspapers and in 1892 founded *Patria*, the official newspaper of the Cuban Revolutionary Party, which continued to be published until 1898. My reasons for choosing Martí as a significant anchor in this cultural analysis of the Americas are twofold: First, it was during the time that he lived in New York that he produced the most important essays about his vision of the American continent, the oppositional relations between the "Anglo" and "Latin" American components, and about the greatness and wretchedness of living in what he referred to as *las entrañas del monstruo* ("I have lived inside the monster and know its entrails," he once said). Second, he was an important figure during the formative years of the New York City *colonia hispana*—a period that is fundamental to the historical reconstruction of U. S. Latino communities as we learn more about the links of solidarity among Cubans, Puerto Ricans, Dominicans, and other Latin Americans living in New York and other U. S. cities during the course of the nineteenth century. The Hispanic Caribbean émigrés' involvement in the independence movements against Spanish colonial rule and the impact of their activities in galvanizing these struggles back in their native islands have not received adequate attention by scholars. Ironically, for both Cubans and Puerto Ricans, the consolidation of nationalist ideals to support their claims for independence did not flourish as strongly among the populations of the islands, where separatist movements were subject to the implacable repression of Spanish colonial authorities, as it did among the exiles of the émigré communities, particularly among those located in the United States. Similar transnational and pan-ethnic connections, collaborations, and alliances would also flourish in the New York metropolis in subsequent decades among Spanish nationals, other Latin American and Caribbean peoples, and various U. S. groups with regard to a wide range of cultural, political, and social issues and concerns, particularly during the years of the Harlem Renaissance, the Great Depression, the Spanish Civil War, World War II, the McCarthy Era, and in more recent decades, during the civil rights, ethnic revitalization, multiculturalist, and women's movements.[5]

From many of the writings that Martí produced while living in the New York metropolis, we learn a great deal about the class and racial conflicts of the United States; about the increasing polarization and the clashes between capital and labor; about the detrimental conditions and the discrimination faced by

Native American and Black populations; and about the mighty threat of an emerging U. S. imperialism which loomed over Cuba and other parts of Latin America. But most importantly, from the perspective of this essay, is what we learn about Martí's continental vision—his efforts at capturing and defining the diversified cultural elements that compose Latin American identity—and his quest for a free and color-blind multicultural society that is not characterized by, as he once said, the "struggle of races" but by the "affirmation of rights" (Martí 1977). Contrary to other intellectuals of his time, who viewed the future of Latin America in the emulation of imported "civilized" European or Anglo-American models, or who contraposed Western civilization to the purported "barbarism" of the native indigenous, black, mestizo, or peasant creole populations, Martí reaffirmed the need to take into account those non-Western elements that are peculiar to the peoples of the Americas. More than any other intellectual of his time, he recognized the need to surmount existing social and racial divisions and to validate the diversity of cultures autochthonous to the region as well as those that result from a creolization process—that unprecedented mixing of races and cultural syncretism that took place in the Americas, and which perhaps has never reached a similar magnitude in any other part of the world. Martí emphatically called "our mestizo America...to show itself as it is" (Martí 1953:141). And what is after all, the true face of *nuestra América*, if not a place depopulated by conquest and colonization and repopulated by uprooted immigrants and African slaves; the stage where the Spanish/European culture, in exerting its domination, converged and blended with the many indigenous and African cultures that participated in this fateful encounter, to produce new and striking cultural configurations. Thus, from Martí's perspective, the process of Latin American nation building required an understanding of the region's social, racial, and cultural plurality and divisions.

> The good governor in America is not the one who knows how government is conducted in Germany or France, but the one who knows the various elements of which a country is made, and how they can be marshaled so that by methods and institutions native to the country the desirable state may be attained...The history of America, from the Incas to the present, must be taught until is known by heart, even if the archons of Greece go by the board. Our Greece must take priority to the Greece that is not ours...Let the world be grafted in our republics, but the trunk will be our own. (Martí 1953:141, 143)

Perhaps one of Martí's most outstanding contributions to the Cuban independence struggle was his frontal attack on the racism that divided his native country and that could affect the common cause for Cuban independence. In 1890, two years before the Cuban Revolutionary Party was founded in New

York City, Martí worked with Afro-Cuban émigrés in the city in the formation of *La Liga* (The League), which focused on the education and advancement of this working-class sector of the community.[6] In this way he helped to lay an important foundation for combating racism and promoting racial harmony and equality, and carried on his efforts to ameliorate social class divisions within the independence movement. When Martí declared that "Whoever foments and propagates antagonism and hate between the races, sins against Humanity" (Martí 1977:150) or when he delivered his oration "With all, and for the good of all" (Martí 1977:249), he was surpassing racial and class barriers in an attempt to unite the heterogeneous elements present within the independence movement. Hence Martí's Latin American national project was not based on legitimizing the hegemony of the white creole elites with their accompanying foreign-looking world views and lifestyles, and their flirtatious relationship with foreign economic interests. On the contrary, it was based on the articulation of a pan-national/ pan-ethnic consciousness of Latin American identity, grounded on a unitary sense of anti-imperialist struggle against denationalizing external and internal forces and on a commitment to the unrealized social and racial emancipatory struggles that confronted each country. Although Martí is generally considered to be one of the main articulators of anti-imperialist thought in Latin America, he was as wary of U. S. imperialism as he was of the racism he witnessed while living in the United States. Through his numerous essays about the two Americas, he articulated his continental political, social, and humanitarian vision about the future of the continent as much as his more specific concerns about the plight of the U. S. Native American and Black populations. His essays "Los indios en los Estados Unidos," "Los últimos indios," "Indios y negros," and "El problema negro" (Martí 1968) admonish Anglo politicians and the U. S. government for their "degrading tutelage" toward these groups, and for "a vilified system" of Indian reservations which he describes as "criaderos de hombres" (hatcheries or breeding grounds for men) (Martí 1968:90, 92). He strongly criticized white ministers for violating God's law and refusing to sit next to Black ministers. Referring to the inferior condition of the African American, he emphatically noted that: "Others may fear him: I love him. Anyone who speaks ill of him I disown, and I say to him openly: 'You lie!'" (Martí 1977: 28).

The idea of equal dignity and harmony among the races was essential to Martí's concept of Latin American nation building and the future of his own country. Yet, his pan-national affirmation of a multicultural and multiracial *nuestra América* also takes on great contemporary significance as we strive to put an end to European and Anglo-American ethnocentrism by decolonizing and deconstructing the cultural mythologies and received knowledge about subaltern groups perpetuated within the dominant Western tradition. There is no question that the essentialist cultural hegemony and parochialism of the West has undermined the many subaltern cultural "others" of the so-called Third World, without properly acknowledging any shared system of cultural interactions or by conceiving Western realities and accomplishments in isolation from the rest of the world.

While Martí developed the concept of *nuestra América* in reference to a nineteenth-century Latin America that was struggling with the evils of tyranny, exploitative economic forces, and social injustice he realized that the destiny of the continent was inextricably linked to the Colossus to the North. From his perspective, U. S. government imperialist aims—its expressed desire to annex Cuba and other overseas territories—and the expansionist economic ambitions of U. S. wealthy investors, made Cuba, Puerto Rico, and other Latin American territories vulnerable to military and economic intervention and domination. Man of vision that he was, however, Martí could not have anticipated the extent to which, more than a century later, some of those very economic, social, and political forces that he so feared are pushing the peoples of Latin America and the Caribbean out of their own countries and into the United States in unprecedented numbers. Ironically, more than ever before, the citizens of Martí's *nuestra América* are caught in an intricate and complex web of international (im)migration and labor flows that are causing multiple population displacements from the peripheral to the advanced capitalist nations. The economic destitution, social inequalities, political repression, and dependence that continue to plague many Latin American and Caribbean countries, make the journey to the prosperous *norte* a viable and alluring alternative. *Nuestra América* has become a very palpable presence *in* the United States itself. This dramatic diasporic reality, and the ongoing and projected changes in the demographic composition of the U. S. population, is forcing us not only to come to terms with but also to expand the terms in which Latino identity is being defined by scholars, artists, and community activists. More accurately, these realities underscore the need for a better understanding of how multiple and fluid Latino(a) identities are constructed and juggled in the new transnational context; identities which are reconstituted or remolded from generation to generation from the cultural inter- and cross-connections with the respective native cultures, with the U. S. mainstream culture that marginalizes ethnoracial minorities, and with the cultures of other subordinate groups.

CONSTRUCTING THE HISPANIC/LATINO NATION FROM WITHIN THE UNITED STATES

Hispanics, as they are officially classified by government agencies, or Latinos, as they increasingly prefer to be collectively identified, have been lumped together under an imposed bureaucratic label that tends to eclipse the many different nationalities, cultural experiences, and histories shared by the many individual groups. Thus the accuracy and use of a label that homogenizes such a diverse conglomerate of individual nationalities is still strongly contested.[7] The Hispanic category used by the U. S. Census includes the descendants of early Spanish settlers of the colonial period as well as the newcomers of our time; many were born in what was once part of Mexico and later became U. S. territory, and others have arrived from other parts of Latin America and the Caribbean as immigrants or migrants, or as undocumented workers. Hence, the Hispanic/ Latino presence in the United States is inextricably linked to the past and present realities of this nation (see Oboler, chap. 4).

The influx of Hispanics or Latinos from diverse cultural backgrounds into the United States has, therefore, a long historical tradition as well as being a current and vital part of U. S. society. This reality is underscored by the 1980 and 1990 census data, which demonstrate that Latinos constitute the fastest-growing minority in U. S. society. The importance and magnitude of demographic changes in the composition of the U. S. population continues to be highlighted by more recent U. S. Census projections.[8] Figure 5.1 shows the current and projected growth in the Hispanic population of the United States. Currently numbering over 29.5 million, if prevailing growth rates continue,

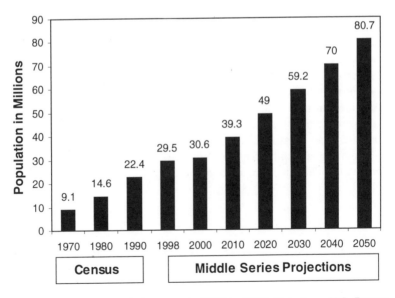

Fig. 5.1. Hispanic population growth: 1970 to 2050. Data from U.S. Bureau of Census (1993, 1994, 1996).

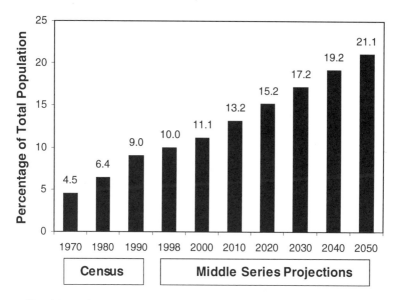

Fig. 5.2.   Hispanic population growth by, percentage of total population:
1970 to 2050. Data from U.S. Bureau of Census (1993, 1994, 1996).

Hispanics could well become the largest minority group in the United States in
the first part of the twenty-first century. Figure 5.2 illustrates the dramatic
growth in the Hispanic percentage of the total U. S. population from 1970
to 1990 and also shows U. S. Census projections for the next six decades.
While the total non-Hispanic U. S. population grew by 7 percent between 1980-
1990 and 9 percent between 1970-1980, the Hispanic population increased by
53 percent and 60 percent respectively, about seven times more than the non-
Hispanic population. Figure 5.3 provides the percentages of population growth
for each of the major Latino groups between 1980-1990 and compares them
with that of the non-Hispanic population. Most scholars agree that the
unprecedented growth of the Hispanic population during the last few decades,
together with the U. S. Census's future growth estimates, has brought more
attention to bear upon the U. S. Latino experience.

That the U. S. Latino groups may prefer to identify themselves by their
individual nationalities rather than by the Hispanic or Latino label, does not
preclude the manifestation of a growing pan-ethnic consciousness, nor the construction of a collective Latino identity within the United States. Nor does it
inhibit the influence that collective identity exerts over the shaping of specific
social, political, educational, and cultural agenda. The umbrella term represents a symbol of collective cultural affirmation and distinctive identity in a
society that for a long time promoted the myth of being a cultural "melting

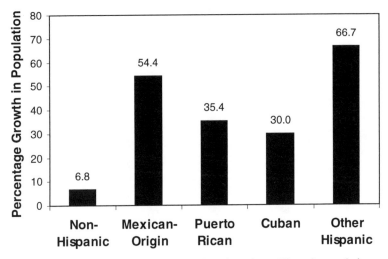

Fig. 5.3.   Percentage growth of the Hispanic and non-Hispanic populations.
Data from U.S. Bureau of Census (1993, 1994, 1996).

pot." The assimilationist melting pot ideology advocated the suppression or re-nunciation of cultural, racial, and linguistic differences and the incorporation into a presumably unified American ethos that tended to ignore or downplay the long history of exclusion, racial discrimination, and segregation as well as the social and civil rights struggles and contributions of people of color in U. S. society. The Hispanic/Latino collective pan-ethnic label also has proved to be useful in the political articulation of the pressing socioeconomic and educational needs and priorities of the various Latino communities. Thus, even though individual Latino groups have differing senses of their own national origins and identity and of their particular relationship with U. S. society, Latinos increasingly find that their commonalties and potential to build coalitions provide them with a more effective political voice.

The last few years have witnessed the proliferation of scholarship on U. S. Latinos, especially works that acknowledge their heterogeneity—the significant racial, social, national, and generational differences among them—but at the same time, recognize the presence of a pan-ethnic "Latino imaginary" (Flores 1995; chap. 6 this volume), a "Hispanic condition" (Stavans 1995), or the forging of a "Hispanic nation" (Fox 1996) within the United States. Leaving aside ongoing debates about the appropriateness of the aforementioned conceptualizations or, for that matter, the adequacy or contested nature of the Hispanic/Latino label, we cannot ignore the spreading manifestations of a pan- or trans-Latino identity, which are continuously reinforced by different forms of cultural expression and the media (Flores 1996). Without a doubt, this ongoing construction of a pan/trans-Latino identity compels us as scholars to transgress the artificial boundaries that for a long time separated the study of the Latin American and Caribbean regions from their respective U. S. diasporas. The articulation of a Latino pan-ethnic consciousness within U. S. society and of a transnational hemispheric Latino consciousness are not, however, contemporary phenomena. On the contrary, there is a long and vigorous intellectual tradition in Latin America and the Caribbean that promoted the notion of continental and regional identities that transcended individual nationalities. Moreover, it is not difficult to document in different historical periods many examples of the pan-ethnic political alliances, cultural interactions, and exchanges that, although rooted in the U. S. Latino communities, also achieved both national and continental dimensions (see Sánchez Korrol 1988). For contemporary U. S. Latinos, the processes of learning about the pioneer communities and reconstructing a tradition within U. S. society provide a sense of origin and continuity with the past and a vital source of collective identity and empowerment that counteract some of the negative effects of their current marginal status. This is particularly important for Latinos born or raised in the United States, who may have fewer ties or less contact with their families' countries of origin.

During the nineteenth century, the United States, following its policies of territorial expansion, made its first incursions into Latin America and took possession of about half of the territory that was part of the nation of Mexico. The 1848 Treaty of Guadalupe Hidalgo transformed Northern Mexico into the U. S. Southwest. The contemporary Chicano playwright and filmmaker Luis Valdez summarized the disastrous outcome of this armed conflict with his famous quote: "We did not come to the United States at all. The United States came to us."

It was also in this century that the Colossus to the North appropriated the name "America" to signify the United States. In his book *The End of American History* (1985), historian David Noble argues that implicit in this change in the use of the name America is a profound commitment to isolating the Anglo-Saxon national culture and minimizing any major claims of cultural interdependence with other nations or groups when defining the country's national identity. Thus the construction of the historical narrative of the U. S. nation was guided not only by the political independence claimed in 1776, but also by the concept of a Chosen People coming into a Promised Land who developed "a unique national culture that modified its colonial inheritance from its mother country, England…But American historians…have not used a concept that combines political independence with cultural interdependence to define [their] cultural identity. They have thought and written as if the United States was absolutely independent, standing apart in its uniqueness from the rest of the human experience" (Noble 1995:7).

Noble's interpretation is particularly illuminating if we consider that the United States always has been a necessary or unavoidable point of reference for the rest of the continent, while, in contrast, the presence and importance of Latin America and the Caribbean in the U. S. national discourse is usually minimized or dismissed by claims about their inferior status of economic dependency and political turmoil, despite these regions' historic economic and strategic geopolitical importance. Even in its territorial expansionist enterprise, the United States separated itself from Europe. In *Cultures of United States Imperialism*, Amy Kaplan and Donald Pease (1993) document the absence of the concept of empire in the study of U. S. culture. They persuasively argue that U. S. historiography has portrayed the nation as inherently anti-imperialist and has been reluctant to acknowledge that the country has engaged in imperialist practices. This paradigm of denial explains the exclusion of the many historical episodes of continental and overseas expansion, of the conquest of and resistance by the original populations and settlers of the West and the Southwest, and of the over five million U. S. citizens, including Puerto Ricans, currently living in overseas colonial territories acquired from Spain in 1898. These prevailing standpoints in the historical narrative of the U. S. nation achieve significant contemporary relevance if we consider the current national debates over multiculturalism. Those who oppose multiculturalism assert that it produces a state of "culture wars," and they indicate clearly that they consider any claims to a U. S. national identity that deviate from the dominant Anglo-Saxon narrative of the nation's history or from the mythical melting pot to be disuniting, divisive, and essentially un-American (Glazer 1997; Schlesinger 1991).

Conventional historical accounts of the formative years of the United States tend to regard everything that preceded the establishment of the British thirteen colonies as unimportant. They pay little attention to other groups such as Native Americans and Hispanics who occupied North American territory long before the British settlers and whose presence is interwoven into the historical fabric of the nation. The nineteenth-century westward territorial expansion of the United States from the original thirteen colonies to the Pacific Coast and south to the Rio Grande and the Gulf Coast was the fulfillment of the nation's Manifest Destiny. But this confined view of U. S. territorial expansion and the formative years of the nation, tends to fragment or obscure the entire history of the past and its links to the present, and leaves us with an impoverished understanding of how other groups, including those of Hispanic extraction or descent, have been and continue to be an integral part of this country's multicultural patrimony and have at different times played a perceptible role in the shaping of U. S. history and society. Moreover, seeking to understand the larger meaning of the U. S. Latino heritage allows us to recognize how the different parts of the American hemisphere are inexorably linked, more so than U. S. and Latin American historical accounts have been willing to acknowledge. Not only must we begin to fill in these gaps in the construction of the United States' formative years as a nation, but we must also acknowledge the complexity of the cultural interactions and amalgamations among the various peoples—indigenous, Spanish, British, other European, and African enslaved populations—that took place in what is today U. S. territory as well as throughout the Americas. The increased population growth and visibility of U. S. Latinos in recent decades and the work that is being produced by many Latino writers and scholars is leading scholars to pay more attention to the common denominators and the cultural bridges that have existed during various historical periods between the United States and Latin America. Other non-Latino scholars also have suggested innovative ways of looking at the interconnections between different parts of the hemisphere. A good example is Immanuel Wallerstein's concept of "the extended Caribbean" (1980), which emphasizes the geographic linkages among the U. S. South, the Caribbean islands, and the coastal areas of Central and South America all the way down to Brazil—areas where societies supported by enslaved African labor and the plantation system developed and which thus share strong commonalties. More recently, the anthropologist Constance Sutton (Sutton and Chaney 1987) has introduced the notion of a transnational sociocultural system that allows Puerto Ricans and other Caribbean migrants to reconstitute their lives in New York City and affirm a distinct cultural identity while maintaining strong interactions with their countries of origin. This process further creolizes Caribbean cultures and identities in both New York City and in the countries of origin, challenging conventional notions of immigrant assimilation and marking new possibilities in the struggles for social, cultural, and political empowerment of these marginalized groups.

The historiography about the evolution of most U. S. Latino communities, particularly those in the Northeast, and the linkages that these groups maintained with their countries of origin during earlier periods is still scarce. Until recently, very few scholars have taken an interest in reconstructing the histories of specific Latino communities. Most of the available research is about communities in the large urban centers, such as New York City, Los Angeles, and Chicago. Nonetheless, community microhistories along with oral histories, testimonies, memoirs, and nonmainstream periodicals are some of the major sources that now are being used to reconstruct what Eric Wolf (1982) called the forgotten or ignored contributions of "the people without history."

One major figure who attempted to disprove fully the notion that peoples of African descent did not have any history was Arturo Alfonso Schomburg, an Afro-Puerto Rican who arrived in New York City in 1891 at age 17, and lived there until his death in 1938. In New York, Schomburg joined Martí and other members of the Cuban and Puerto Rican community of intellectuals and political émigrés, who along with working-class *tabaqueros* (cigarmakers) were engaged in the independence struggles of the two Caribbean islands. During his early years in New York, Schomburg became a founding member and secretary of the Club Dos Antillas (The Two Antilles) formed to actively assist in the independence of Cuba and Puerto Rico. Martí's death in 1895 and the Spanish-Cuban-American War of 1898 changed the circumstances for the possible independence of Cuba and Puerto Rico, and many of these organizations disbanded shortly thereafter. The fervor and devotion that Schomburg had demonstrated to the independence cause was then transferred to a different, but equally worthy, cultural endeavor to which he would make a lifelong commitment. He undertook the monumental task of collecting and preserving the heritage of the African diaspora worldwide, adhering to the ideology of pan-Africanism promoted by some African American and Afro-Caribbean intellectuals of his time. In her explanation of Schomburg's lifelong passion for book collecting, Elinor Des Verney Sinnette (1989), one of Schomburg's biographers, refers to an anecdote about his childhood years in Puerto Rico: a teacher is said to have told him that black people had no history, heroes, or great events to be studied. This remark impressed upon the young Arturo a desire to learn more about his African ancestry.

After his years of involvement with the Cuban and Puerto Rican separatist organizations, Arturo Alfonso Schomburg developed strong affinities and close friendships with members of the African American community, to the extent that he eventually anglicized his name to Arthur. His ties and contributions to the New York Puerto Rican community remained generally unknown until recent decades. Schomburg, the tireless and consummate bibliophile who collected documents about the African experience around the world, ultimately became curator of his own collection, which he turned over to the New York Public Library and which forms the core of today's Schomburg Center for Research in Black Culture. In an essay he wrote in 1913, Schomburg advocates the establishment of a Chair of Negro history in a U. S. university, turning into a precursor of the contemporary African American Studies movement.

> We have reached the crucial period of our educational existence...The white institutions have their chair of history; it is the history of their own people, and whenever the Negro is mentioned in the text-books it dwindles down to a footnote...Cases can be shown right and left of...palpable omissions.
>
> Where is our historian to give us our side [sic] view and our Chair of Negro history, to teach our people our own history? We are at the mercy of the 'flotsam and jetsam' of the white writers...
>
> We need in the coming dawn [someone]...who will give us the background for our future; it matters not whether...[this person]...comes from the cloisters of the university or from the rank and file of the fields. (Cunard 1970: 77-78)

It is quite revealing that individuals from a self-educated working class, such as Schomburg—or for that matter, other figures of the time such as the

Puerto Rican *tabaqueros* Bernardo Vega (1885-1965) and Jesús Colón (1901-1974) who also left valuable historical legacies—clearly understood that the dominant white cultural elite would not make room for them in their official histories. Thus, it would be necessary for working class individuals like themselves to undertake the task of recovering and preserving their own historical legacies. Schomburg recognized the cultural bonds among the Black peoples of the United States, the Caribbean, and Africa, and the pressing need for all peoples of African descent to appropriate their history, to build a body of knowledge that would serve as "a background for [the] future...providing useful and inspiring models for [our] children to have before them" (Cunard 1970:76).

Two admirers of the legacy their compatriot Arturo Schomburg had bestowed upon the African American community, and whose work is also informed by a consciousness of what needs to be transmitted to future generations, are Bernardo Vega, a white Puerto Rican who came to New York in 1916, and Jesús Colón, an Afro-Puerto Rican who arrived in New York a year later. Both were from the tobacco-growing countryside of Cayey, Puerto Rico, and after leaving the island, both remained most of their adult lives in the New York metropolis.

In New York, Vega became publisher of *Gráfico*, "semanario defensor de la raza hispana" (a weekly newspaper defender of the Hispanic race), published between 1927-1931. In addition to his journalistic contributions and community activism, Vega wrote his memoirs, which provide a meticulous and detailed account of the development of the New York Puerto Rican community during the early part of the century. Although Vega wrote his memoirs during the 1940s, they did not see the public light until more than a decade after his death in 1965. In 1977 they were edited and published for the first time by Puerto Rican writer César Andreu Iglesias. In his *Memorias*, Vega, as if trying to forge a historical record, provides valuable information about grassroots activism and the many community organizations and publications that flourished during the early years of New York's *colonia hispana*.

Jesús Colón was an avid collector of articles, newsletters, leaflets, newspaper and magazine clippings, reports, photographs, and personal correspondence that now form part of the Jesús Colón Papers Collection at the Centro de Estudios Puertorriqueños Library of Hunter College. Colón's passion for writing is substantiated by his prolific output of journalistic articles during the more than five decades that he lived in New York City. His writings, however, were relatively unknown since they were scattered over more than thirty different newspapers, magazines and newsletters of community, labor and political organizations. Not being a mainstream press writer, Colón's only published book *A Puerto Rican in New York and Other Sketches* (first published in 1961) remained forgotten until Puerto Rican scholar Juan Flores brought it to public attention in a 1982 edition. A few years ago, historian Virginia Sánchez Korrol and I undertook the exciting task of recovering and identifying over four hundred pieces of Colón's writing, including an unfinished manuscript entitled *The Way It Was*, which was found among his papers. This manuscript was intended to be a history of the development of the New York Puerto Rican community. Some of these writings were collected and published with the support of the *Recovering the U. S. Hispanic Literary Heritage Project*, a project directed by Professor Nicolás Kanellos at the University of Houston.

In the last few years, the *Recovering the U. S. Hispanic Literary Heritage Project* has brought together about twenty Latino scholars in search for the legacy of literary and historical writings by Hispanics, published from colonial times to the present, in what is today the United States. A noteworthy aspect of the *Recovery Project* is the indexing and annotation of texts selected by scholars from a wide array of periodicals. These periodicals were published in the diverse Hispanic communities throughout the United States since the early part of the nineteenth century. It is difficult to anticipate what the process of recovery and (re)discovery of a cultural and historical heritage represent for the U. S. Latino communities. The truth is that the project's full promise and impact probably will not be realized until many years from now. There is a plethora of information that still needs to be processed and of writings by community figures, including several women, that still are being recovered and require study and contextualization.[9]

Hispanic periodicals have proven to be quite valuable in reconstructing a chronicle of the past and have provided glimpses into the everyday life of the various communities at different historical periods. Of primary interest are the linkages and reciprocal interactions that previous generations of U. S. Latinos developed among themselves or maintained with their diverse countries of origin. These periodicals also facilitate, for instance, the exploration of the connections, relations, and tensions between African American and Spanish Harlem during the 1920s and 1930s. Although there were other Puerto Rican or Hispanic colonias that formed in other parts of the New York metropolis, in the 1920s East Harlem had the largest concentration of Puerto Ricans in New York. For this reason it eventually became known as *el Barrio* or Spanish Harlem. The 1920s were the years of the Harlem Renaissance, a period of cultural affirmation and effervescence of a Black consciousness within U. S. society, the Caribbean, and other parts of the world. The Harlem movement coincided with the Afro-Antillean and *négritude* cultural and literary movements in the Hispanic and French Caribbean, and together provide evidence of a strong continental pan-African consciousness during this period. Indeed, many notable figures of the Harlem Renaissance were from the Caribbean—Marcus Garvey, Claude McKay, Richard Moore, and Arthur Schomburg to mention a few—and these connections await further examination (see Watkins-Owens 1996). From Vega and Colón's testimonial accounts, we have learned a great deal about the shared interethnic solidarities within the organized labor movement during the

1920s and 1930s. We also have learned that this was a community in which intellectual pursuits often went hand in hand with sociopolitical activism, and in which prominent members of the intellectual elite often stood side by side with members of the working class in their struggles for social justice.

Two other weekly periodicals, *Pueblos hispanos*, published from 1943-1944, and *Liberación*, published from 1946-1949, confirm widespread continental, international, and Latino pan-ethnic and antiassimilation viewpoints. These viewpoints are reflected in many of the articles published as well as in the overall cultural vision and political goals of each periodical. *Pueblos hispanos*, for instance, described itself as a progressive weekly that strived for: (1) the unification of all the Hispanic colonias in the United States to defeat Nazi-fascism and in solidarity with all democratic forces; (2) the defense of all the rights of Hispanic minorities; (3) the combat of prejudice against Hispanics based on race, color or creed and the denunciation of prejudice against minorities (1943:1). While these goals were enunciated back in 1943, it is worth noting the contemporary resonance of this discourse. There were several other periodical publications, for example, the *Revista de Artes y Letras* (1933-1945) which was directed and owned by Puerto Rican journalist and civic leader Josefína Silva de Cintrón. The *Revista* achieved international circulation and still awaits careful examination from the perspective of women's concerns and the struggles of the time. These and many other periodicals injected a transnational dimension into the cultural life of the New York Latino community that clearly contradicts the image of the *barrios* as closed and hopeless spaces submerged into a "culture of poverty" and thus a "poverty of culture."

The above examples support the argument that the emergence of a Latino consciousness in the United States as an expression of a wider pan-ethnic and transnational identity and the fostering of bonds of solidarity among Latino groups have a long and vigorous historical tradition. Their presence in earlier periods of development within the many U. S. Latino communities is now being extensively documented. The consciousness-raising decades of the 1960s and 1970s, the civil rights and women's movements, and other struggles for social justice during these times allowed Chicanos and Puerto Ricans to join African Americans in their efforts to revitalize and reaffirm their respective ethnic and racial identities. This movement was led by U. S. ethnoracial minorities who were attempting to rid themselves of the negative self-images and stigma they had internalized from the racism and marginalization they experienced within U. S. society and which had denied them a collective positive identity. The results of the explosion in grassroots ethnic activism and organizing that characterized the 1960s and 1970s, eventually reached the walls of academia and African American, Chicano, Puerto Rican, and Native American ethnic studies and bilingual education programs began to proliferate across U. S. colleges and universities.

BORDER CULTURES

There is no better illustration of the cultural and literary continuity of a Latino consciousness in the United States than the work being produced by Chicano, Puerto Rican, Cuban, Dominican, and other Latino writers and artists during the last few decades. Each major group has its own distinctive body of literature reflecting the interactions of their respective cultural worlds. These bodies of literature, written primarily in English, but frequently in Spanish or bilingually, were, until recently, ignored by scholars of U. S. and Latin American literatures alike. The language issue, the working-class character of these writings, and the publication of many of them by small ethnic presses have further limited their diffusion and marketing, and hence their possibilities for critical acclaim.

In their book *Breaking Boundaries: Latina Writings and Critical Readings* (1989), Asunción Horno-Delgado, Eliana Ortega, and Nancy Saporta Sternback underscore ways in which *latinismo* or a Latino consciousness among Latina writers constitutes a unifying element in their works that incorporates elements of solidarity with other women's liberation movements in the United States, Latin America, and other parts of the Third World. Adopting the term "women of color" reflects a wider internationalist and humanitarian consciousness and symbolic identification with the working class and other Third World women's struggles. The collections *This Bridge Called My Back* (Moraga and Anzaldúa 1981), *Este puente, mi espalda* (Moraga and Castillo 1988), *Cuentos: Stories by Latinas* (Gómez et al. 1983), and *Compañeras: Latina Lesbians* (Ramos 1987) were some of the pioneering efforts that attest to the emergence of a literary discourse based upon a cultural subjectivity of being a Latina. This intersection of feminist, ethnoracial, and class consciousness articulates shared experiences of oppression both at an individual and at collective levels. The particular discourse forged by Latinas also transcends national origins and reflects a spirit of solidarity and identification with other worldwide liberation movements constituted of women and other groups marginalized by their class position, race, ethnicity, or sexual preference.

Anthropologist Ruth Behar in her two volume edited collection of writings (co-edited with Juan León), *Bridges to Cuba/Puentes a Cuba* (1994) juxtaposes the metaphors of "bridges" (points of connection), and "borders" (points of separation), between Cubans in the United States and those back on the island in her "personal quest for memory and community" (Behar 1994:401-402). In doing so, she reveals the tensions, contradictions, and need for Cuban Americans to reconnect to their roots, to the island community. Puerto Rican writer Luis Rafael Sánchez invented the metaphor of "la guagua aérea" (the airbus)—that space where we find a nation floating or commuting between two ports—to refer to the movement of people between the island of Puerto Rico and the U. S.

metropolis. After all, as the author would say, "Nueva York sería la otra capital de Puerto Rico, si no lo fuera de toda Hispanoamérica" (Sánchez 1994:23) [New York would be the other capital of Puerto Rico if it were not already the capital of Spanish America].

More than any other group Latino(a) writers and artists continue to span the distance between the Americas. They, as many other Third World peoples around the globe, are caught in a state of displacement that Angelika Bammer (1994) accurately describes as "one of the most formative experiences of our century" (Bammer 1994:xi). This displacement is produced by the physical dislocation from their native cultures that is experienced by (im)migrants, refugees, and exiles, or by the colonizing experience. From that constant commuting—*el ir y venir* (the back and forth movement) of those from "here" and "there" (*los de aquí y los de allá*)—emerge the tensions, contradictions, and reconfigurations that influence and mold the construction of contemporary Latino identities. These identities are marked by absence, loss, fragmentation, estrangement, reclamation, and an inscribing presence. The words of the poet Lourdes Casal (1994) recreate what she views as the unresolved nature of this process:

> This is why I will always remain on the margins,
> a stranger among the stones,
> even beneath the friendly sun of a summer's day,
> just as I will remain forever a foreigner,
> even when I return to the city of my childhood
> I carry this marginality, immune to all turning back,
> too *habanera* to be a *newyorkina*,
> too *newyorkina* to be
> —even to become again—
> anything else.
>
> ("For Ana Veldford", p. 416)

The voice of Puerto Rican poet, Sandra María Esteves (1984), captures the same sense of straddling between cultures and languages:

> Being Puertorriqueña Americana
> Born in the Bronx, not really jíbara
> Not really hablando bien
> But yet, not Gringa either
>
> ("Not neither". In *Tropical Rains*, p. 26)

Some Chicano writers have introduced the notion of "border cultures" to refer to U. S. Latino identities, which are bilingually described by the writer and performance artist Guillermo Gómez-Peña (1993) in his artistic manifesto "The Border Is":

> Border culture means boycott, complot, ilegalidad, clandestinidad, contrabando, transgresión, desobediencia binacional...
> But it also means transcultural friendship and collaboration among races, sexes, and generations.
> But it also means to practice creative appropriation, expropiation, and subversion of dominant cultural forms.
> But it also means a multiplicity of voices away from the center, different geo-cultural relations among more culturally akin regions...
> But it also means regresar, volver y partir: to return and depart once again...
> But it also means a new terminology for new hybrid identities and métiers constantly metamorphosing...
> But it also means to look at the past and the future at the same time.
> ("The Border Is". In *Warrior for Gringostroika*, pp. 43-44)

In her book *Borderlands/La frontera*, Chicana writer Gloria Anzaldúa (1987) adds a gender dimension to the oscillation and struggle between two cultural worlds and claims an emerging new consciousness, "a new mestiza consciousness, *una conciencia de mujer*. It is a consciousness of living at the Borderlands" (Anzaldúa 1987:77).

> Because I, a *mestiza*,
> continually walk out of one culture
> and into another,
> because I am in all cultures at the same time...
> ("Una lucha de fronteras/A Struggle of Borders".
> In *Borderlands/La frontera*, p. 77)

Yo soy un puente tendido
    del mundo gabacho al del mojado,
lo pasado me estirá pa' 'tras
    y lo presente pa' 'delante.
Que la Virgen de Guadalupe me cuide
Ay ay ay, soy mexicana de este lado
    ("The Homeland, Aztlán," In *Borderlands/La frontera*, p. 3)

Other Latino writers proclaim a new cultural synthesis that emerges from this cultural and linguistic straddling by affirming a new hybrid or syncretic identity that incorporates multiple forms of consciousness based on the multi-, inter-, intra-, and cross-connections among the cultures shared as well as from the multiple marginalities that arise from gender, racial, and class differences. All of these elements come together to form what Puerto Rican author Aurora Levins Morales (1981) describes as a new hybrid but holistic sense of identity borne out of the historical marginalization and multiple oppressions experienced by certain groups:

> I am a child of the Americas
> a light-skinned mestiza of the Caribbean
> a child of many diaspora, born into this continent at a crossroads.
> I am not African. Africa is in me, but I cannot return.
> I am not taína. Taíno is in me, but there is no way back.
> I am not european. Europe lives in me, but I have no home there.
> I am new. History made me. My first language was spanglish.
> And I am whole.
> ("Child of the Americas," In *Getting Home Alive*, p. 50)

At the cultural crossroads described in these texts, languages also intermingle and *Spanglish* emerges as a creative force of hybrid interlinguality.[10]

> assimilated? qué assimilated,
> brother, yo soy asimilao,
> así mi la o sí es verdad
> tengo un lado asimilao.
> (Tato Laviera, "asimilao," In *AmeRícan*, 1985:54)

> we gave birth to a new generation,
> AmeRícan salutes all folklores,
> european, indian, black, spanish,
> and anything else compatible...
> AmeRícan, defining myself my own way any way many
> ways Am e Rícan, with the big R and the
> accent on the í!
> (Tato Laviera, "AmeRícan," In *AmeRícan*, 1985:94-95)

The voices of Latino writers are, therefore, powerful examples of how geographic, cultural, and linguistic borders are being transgressed, perhaps until they become meaningless or until the American continent ceases to be not just Anglo/European, not just white, not just the place where the "Otherness" of the subaltern subject remains at the margins.

CONCLUSION

By revisiting the more than a century-old concept of *nuestra América*, I am arguing for the need to "reinvent" it in view of contemporary Latino realities. Any continental vision of Latino(a) identities can no longer ignore the cultural and historical realities and legacies bestowed by those generations of Latinos who have forged their lives in the United States, but who remain interconnected with their countries of origin. Thus, the historical and cultural experience of U. S. Latinos is forcing scholars also to transgress the barriers imposed by national frontiers and by conventionally defined parameters about what constitutes Latin American or Caribbean cultural authenticity. Ultimately, this means breaking away from purist notions of both cultural and linguistic processes.

Moreover, in the postmodern world of expanding transnational interconnections, it is no longer tenable to talk about the concept of *nuestra América* without, as I suggest here, including the U. S. Latino population. More than ever before, the two Americas intertwine, at a time when, paradoxically, some sectors of U. S. society view with increasing disdain and hostility the more visible presence of minorities and (im)migrants. The current U. S. anti-immigration backlash is fostering a polarizing discourse that appeals to deeply ingrained prejudices and fears, and attempts to reverse many of the modest gains of recent decades in the battle against social, racial, and gender inequalities. This environment is turning into fertile ground for the spread of xenophobic attitudes aimed at the closing of borders to labor while, ironically and contradictorily, they remain widely open to the global circulation of capital.

The decade of the 1990s has witnessed to the Quincentennial commemoration of the encounter between the Old and New Worlds, and the centennial of the Spanish-Cuban-American War, which ended Spanish imperial domination in the Americas, but established the United States as the dominant power within the hemisphere. Rather than fall into the "fin de siécle" malaise or recriminations that so predominated the Spanish and Latin American worlds a century ago, Latinos should take this opportunity to reexamine the multifaceted interactions between the interconnected, multicultural worlds of the North and South. More than any other group, Latinos are bridging the Americas and, in so doing, are restoring the original hemispheric sense to the name America by producing the kind of emancipatory knowledge that recognizes multiple cultural citizenships, experiences, and alliances. They also are promoting a liberating dialogue about the hemisphere based not on one dominant country's exceptionalism, but on the many identities most of us share. Only when the multicultural and multiracial wealth of all the American nations are fully recognized will societies move closer to achieving the human equality and dignity that so many groups are struggling for.

NOTES

1.   Immigrants are those individuals that come to the United States from foreign countries. Migrants are populations that move within the same national territory or have established back and forth patterns of movement between the host society and their countries of origin. For instance, since Puerto Rico is a U. S. territory and Puerto Ricans are U. S. citizens by birth, technically, they are considered migrants and not immigrants.

2.   For a discussion of the origins and shortcomings of the term Latin America, see Daniel Mato, "Problems in the Making of Representations of All-Encompassing U. S. Latino(a)-"Latin" American Transnational Identities," *Latino Review of Books* 3.1-2 (1997): 2-7. This dichotomized Anglo-Latin view of the Americas has been common in the literature since the early nineteenth century.

3.   See *Idea y cuestión nacional latinoamericanas* by Ricaurte Soler (Mexico City: Siglo Ventiuno, 1980). Among the Latin American figures who have used the concept of *nuestra América* in their writings prior to Martí are Francisco Miranda, Fray Servando Teresa de Mier, and Simón Bolívar.

4.   I use the terms pan-national and pan-ethnic to mean those ideologies that transcend the nationalities or ethnicities of individual groups who share certain commonalties and promote a unified sense of collective identification. The term transnational refers to reciprocal or bi-directional cultural exchanges and interactions between the (im)migrants' host society (in this case, the United States) and their countries of origin.

5.   Irma Watkins-Owens (1996) begins an explanation of the relations between African Americans and Afro-Caribbeans in Harlem in her book, *Blood Relations.*

6.   Martí also helped found the Liga de Instrucción de Tampa, modeled after the one in New York. See Nancy Raquel Mirabal (1995), "'Más que negro': José Martí and the Politics of Unity," in *José Martí in the United States: The Florida Experience,* edited by Louis A. Pérez, Jr., pp. 57-70, Arizona State University Center for Latin American Studies, Tempe.

7.   The terms used to identify U. S. ethnic groups may differ or may be accorded different meanings depending on the historical period. Since the 1970s, U. S. government agencies have used the umbrella term Hispanic to identify the sector of the U. S. population with origins in Spanish-speaking nations. In prior decades, however, these groups were mostly identified by or preferred to identify themselves by their individual nationalities (e.g., Mexican American/Chicano, Puerto Rican, Cuban). In the 1980s, the groups themselves showed an increased preference for using the Spanish term Latino over the U. S. government's English term Hispanic for collective identification purposes. Individual nationalities are still commonly used and often preferred in differentiating the experiences of the many groups that are included under the Hispanic/Latino umbrella. Recognizing the contested nature and fluidity of many ethnic identification labels, I have chosen to use the more contemporary term Latino here and to introduce the term Hispanic only when citing official U. S. Census data or when referring to past historical periods.

According to the U. S. Census official definition, the Hispanic category includes individuals born in any of the nineteen Spanish-speaking countries of Latin America and the Caribbean, or in Spain. Thus the official definition excludes non-Spanish-speaking Latin Americans such as Haitians and Brazilians. It also should be noted that despite its current use as a collective identifier for U. S. Latinos, the terms Latino and *latinoamericano* are generally used outside the United States to refer to the people of Latin America and the Caribbean.

8. See National Association of Hispanic Publications and U. S. Bureau of the Census (1995), *Hispanics Latinos: Diverse People in a Multicultural Society,* National Association and Bureau of the Census, Washington D. C.

9. See Acosta-Belén (1993). The Center for Latino, Latin American, and Caribbean Studies (CELAC) at the State University of New York at Albany, collaborated with the University of Houston's *Recovery Project* in the indexing, annotation, and analysis of Hispanic periodicals.

10. For a discussion on the concept of interlinguality, see Bruce-Novoa (1980:27-30).

REFERENCES CITED

Acosta-Belén, Edna
  1993   The Building of the Community: Puerto Rican Writers and Activists in New York City, 1890s-1960s. In *Recovering the U. S. Hispanic Literary Heritage,* edited by Ramón Gutiérrez, and Genaro Padilla, pp. 179-195. Arte Público Press, Houston.
Acosta-Belén, Edna, and Carlos E. Santiago
  1995   Merging Borders: The Remapping of America. *The Latino Review of Books* 1:2-12.
Andreu Iglesias, César (editor)
  1977   *Memorias de Bernardo Vega.* Ediciones Huracán, Río Piedras, Puerto Rico.
  1984   *Memiors of Bernardo Vega.* Translated by Juan Flores. Monthly Review Press, New York
Anzaldúa, Gloria
  1987   *Borderlands/ La frontera: The New Mestiza.* Spinsters/Aunt Lute, San Francisco.
Bammer, Angelika
  1994   *Displacements: Cultural Identities in Question.* Indiana University Press, Bloomington.
Behar, Ruth, and Juan León (editors)
  1994   *Bridges to Cuba/Puentes a Cuba. Special Issue of Michigan Quarterly Review* 33:3-4.
Bruce-Novoa, Juan
  1980   *Chicano Authors: Inquiry by Interview.* University of Texas Press, Austin.
Casal, Lourdes
  1994   For Ana Veldford. *Michigan Quarterly Review* 33:415-416.
Colón, Jesús
  1961   *A Puerto Rican in New York and Other Sketches.* Mainstream Publishers, New York. Second Edition 1982. International Publishers, New York.
Cunard, Nancy
  1984   *Negro: An Anthology.* African Caribbean Poetry Theatre, New York.

Esteves, Sandra María
1984 *Tropical Rains*. African Caribbean Poetry Theatre, New York.
Flores, Juan
1995 The Latino Imaginary: Dimensions of Community and Identity. In *Polifonía salvaje: Ensayos de cultura y política en la postmodernidad*, edited by Irma Rivera Nieves, and Carlos Gil, pp. 108-120. Editorial Posdata, San Juan, Puerto Rico.
1996 Pan-Latino, Trans-Latino: Puerto Ricans in the New Nueva York. *Centro* 8:170-186.
Fox, Geoffrey
1996 *Hispanic Nation: Culture, Politics, and the Constructing of Identity*. Birch Lane Press, New York.
Garcia Canclini, Néstor
1995 *Hybrid Cultures: Strategies for Entering and Leaving Modernity*. Translated by Christopher L. Chiappari, and Silvia L. López. University of Minnesota Press, Minneapolis.
Glazer, Nathan
1997 *We are all Multiculturalists Now*. Harvard University Press, Cambridge.
Gómez, Alma, Cherríe Moraga, and Mariana Romo-Carmona (editors)
1983 *Cuentos: Stories by Latinas*. First edition. Kitchen Table Press, New York.
Gómez-Peña, Guillermo
1993 *Warrior for Gringostroika*. Graywolf Press, Saint Paul, Minnesota.
Horno-Delgado, Asunción, Elianda Ortega, and Nina M. Scott
1989 *Breaking Boundaries: Latina Writings and Critical Readings*. University of Massachusetts Press, Amherst.
Kaplan, Amy, and Donald Pease (editors)
1993 *Cultures of United States Imperialism*. Duke University Press, Durham.
Laviera, Tato
1985 *AmeRícan*. Arte Público Press, Houston.
Levins Morales, Aurora, and Rosario Morales
1981 *Getting Home Alive*. Firebrand Books, Ithaca, New York.
Martí, José
1953 *The America of José Martí*. Translated by Juan de Onís. Noonday Press, New York.
1968 *En los Estados Unidos*. Edited by Andrés Sorel. Alianza Editorial, Madrid.
1977 *Our America*. Edited by Philip S. Foner. Translated by Elinor Randall, with additional translations by Juan de Onís, and Roslyn Held Foner. Monthly Review Press, New York.
Moraga, Cherríe, and Gloria Anzaldúa (editors)
1981 *This Bridge Called My Back*. Kitchen Table Press, New York.
Moraga, Cherríe, and Ana Castillo (editors)
1988 *Este puente, mi espalda*. Translated by Ana Castillo, and Norma Alarcón. ISM, San Francisco.
Noble, David W.
1985 *The End of American History*. University of Minnesota Press, Minneapolis.
Pérez, Louis, Jr. (editor)
1995 *José Martí in the United States: The Florida Experience*. Special Study no. 28. Center for Latin American Studies, Arizona State University, Tempe.

Portes, Alejandro, and Rubén G. Rumbaut
   1990   *Immigrant America: A Portrait*. University of California Press, Berkeley.
Ramos, Juanita (editor)
   1987   *Compañeras: Latina Lesbians*. First edition. Latina Lesbian History Project, New York.
Sánchez, Luis Rafael
   1994   *La guagua aérea*. Editorial Cultural, Río Piedras, Puerto Rico.
Sánchez Korrol, Virginia
   1988   Latinismo Among Early Puerto Rican Migrants in New York City: A Sociohistoric Interpretation. In *The Hispanic Experience in the United States*, edited by Edna Acosta-Belén, and Barbara R. Sjostrom, pp. 151-162. Praeger Publishers, New York.
   1994   *From Colonia to Community: A History of Puerto Ricans in New York City, 1917-1948*. Second Edition. University of California Press, Los Angeles.
Schlesinger, Arthur
   1991   *The Disuniting of America: Reflections on a Multicultural Society*. Whittle Direct, Knoxville, Tennessee.
Schomburg, Arthur
   1970   From Racial Integrity: A Plea for the Establishment of a Chair of Negro History. In *Negro: An Anthology*, edited by Nancy Cunard, pp. 74-78. Frederick Ungar, New York.
Sinnette, Elinor Des Verney
   1989   *Arthur Alfonso Schomburg: Black Bibliophile & Collector*. New York Public Library and Wayne State University Press, New York and Detroit.
Stavans, Ilan
   1995   *The Hispanic Condition: Reflections on Culture and Identity in America*. Harper Collins, New York.
Sutton, Constance R., and Elsa M. Chaney (editors)
   1987   *Caribbean Life in New York City*. Center for Migration Studies, New York.
U. S. Bureau of the Census
   1993   *Hispanic Americans Today*. Current Population Reports, Series P23-183. Government Printing Office, Washington D. C.
   1994   *Current Population Survey*. Government Printing Office, Washington D. C.
   1996   *Population Projections of the United States by Age, Sex, Race, and Hispanic Origin: 1995-2050*. Current Population Reports, Series P25-1130. Government Printing Office, Washington D. C.
Wallerstein, Immanuel
   1980   *The Modern World System II: Mercantilism and the Consolidation of the European World-economy, 1600-1750*. Academic Press, New York.
Watkins-Owens, Irma
   1996   *Blood Relations: Caribbean Immigrants and the Harlem Community, 1900-1930*. Indiana University Press, Bloomington.
Wolf, Eric R.
   1982   *Europe and the People Without History*. University of California Press, Berkeley.

6

Pan-Latino / Trans-Latino

Puerto Ricans in the "New Nueva York"

Juan Flores

One of the most dramatic and visible changes in the face of New York City over the past 20 years or so has been the growing diversity of its Latino presence. Of course Puerto Ricans have never been the lone Spanish-speaking group here; earlier chapters of that history, as told by chroniclers like Bernardo Vega and Jesús Colón, abound with accounts of Cubans, Dominicans, Spaniards, Mexicans, and many other "Hispanos" making common cause with Puerto Ricans in everyday life and in social struggles on many fronts. But over the decades, and especially with the mass migration of the 1950s, Puerto Ricans have so outnumbered all other Latinos that they have served as the prototype or archetype—certainly the stereotype—of Latino/Hispanic/ "Spanish" New York. Increasingly since the 1920s, and indelibly with influential representations of Puerto Rican culture such as *West Side Story* and Oscar Lewis' *La Vida*, the overlap has been nearly complete, the terms "Latin New York" and "Puerto Rican" ringing virtually synonymous in the public mind.

By the 1990s that image—based of course on unambiguous demographic realities—has waned significantly, especially as the media and many research efforts tend to find greater delight in the novelties and anomalies of "other," more exotic newcomers than in the more familiar Puerto Rican culture. And

Reprinted, with changes, from the *Centro Journal* 8, no. 1/2 (1996):170-186, by permission of the publisher.

yet, the growth, quantitative and qualitative, of the Dominican community, especially in New York City and in urban Puerto Rico, has been nothing short of sensational; the political and cultural consequences of such growth, for New York, the Dominican Republic, Puerto Rico, and perhaps most of all for the Puerto Rican community in New York, are already highly visible and promise to increase over time.

The "Mexicanization" of New York has also proceeded apace, especially over the past decade; in fact, for some years the proportional arrival rates of migration from the Mexican state of Puebla may even exceed those from the Dominican Republic. Add to them the huge numbers of Colombians, Salvadorans, Ecuadorians, Panamanians, Hondurans, Haitians, Brazilians, and the "new" New Yorkers from nearly every country of Latin America and the Caribbean, and it is clear why "Latinos in New York" no longer rhymes with Puerto Rican.

This momentous pan-Latinization over the course of a single generation makes it necessary to rethink the whole issue of Puerto Rican culture and identity in the United States. How does Puerto Rican/Nuyorican (self) identification and cultural history interface with and elude the pan-ethnic "Latino" or "Hispanic" label? We must remember that such an identification has by now become stock-in-trade of most media, government, commercial, social science, and literary-cultural "coverage," so that Puerto Ricans themselves have constant recourse to the term in extending their political, cultural, and intellectual reach in accord with changing social realities. For while we may be appropriately critical and even suspicious in the face of the catchall categories, a contemporary analysis of Puerto Rican culture and politics in New York necessarily invokes a more embracing term and idea such as "Latino" to refer to what is clearly an ensemble of congruent and intertwining historical experiences. Most of the deliberation over the Latino/Hispanic label thus far has been national in reference, or with a mind to areas, mostly cities, witnessing ample interaction among more or less equally sizeable Latino groups (Chicago is the first example to come to mind, though Los Angeles and Miami are also pertinent). But in many ways it is New York which has become the pan-Latin city par excellence. And it is perhaps here, in the "new," post-Nuyorican Nueva York, that the Latino concept of group association stands its strongest test.

THE NEW MIX

The first signs of imminent change can be traced to the early 1960s. The aftermath of the 1959 Cuban Revolution brought a huge new influx of Cuban exiles, many of them settling in the New York area. The death of Trujillo in 1961 marked an easing of the restrictive emigration policies that had prevailed in the Dominican Republic throughout the Trujillo era (1930-1960). Pressing economic conditions and ongoing political strife, especially the civil war and American military invasion in 1965, have propelled growing numbers of Dominicans to immigrate to the United States ever since. The overwhelming majority of them—by 1990 a full two-thirds—came to New York City.

But what is considered the single most important factor to usher in the "new immigration" was the change in the U. S. immigration law in 1965, which put an end to the national origins quota system, in effect since the 1920s, favoring northern and western Europeans. This policy shift, which placed a ceiling of 120,000 people each for Asia and the Western Hemisphere, literally opened the floodgates to a massive immigration from many parts of Asia and most countries of Latin America and the Caribbean. True to its longstanding historical role, New York City has continued to be a favored destination for these new arrivals, and the figures for the post-1965 period are indeed telling. "In the past two decades," it was reported in 1987, "more than a million immigrants have settled in New York City, most from the West Indies, Latin America, and Asia" (Foner 1987:1). According to the 1980 U. S. Census, 80 percent of the Asian-born, 82 percent of the Jamaican-born, and 88 percent of the Trinidad-born residents in the New York metropolitan area had arrived since 1965 (Foner 1987:3). That was how things stood a decade before the 1990 count, which recorded an even greater increase of new arrivals.

New New Yorkers from Spanish-speaking countries, increasingly referred to in official parlance as "Hispanics," figure prominently in this demographic explosion, and their numbers are true to the pattern. With the exception of Puerto Ricans and Cubans, representation from nearly all countries of Latin America and the Spanish Caribbean has increased geometrically over the decades since 1960. Already numbering nearly a million according to official count by 1960, the size of the composite New York Latino population has more than doubled by 1990 to make up a full fourth of all New Yorkers, equal in proportion to African Americans. National groups with only a minor presence of one or two thousand in 1960 (for example, Salvadorans, Guatemalans, Hondurans, and Peruvians) have grown to around 20,000 by 1990, while the ranks of Colombians, Ecuadorians, and Mexicans have swelled to well over 50,000 each within the thirty-year period. The most dramatic increase, of course, is among the Dominicans, who at 13,293 represented 1.7 percent of the city's Latino population in 1960; by 1990, Dominican New Yorkers totaled 332,713 or 18.7 percent of Latinos in New York, making them by far the largest Latino community after the Puerto Ricans (Haslip-Viera 1996).

But while the legislative change of 1965, and for the sake of statistical contrast the 1960 U. S. Census, may serve as convenient signposts for marking

off the "old" from the "new" immigration period, the most dramatic demographic leaps among New York Latino groups actually occur a decade later
and thereafter. The "New Nueva York," as *New York Newsday* titled a lengthy
supplement on the city's Latinos in October 1991, is really a phenomenon of
the 1980s and 1990s, though trends did point clearly in that direction by the
later 1970s. If one looks at the overall Latino population, it is true that growth
has been roughly the same per decade since 1960. But when it comes to the
diversification of New York's Latinos, and the emergence of the "pan-Latino"
face by which the city is now recognized, the last quarter of the twentieth century makes for a more accurate time frame. For, to begin with, it was in the
1970s that the Puerto Rican migration, having reaching a benchmark around
1970, leveled off significantly. Puerto Ricans continued to arrive by the thousands, but their numbers were more than offset by a continually growing return
migration and by diaspora-like dispersion in the United States.

Relative to many other Latino groups, and to the composite Latino population, the proportion of Puerto Ricans has been on a steady decline: over eighty
percent in 1960. Latin New York is now only half Puerto Rican, with a full ten
percent drop in the 1980s. Cuban New Yorkers, after doubling in size in the post-
Revolution 1960s, have been declining substantially ever since; long the city's
second largest Hispanic group, and still so in 1970, they were far surpassed by
Dominicans during the 1970s; by 1980 there were twice as many Dominicans
as Cubans, and by 1990 over six times as many. By 1990, in fact, Cubans no
longer even counted among the five largest Latino groups in the city: in 1980
they were still a comfortable third, but by the latest of fiscal tabulation they
have come to be outnumbered by Colombians, Ecuadorians, and Mexicans, with
Salvadorans, Panamanians, and Peruvians ranging not too far behind.

This radical reconfiguration of the Latino mix in New York is of course
a highly complex, conjunctional process, with layers and levels of explanation
as diverse as the range of Latin American nationalities that have come to reside
in the city in the present generation. Rather than one, pan-Latino story of
arrival and settlement in New York, there are clearly Cuban, Puerto Rican,
Dominican, Salvadoran and Colombian stories, each of them bearing varied
and sometimes jarring internal narratives of their own. Still, the stories all con-
verge in "Nueva York," achieving full hemispheric representation, including even
that crucial Mexican component, by 1990. The common locus of new social
experience and identity formation is New York City, just at a time when it is
being christened a "global city" in the contemporary sense.[1]

It is in the story of present-day New York City, and its restructuring in
accord with its global geo-economic role, that it is possible to find a framework
in which to interpret the huge and diverse Latino presence. The history of the
"new" immigration takes on a different range and contour when viewed from
the perspective of Latinos in New York. Rather than stretching from 1965 to the

present, the change-over from "old" to "new" immigration is comprised of two periods corresponding with two phases in the restructuring of the city's economy since mid-century, with the turning point marked by the fiscal crisis of the mid-1970s. The first phase, from 1950 to 1975 (but especially since the early 1960s) amounted to a time of "dashed hopes" of Puerto Ricans; the second, since 1975, is characterized by their "re-placement" in both senses of the word—to other places, and by other groups.

When Puerto Ricans began flocking to New York by the tens and hundreds of thousands in the late 1940s and early 1950s, hopes were high, and expectations only reasonable, that over time they would find their place in the local economy. There would be gaps to fill in the city's postwar labor market, the thinking went, and adequate employment opportunities for newcomers, which in those years meant predominantly Puerto Ricans and African Americans. "Assuming continued regional vitality and an effective educational system, there was no a priori reason to doubt the likelihood of successful incorporation of these groups into the economic mainstream" (Torres and Bonilla 1993:98-99). The shared historical experience between Latinos and African Americans warrants particular emphasis: New York's "Negroes and Puerto Ricans" were, after all, the "newcomers" in Oscar Handlin's influential 1959 book of that title (Handlin 1959).

But "continued regional vitality," presupposing as it does for the "global city" continued national and international economic vitality, was decidedly not in the offering. The stagnation that set in by the late 1950s, combined with the disastrous aftermath of the Operation Bootstrap experiment, dashed whatever hopes Puerto Ricans might have held to strike a more stable and favorable foothold in New York life. "For Puerto Ricans the principal outcome of this period was labor force displacement, manifested in a sharp decline in labor force participation and a rise in unemployment from 1960 to 1970" (Torres and Bonilla 1993:99). In 1976, in what amounts to a taking stock of this phase, the United States Commission of Civil Rights released its alarming report, *Puerto Ricans in the Continental United States: An Uncertain Future,* which put Puerto Ricans on record as the exception to the rule of immigrant incorporation and advancement (U. S. Commission of Civil Rights 1976).[2]

The second phase, beginning in the mid-1970s, brought a continuation of these developments, but at more intense levels and in different ways. Unemployment levels among Puerto Ricans magnified as stable jobs in both the corporate and public sectors became ever scarcer. Public employment opportunities, which had expanded consistently since mid-century and absorbed increasing numbers of Puerto Rican and African American workers, were curtailed sharply as a result of the fiscal crisis of 1975-76, with Puerto Ricans being the heaviest casualties in this shrinkage. The replacement of relocated corporations by service industries and light manufacturing harbored little hope, as both "established a new profile of occupations and labor process" largely inaccessible to African Americans and Puerto Ricans. The reorganization of light manufacturing since the mid-1970s in particular spelled the large-scale "re-placement" of Puerto Ricans by more recent immigrants, mostly other Latinos: "The labor force attached to the earlier manufacturing complex, which had been displaced to a significant extent, was not redeployed into the newly evolving sector. The growth of the new sector was dependent on a lower cost of labor, a condition met by the use of new sources of immigrant labor." And further, "It is a considerably revamped manufacturing sector [in which Puerto Ricans have had a historically high representation], dependent on lower labor costs, that has largely absorbed Dominican labor," though it is added that "since the mid-1980s, the garment industry has suffered a new period of decline" (Torres and Bonilla 1993:102-3).

"Decline within Decline," the title of the article cited, seems an apt description of what New York's huge Latino population has experienced in recent decades, at least when it comes to its fit into a sharply fluctuating labor market. For the critical socioeconomic hardships confronting the New York's "new" Latinos in the 1990s are an extension, a further stage, in a local, regional and global restructuring process extending back to the 1950s and experienced at its onset by an overwhelmingly Puerto Rican population. In important ways, adjustments in the city as a postindustrial command center propelled the demographic movements leading to its most recent repeopling. The emergence of a "pan-Latino" New York comes in the wake of a prior move to import and incorporate Puerto Ricans.

Whatever the parallels and differences, though, the pan-ethnic diversity of the current Latino population is in large measure a reflex of major structural shifts as manifest in the regional political economy of the "global city." The history of this adjustment extends back to the immediate postwar years and has entailed a paradigmatic change in the immigrant experience from the "old," mainly European, to the "new," mainly Hispanic. Viewed in its full trajectory, the Latinization of New York centers on the congruencies and contrasts between Puerto Ricans and the other Latino groups, individually and as a composite. With a century of experience here, New York Puerto Ricans actually straddle the "old" and the "new," and their emigration en masse in the 1950s and 1960s was clearly the first wave of the "new" non-European flow. Rather than just one more among the many Latino groups, receding in relative prominence as the others expand and dig in, the Puerto Rican community remains at the crux of any consideration of Latinos in New York, the historical touchstone against which all that follows must be considered.

The embattled concept of "Latino" or "Hispanic" is once again at issue in present-day public discourse, and by extension the policy and practices of pan-ethnic categorization. Within the same generation in which New York came to join Chicago, Miami, Houston, and Los Angeles as "pan-Latino" cities on a contemporary scale, the terms Latino and Hispanic have established themselves firmly in everyday U. S. parlance. The debate over the relative validity and limitations of the terms—connected to the volatile questions of race and immigration—rages close to the combat zone in the culture wars of our time. Before returning to the "New Nueva York" and assessing the new issues of Puerto Rican cultural identity raised by its recent reconfiguration, a critical engagement of that discourse may suggest an appropriate theoretical framework.

ETHNIC, PAN-ETHNIC

The terms Hispanic and Latino have come into such wide currency since the 1970s, and especially since the official use of "Hispanic" in the 1980 U. S. Census, that they have the ring of neologisms, fresh coinages for a new, as yet unnamed presence on the social scene. Historical memory seems to stop short at the height of the Chicano and Puerto Rican movements, when it comes to a genealogy of these new labels. Yet the people thus labeled have been using these and similar terms, in English and Spanish, to identify themselves at least since the 1920s and probably much earlier. For example, in New York—which when compared to the Southwest is the younger and smaller of the two major concentrations of Hispanic peoples—there were as many organizations, periodicals, movements and events with "Latino," "*Hispano,*" "Latin," "Spanish," and "Spanish-speaking" in their titles as there were "*Puertorriqueño,*" "Puerto Rican" or "*Boricua.*"[3] Indeed, what could be more "Latino" in the sense of pan-ethnic solidarity than the Partido Revolucionario Cubano with its "Sección de Puerto Rico," which united the two Caribbean nationalities in joint struggle against Spanish colonialism? The Partido, and its affiliated Club Dos Antillas, which included Dominicans and sundry "others," were active in New York City over 100 years ago.

The sense and practice of a Latino/Hispanic unity across national lines thus has a long and complex history, as does the recognized need for names to designate such tactical or enduring common ground. Even the government bureaucracy was not without its earlier pan-group usage: before "Hispanic" the traditional entry had been "Spanish Origin," with "Spanish/Hispanic origin or descent" cropping up frequently in explanatory memos prior to the 1980 U. S. Census (see Forbes 1992). And there are continuities between the older and the more recent (self)-identifications, not the least of which is their consistent Eurocentric connotation. Though surely outnumbered by the casualties of time and renaming, there are pan-Latino organizations, newspapers, neighborhoods, and of course people from the earlier decades who attest to the longevity of the cross-ethnic newborn whose baptism we are now asked to celebrate, or at least acknowledge. Scholars have argued that the "racialization" of Latin American and Caribbean peoples in the United States (the "othering" process for which the label "Hispanic" provides an official seal) spans the full twentieth century, and much of the nineteenth century as well if we extend the frame to include hemispheric relations (Forbes 1992; Giménez 1992; F. Padilla 1990; Robinson 1992). What is new, if not the object or act of signification, is the discursive context and sociohistorical climate in which the (self-) naming is enacted. The quantum growth, diversification, and dispersal of the Latino populations over a single generation are surely at the base of this change, though the many Latino social and cultural movements since the late 1960s also resonate strongly in the new semantic reality. More than the census count itself, it is the echoing cries of "Brown Power" and the alarm signals about "America's fastest growing minority" that have set the temper for the present discourse—a collective mood ranging from radical defiance to a national anguish bordering on hysteria. By the 1990s, "Hispanic" and "Latino" are everywhere. The terms, like the people themselves, have proliferated in numbers and locations, and assumed an emotional charge and connotative complexity unknown in their previous historical usages.

And the "coverage," in the form of media specials and academic studies, also abounds. In the 1980s and 1990s, most major newspapers and magazines dedicated investigative surveys and extensive portraits of the "new Americans" from south of the border, while in the same period dozens of books and hundreds of journal articles have focused on the "sleeping giant" of U. S. cultural and political life. The subject has shifted from the experience of a single national or regional group—Caribbeans, Mexicans or Central Americans—to the "Hispanic" or "Latino" experience, with an emphasis on commonalties and interactions across groups. The first half of the 1990s alone saw the publication of the following book titles: *Latinos: Biography of a People* (Shorris 1992); *Latinos in a Changing U. S. Economy: Comparative Perspectives on Growing Inequality* (Morales and Bonilla 1993); *Out of the Barrio: Toward a New Politics of Hispanic Assimilation* (Chavez 1991); *Ethnic Labels, Latino Lives: Identity and the Politics of (Re)Presentation in the United States* (Oboler 1995); *The Hispanic Condition: Reflections on Culture and Identity in America* (Stavans 1995); and even, *Everything You Need to Know about Latino History* (Novas 1994). Even though these works vary along political, methodological and stylistic lines they all tend to accept the validity of the pan-category and proceed to make their observations, analyses, and policy proposals on that basis. Disclaimers and qualifiers abound, of course, and a book like Earl Shorris' (1992) *Latinos: A Biography of a People* actually discusses more differences among the groups than their similarities, and the promised story line ends up splintering into what are really "biographies of people." There is little effort to scrutinize the category itself. The theoretical options that are offered often amount to a stereotyped counter-position of "Hispanic" vs. "Latino," with no evidence of a consensus as to the preferred term.[4] All of these writings, however, assume that the terms refer to something real or in the making, whether it is a demographic aggregate, a voting bloc, a market, a language or cultural group, a "community" or, in Ilan Stavans' grandiloquent phrase, a "condition." Given the xenophobic tenor of mainstream politics in the 1990s, which perceives "Hispanic" and "Latino" most of all as a "problem" ("HisPANIC Causing Panic"), such conceptions are necessary and contribute to the social construction of a major group identity.

A consensus of these writings would probably settle on ethnicity as the concept that most closely approximates the bond among Latinos, and the boundary that marks them off from "others" in U. S. settings. Though the phrase "Hispanic ethnic group" does not always appear as such, the underlying premise throughout America today is that, insofar as Latinos comprise a definable group, they are an ethnicity. But even in the cultural and demographic literature that does lump Hispanics together, there is an abiding awareness that this is an ethnicity of ethnicities, an "ethnic group" that only exists through its constituent "subgroups."

A more circumspect line of thinking therefore refers to Latinos as a pan-ethnicity; a group formation that emerges out of the interaction or close historical congruence of two or more culturally related ethnicities. Writers like David López, Yen Espiritu, and others have advanced a pan-ethnic approach[5] which has the distinct advantage of centering analysis on the dialectic between the parts and the whole, the discrete national groups and the "Latino" construct. The focus is necessarily on interaction, while the social group itself, along with its "discourse," is understood as process rather than as a fixed entity or meaning.

An early instance of such an approach, though predating concepts like pan-ethnicity by over a decade, is Félix Padilla's *Latino Ethnic Consciousness: The Case of Mexican Americans and Puerto Ricans in Chicago*. Published in 1985, the book is actually based on case studies from the early 1970s, when Chicago was still the city with the nation's most substantial multi-Latino population, and the two largest groups were Mexican Americans and Puerto Ricans. Padilla's aim is to analyze "the process of Latino/Hispanic ethnic group formation in the city of Chicago" (F. Padilla 1985a:7). He is interested in the "conditions that have enabled Mexican Americans and Puerto Ricans to transcend the boundaries of the respective nationally and culturally based communities and adopt a new and different collective 'Latino' or 'Hispanic' identity during the early years of the 1970s." By studying the "interaction process involving Puerto Ricans and Mexican Americans," he seeks to understand the emergence of a "Latino or

Hispanic ethnic-conscious identity and behavior, distinct and separate from the groups' individual ethnic identities" (F. Padilla 1985a:7). The strength and the weakness of Padilla's book, looked at now with the advantage of hindsight, lie in its pragmatism. On the positive side, it is a serious study of an imperative issue in pan-ethnic analysis: the actual social interaction between and among Latino groups. Focusing on the lived experience of distinct but kindred communities coming together to act and feel as one, Padilla avoids cultural essentialism before that pitfall was being talked about, at least in present-day terms. To this end, he argues well for an understanding of Latino unity as "situational"—and also "political" in the sense of being grounded in the recognition of shared social interests.

The problem with this on-the-ground, pragmatic concept of Latinismo, however, is that it reduces the object of study, "ethnic consciousness," to "behavior" (the words are coupled throughout, often as synonyms). And because the emergent Latino identity is taken in such explicit and deliberate separation from Mexican American or Puerto Rican identity, the process of pan-ethnic formation is disengaged from the historical trajectories of each group. The book is notably sparse, in fact, on such background, and on any sustained attempt to explain how so many Mexicans and Puerto Ricans got to Chicago in the first place. Contrary to his own expressed political sentiments, and his views about "Latinismo" that appear in his subsequent writings (F. Padilla 1985b, 1990), Padilla effectively divorces the formation of pan-Latino unity from its larger international context, Latin America.

Many of these limitations are averted, and the terms of analysis significantly updated, in Suzanne Oboler's recent book, *Ethnic Labels, Latino Lives: Identity and the Politics of (Re)Presentation in the United States* (1995, see also chap. 4 this volume). Here the hemispheric sensibility is more alive, as would befit a Peruvian American writing in the years when "Latino ethnic consciousness" is being infused with perspectives and experiences from all over nuestra América. Oboler treats the conceptualization of Latino identity in much broader theoretical and historical terms than does Padilla. Indeed, her treatment is broader than other writings on the subject to date. And while expansive, her account of "the Hispanic condition" wisely avoids the presumptuousness, and the glaring errors, of Ilan Stavans in his book of that unhappy title (Stavans 1995).[6] Most important, Oboler is writing after the term "Hispanic" had been made official as a census category and during its commercial circulation as an item of semantic consumption.

Oboler's major contribution, as her title indicates, is the critical scrutiny of that clash between labels and lives; that is, between imposed and assumed identities. She traces the genesis of and motives behind the newfound policy toward Hispanics, and relates it to a larger process of racialization (*Latin American Perspectives* 1992).[7] The sharp dramatization of the crisis of

Latino "(re)presentation," the inclusive yet critical sense of a fully pan-Latino identity, and the sustained attention to gender and class differentiations make *Ethnic Labels, Latino Lives* (Oboler 1995) an important and welcome advance beyond the methodological and theoretical limitations of Padilla's earlier study.

Nevertheless, when it comes to the Latino concept itself, Oboler remains within Padilla's universe of discourse, or at least in close proximity to it. Ethnicity, as a reliable category of social differentiation, still reigns supreme. She also uses the inevitable equivocation, when referring to Latinos, about the two "levels" or kinds of ethnic affiliation: the single group and the pan-ethnic. Oboler repeatedly points out the lazy relativism and arbitrariness of the ethnic concept, and calls for a historical and structural differentiation among the "Latino" groups. At points she even sides with skeptics, such as Martha Giménez and David Hayes-Bautista (*Latin American Perspectives* 1992), and would seem to do away with the "Hispanic" category altogether (Oboler 1995:3-6). But she pulls back from the implications of Giménez's distinction between "ethnics" and "minorities" and, especially in the second, ethnographic half of her book, lapses into a "Latino" ethnic relativism of her own.

Oboler conducted her fieldwork—her testing ground for the utility of the Hispanic/Latino label—in New York City in 1988 and 1990. While teaching English as a Second Language classes for a union education program, she interviewed thirteen women and nine men who worked in the garment industry. Her informants, most of them between thirty and sixty years old, come from nine different Latin American countries. It is significant that her sample only includes two Puerto Ricans born in New York ("Juan" and "Teresa") and three Puerto Ricans in all. There were four Colombians, three Dominicans, three Nicaraguans, and two each from Peru, Honduras, and El Salvador. Throughout the book, and when introducing her findings, she emphasizes the main crack in the "Hispanic" front, the difference between the Latin American "immigrant populations" and the "more historically established communities of Chicanos and Puerto Ricans" (Oboler 1995:102). Even though in her conclusions she reminds us: "Again, the study is not representative of the immigrant populations from Latin America nor of the Puerto Ricans in New York City"(Oboler 1995:157), she fails to mention that when she conducted her fieldwork more than fifty percent of New York Latinos were Puerto Rican.

Despite her theoretical intentions, the ethnographic section of *Ethnic Labels, Latino Lives* (Oboler 1995) underplays one of the serious perils in using the Hispanic category, a danger that Martha Giménez for one has identified as potentially "racist". "These labels are racist in that...they reduce people to interchangeable entities, negating the qualitative differences between, for example, persons of Puerto Rican descent who have lived for generations in New York City and newly arrived immigrants from Chile or some other South or Central American country" (Giménez 1992:8). It is clear from her theoretical caveats that Oboler does not exactly "negate" these differences. In fact, it is so significant that she even describes her sample as "a small group of twenty-one Latin American immigrants and one U. S.-born Puerto Rican" (Oboler 1995:102), and when first defining her studies she seems to have been uncertain even about including any Puerto Ricans, especially those from the U. S. (Oboler 1995:110). Her report itself has repeated recourse to such conditionals as "many Hispanics, regardless of country of origin (and again, with the exception of Puerto Ricans)," or "leaving aside the U. S.-born Puerto Rican" (Oboler 1995:111, 122). The irony is that Oboler does not even need these warning signals; her interviews speak for themselves. "Juan," and to some extent "Teresa," her two U. S.-born Puerto Rican infomants, make statements and express views about Hispanic identity and U. S. society that stand out markedly among all the testimony. For example, Juan states, "I'm American only by accident, because Puerto Rico's a territory of the United States. I don't think it's by choice, because they've got American bases there" (Oboler 1995:152). Even "Jorge," a native-born Puerto Rican, responds to the "Latino" category in a way unmatched by the other foreign-born informants: "At the beginning, when I arrived, my boss wanted me to speak English, even though I didn't know the language. I think he thought that I was a Latino" (Oboler 1995:152,154).

A lengthy statement by Juan regarding the contemporary labeling of groups reveals the divide between New York Puerto Ricans and the other Latino views.

> White people have a name for everybody else. From whites you came up with the word Hispanics, and spic. I mean, Puerto Ricans never call each other Hispanic. They never called each other spics…They just count all Latin people in one bunch. They do it to the blacks, too. I mean, come on, they're more than just blacks. You got your American blacks, you got your African, your Jamaican; then you got your Puerto Rican blacks; some guys are darker than me. Then you got your Dominican blacks, you got white people that are dark skinned. …So you got your Hispanics over here which includes whatever race you want to put in it south of the border. Then you got your blacks, anything from the Congo down. Then you got your whites which is Americans. (Oboler 1995:155)

Oboler notes that Juan is voicing his recognition that the ethnic labeling process in the U. S. context involves the conflation of race and nationality, but she does not acknowledge that he is the only one of her informants to pose the issue in those terms. Nor does she make anything of this "exceptional" perspective. Rather, she is so intent on drawing out contrasting class (and to a lesser extent gender) positions across national lines that she leaves unanalyzed the blatant singularity of the "Nuyorican" among the many Latino voices in New York.

PAN-LATINO / TRANS-LATINO

The most serious challenge facing an analysis of Latino identity in the "New Nueva York" is how to conceptualize the converging cultural geography of so many Latino lives. How can an analysis assess the relative validity of a common identifying term for all, while still giving adequate analytical weight to the special position and standpoint of the largest, oldest, and most structurally different group, the Puerto Ricans? And further, can that qualitative demarcation be drawn without the analysis appearing divisive or "exceptionalist," to the point of ignoring important commonalties and new lines of solidarity suggested by changing historical circumstances?

In the reigning public and social science view, of course, New York Puerto Ricans have long been viewed or construed as the "exception"—the extraneous ingredient in the melting pot. The assimilationist thrust involved in ethnic and immigrant analogies has been accompanied by the social pathologies of the "Puerto Rican problem": one thinks of Glaser and Moynihan and Oscar Lewis, or in more benign terms, of C. Wright Mills and Father Joseph Fitzpatrick. And, again, in the 1990s, the Puerto Ricans are still the "exception" to the pan-ethnic rule, the "problem" even among their own kind. United States Puerto Ricans are granted a special chapter all their own in Linda Chavez's controversial *Out of the Barrio* (1991) where they are presented as derailed from the path "toward a new politics of Hispanic assimilation". The chapter titled "The Puerto Rican Exception" says everything. Again the New York Puerto Ricans are stuck in the "barrio," mired in their "culture of poverty," while other Latinos are headed for the mainstream. After fifty years of their massive presence in New York and other parts of the United States, Puerto Ricans have gone from being left out of the sauce to being left out of the salsa.

But even Chavez, from her officialist, neoconservative stance, seems at least dimly aware that a dismissive, blame-the-victim account only gets her so far when it comes to explaining her "exception." Speaking of Puerto Rican nonassimilation into American ways as evident in their apparent political apathy, she notes, "Puerto Rico's status, however, cannot help having some effect on the attitudes of Puerto Ricans toward the political process, particularly since they retain a strong identification as Puerto Ricans first and Americans second, according to public opinion surveys" (Chavez 1991:156). Puerto Ricans have most stubbornly rejected the Puerto Rican-American label despite their long presence here in the U. S., their formal citizenry, and their close historical relationship to U. S. society. Chavez (for many of the wrong reasons of course) stumbles onto the key line of explanation for this phenomenon. "Puerto Rico," she remarks, "is neither fish nor fowl politically, neither a state nor an independent nation" (Chavez 1991:156). By relating the Puerto Ricans' "exceptional," unassimilable position to the issue of the political status of Puerto Rico, Chavez is acknowledging that the pan-ethnic concept needs to be aligned with a knowledge of transnational relations if it is to include its most notable "exception." As expected, she sidesteps the deeper implications of this wider conceptual field, concluding her thoughts, cursory on the status options, with the comforting notion that, "in any event, it is unlikely that a change in Puerto Rico's status will do much to solve the problems that face Puerto Ricans in the United States"(Chavez 1991:158).

But the association between Puerto Ricans and Latinos is made, even though the ideological objective is to deny or minimize its pertinence to generalizations about Latinos as a composite group. The bracketing of Puerto Ricans among the Latino aggregate is necessitated by the abiding colonial relationship between the United States and Puerto Rico, which even the most internally focused, U. S. ethnicity-framed discussion cannot altogether ignore. Interestingly, Oboler's South American informants voice an awareness of this difference at some points in their conversation. When "Soledad," who is from Colombia, hears some of her fellow workers saying that they don't know why Puerto Ricans are "separated" from the other groups, she volunteers an explanation: "Oh, I do. It's because they're undecided about Puerto Ricans. They don't really know if they're American or if they're Puerto Rican. See, they have a problem with Puerto Ricans because they can't believe that they can be Americans and still speak Spanish. So they catalogue them as Americans for some things, but for others they're Puerto Ricans. When they count for something they're Americans, but when they don't need them to count for anything they're boricuas" (Oboler 1995:140). Soledad does not explicitly attribute the ambiguity she notes in the identification of Puerto Ricans in New York to the machinations of colonial control, but she is clear that the ambivalence results from a political opportunism at levels far transcending the confines of the New York barrios and factory floors. Here again, the full range of the pan-ethnic category implies transnational relations and perspectives.

Soledad also recognizes that such treatment is not so particular to Puerto Ricans after all, but is perhaps only more evident and intense in their case. The "exception" may also be the paradigm. "But in different ways," she concludes her remarks, "they do that with all of us who speak Spanish. You know, if an American is running, he's just doing exercise; but if one of us is running, we've just committed a robbery" (Oboler 1995:140). With this common experience in view, what would seem to distinguish the situation of Puerto Ricans—the direct structured link between their "ethnic" placement and the political reality of their homeland—is actually a more graphic and prominent version of the Latino experience in general. The reason for differentiating, and perhaps privileging, a Puerto Rican perspective when analyzing the pan-Latino concept does not rest, therefore, on an appeal to the size and longevity of the New York community, though a much longer historical view than that provided by Oboler is clearly

called for. There is, after all, some solid and heartfelt truth in the angry response of salsero Willie Colón to the description of Puerto Ricans in *Out of the
Barrio* (Chavez 1991), which he suggests calling "out of left field." "Perhaps
Chavez thinks Puerto Ricans have a genetic problem," he notes, and draws a
parallel to the pitiful situation of Native Hawaiians. "Just change Hawaii to
Puerto Rico. This is what happens to people who become guests in their own
home" (Colón in Serrano 1991:86). Stressing the price Puerto Ricans have paid
for their ground-breaking role in the history of Latin New York, Colón goes on:
"The fact that, in the east, people tolerate Spanish speakers, the reason there are
Spanish newspapers, TV and radio shows, bilingual driver's license tests, and
salsa music is because Puerto Ricans gave their hearts and souls to earn their
place here. Puerto Ricans created an environment that makes it easy for other
Latinos to succeed. I hear many new Latino immigrants say, 'In this country
any little job is a profession.' That's because they weren't here when they would
beat you with a baseball bat for trying to sell piraguas or put you in jail for
playing dominoes" (Colón in Serrano 1991:86).

Again, this "we-were-here-first" and "there's-more-of-us" reaction, though
a valid response to an ahistorical pathology, is not enough to account for the
"Puerto Rican exception" among Latino groups. A more adequate explanation,
which addresses the seeming paradox of Puerto Ricans having more, as citizens, yet accomplishing less than other Latinos, is suggested in the response to
Chavez's book (1991) by another public figure, Bronx Congressman José Serrano:
"She blames us for not capitalizing on our citizenship," Serrano remarked. "How
do you capitalize on a second-class citizenship? What she doesn't understand is
that in the same way slavery's legacy remains with African Americans, colonialism has affected Puerto Ricans" (Serrano 1991:83). Serrano insists on the
long historical view and on the enduring impact of international power relations
on the life and domestic status of Puerto Ricans in U. S. society. Pan-ethnicity
only stands up as a reliable group category if it is recognized that each group
that makes up the aggregate is at the same time participating in a transnational
community—the example of the Puerto Ricans as colonial Latino immigrants
being the most salient.

Losing sight of this exception-as-paradigm location of the Puerto Ricans
within the pan-Latino geography can lead to serious misconceptions and omis-
sions, as Oboler's "situational" ethnography illustrates. Such blurring abounds,
of course, in the more cosmic, essentialist accounts (usually of a journalistic
kind) where "lo Latino" appears as a glorious new "race," united by a primordial bond forged of the Spanish language and Catholicism, a glorious spirit on
the verge of a cultural takeover of Nueva York. Enrique Fernández, for example,
the Cuban-American journalist for the *Village Voice*, *Más* magazine, and the
Daily News, moans that "'Hispanization' was a figure of speech at the beginning of the decade. Today, it's an astonishing reality. We're already a majority

in San Antonio and Miami. Ay, Nueva York! How soon before we need a 'Festival Americano' to meet minority needs?" (Fernández 1988:19). Differentiations of a socioeconomic or political kind are a matter of indifference for such triumphant rhetoric, with the *nuestros hermanos boricuas* [our Puerto Rican brothers] being but one more condiment in the festive *sancocho* [stew]. (That's "boricuas," for Ilan Stavans' information, or "borincanos," but never "Borinquéns," [Stavans 1995:42]).

Such imprecision in posing the notion of Latino "ethnicity," with its characteristic attention to particularities and exclusions, is rampant in the abundant empirical work on New York's Latinos as well. Demographic and socioeconomic profiles generally take the Hispanic aggregate and other census designations for granted and proceed to amass evidence and generate analysis and policy proposals accordingly. The recent report by Fordham's Hispanic Research Center promisingly entitled *Nuestra America en Nueva York: The New Immigrant Hispanic Populations in New York City 1980-1990* (1995), does disaggregate data findings according to national group; however, nowhere does it reflect on the differential placement and historical experience of Puerto Ricans, and consistently takes "non-Hispanic whites" (NHW) as the only operational control variable. This conflation of racial, national, and ethnic categories does not seem to concern the researchers, nor does the potential value of comparisons and contrasts with other groups, particularly African Americans and Asian Americans. As for any resonance of the José Martí vision taken by the title, "Nuestra América en Nueva York," the report lacks a hemispheric, transnational frame of analytical reference.

The same criticism applies to the earlier report by Department of City Planning demographers Evelyn S. Mann and Joseph J. Salvo, *Characteristics of New Hispanic Immigrants to New York City: A Comparison of Puerto Rican and Non-Puerto Rican Hispanics* (1984). Though the title of this paper would suggest a closely focused look at the differences between discrete aggregates, Puerto Ricans and "other Hispanics," their results prove to be of limited value, for they do not make a comparison between Puerto Ricans and each of the "other" groups taken separately, and between Puerto Ricans and the entire "Hispanic" aggregate including Puerto Ricans. Further, the explanatory power of their conclusion is minimal, as is evident in their attribution of the reported differences, which they recognize are "wide," to "basic disparities in fertility, labor force participation and most of all family structure and composition" (Mann and Salvo 1984:abstract). Once again, ideological assumptions and ahistorical treatment of the "Puerto Rican exception" land us right back at the culture of poverty.

Even analysis undertaken from an explicitly Puerto Rican perspective, where one might expect a more historical cast to the Puerto Rican-"other Hispanic" comparison, can fall short of the mark. The recent essay, *Understanding Socio economic Differences: A Comparative Analysis of Puerto Ricans and Recen*

Latino Immigrants in New York City (1996), for instance, disappoints not because it fails to foreground the particularities of Puerto Rican experience, but because it slides too easily from a contrastive to a pan-Latino project as a result. The weight of the argument and policy orientation ultimately rests more on a Latino-mainstream contrast than one between Puerto Ricans and recent Latino immigrants. Admittedly a first stab at the topic, the essay does draw the pertinent data into play. It is helpful in defining a research and policy agenda on some of the most visible issues raised in assessing Puerto Rican-"other Latinos" relations. But the most pressing of these issues, having to do with questions of race, class, gender, and political positioning, are either muddled or sidestepped in the name of an undefined "unity," "progress," and "integration."

Many of the shortcomings of *Understanding Socioeconomic Differences*—and, indeed, how far we are from such an "understanding"—are evident in the final paragraph:

> The severity of most of the socioeconomic indicators presented above challenges researchers, policy makers, and city officials with a sense of urgency; this is not only a problem for the Puerto Rican or Latino communities. Expected growth in the Latino population coupled with a simultaneous stagnation or decline of socioeconomic position has potentially explosive effects for the entire city—as well as for other areas where Puerto Ricans live. While comparisons between Puerto Ricans and other groups are important to understanding how each group is faring, pitting one against the other does nothing to further the progress of any group—and may actually aggravate intergroup conflicts. It is critical for Puerto Ricans to gain entry into different sectors of the city's economy and regain socioeconomic stability. At the same time, however, lessons learned from the Puerto Rican experience in New York City can be useful in successfully integrating other Latino immigrants into the city's mainstream—and charting the progress of future Latino generations. The problems that affect Puerto Ricans have been identified; understanding their origins is the next step toward devising effective solutions. (1996:35-6)

Perhaps the central question raised in a comparative inter-Latino analysis of present-day New York is the relation between Puerto Ricans and Dominicans, a question that is generally elided because of the frequent official grouping of Dominicans in the "Central and South American" or "Other Hispanic" categories. This absence of Dominicans as a discrete point of comparison is the case in all recent quantitative studies available thus far. Yet it is clearly the Dominicans, already by far the second largest group and rapidly approaching the number of Puerto Ricans by unofficial count, that bear closest resemblance to the Puerto Ricans in terms of both cultural history and socioeconomic placement. The two groups together, sometimes even conjoined within the Latino aggregate because of their common Caribbean background, account for well over 80 percent of the whole. They command the public image of the "New York Latino." In addition to magnitude and cultural affinities, it is in its comparison with the situation of Dominicans that the Puerto Rican experience finds its most direct counterpoint.

Unfortunately, treatment of the Dominican community in a sociological manner has thus far left this kind of contrastive analysis largely unaddressed. Whether the pitch is for the community's bustling "vitality" and rapid progress or for its unequaled "poverty"—accounts tend to oscillate between those two extremes—the reference point is the Latino population as a whole, or non-Dominican society in general. A recent study, *Dominican New Yorkers: A Socioeconomic Profile*, for example, marshals ample tabulations comparing Dominicans with "New York City Overall," "Non-Hispanic White," "Non-Hispanic Black" and "Hispanic, overall," but includes only one parenthetical mention of the Puerto Ricans: "only Puerto Ricans have a greater presence" (Hernández et al. 1995:5). Among other things, the omission of such group-to-group comparison places in question the authors' repeated claim to Dominicans' worst-off status among all New York Hispanics.

Of course the point of these comparative analyses cannot be to establish a socioeconomic pecking order of the "most oppressed" or the "fastest achievers." The main problem has more to do with methodology and theoretical perspective than with the unexplored terrain itself. Another recent essay by some of the same authors, in fact, arrives at a more balanced account of the complex socioeconomic reality of the New York Dominican community (Hernández and Tores-Saillant 1996). But it is another recent publication of the CUNY Dominican Studies Institute, Jorge Duany's *Quisqueya on the Hudson: The Transnational Identity of Dominicans in Washington Heights* (1994), that suggests an analytical framework appropriate to a useful comparative study between the two groups, and to a differentiated consideration of the New York Latino experience overall. Duany makes little mention of Puerto Rican identity—though he has written widely on the subject from many angles—nor does he draw out any parallels or contrasts; his strictly local, neighborhood sample, in fact, is even narrower than that of many other studies. But by placing the issue of the "Dominican York" experience in the context of globalization and the formation of "transnational identities," he speaks in terms that, from a historical standpoint, resonate with parallels to social processes lived through by Puerto Ricans. In addition to the usual socioeconomic characteristics, Duany offers observations and cites attitudes on political and cultural orientation toward the homeland, assimilation and its resistance, bilingualism and race, and a range of other identity issues long of central interest in the study of Puerto Rican life in New York. He frames his discussion with reference to concepts of "transnational communities," diaspora, circular and global migration processes, and other constituents of contemporary cultural theory. When he describes Dominicans, for example, as a transnational community, "characterized by a constant flow of people in both directions, a dual sense of identity, ambivalent attachments to two nations, and a far-flung network of kinship and friendship ties across state frontiers" (Duany 1994:2), he could just as well be speaking of Nuyoricans, the prototype of that kind of community among Latinos in New York. *Quisqueya on the Hudson* (Duany 1994), seen in these terms, bears more than a casual resemblance to El Barrio on the East River some thirty or forty years ago, a parallel also noted by other seasoned observers (e.g., Torres and Bonilla 1993:102).

THE COLONIAL "EXCEPTION"

"Mex-Yorkers," the latest group to appear en masse on the city's Latino landscape, are also very much a transnational community, as creative ethnographic research has established in convincing detail (Millman 1992; Smith 1992). Colombians, Ecuadorians, Salvadorans, all of New York's major Latino groups partake of a "transnational sociocultural system" in their everyday lives, "here" or "there," and in their increasingly hybrid forms of self-identification.[8] Individually and as a composite they are more a "diasporic transnation" than anything resembling an ethnic immigrant group. As much as the familiar immigrant narrative may accompany them as they settle into their niches and enclaves, the prospects of their ready or eventual incorporation into New York life remain dim at best under conditions of global economic restructuring. The formation of systemic transnational linkages with economic, political, and cultural dimensions is thus a matter of historical necessity in both locations; the linkages are structured into the very relations between country or region of origin and the United States, and into the very conditions of migration in the first place. In this respect, the transnational quality of the Latino presence in New York follows the pattern set over the course of decades, and in the most intricate way, imitates the Puerto Rican emigrant experience.

But even as "Latino transnationals," Puerto Ricans remain the "exception" among the New York groups, distinct even from their closest cousins, the Dominican Yorks. This difference is marked off, in a formal sense, by U. S. citizenship, and in the practical social arena, as Congressman Serrano is quick to add, by the second-class nature of that supposedly privileged status. Direct colonial relations, as an uninterrupted legacy and ever present reality, govern the motives and outcomes of the whole migratory and settlement process, and fix a consistently low ceiling on the group's expectations and opportunities. For

Puerto Ricans, the "blessings" of American citizenship have been even worse than mixed. Under the constant sway of colonial machinations, citizenship has been a set-up for stigmatization and pathological treatment, more than outweighing, over the long haul, any advantageous exemption from the most pressing of immigrant woes. As Willie Colón has it in the title of a recent album, Puerto Ricans are "legal aliens." And other Latinos, most of whom have indeed endured the deathly humiliations of undocumented status, recognize this difference themselves; as a correspondent for the *Christian Science Monitor* reported in a survey of Hispanic communities, "whenever Puerto Ricans came up for discussion, Chicanos and Cubans repeatedly said that Puerto Ricans had an extra burden to bear, in addition to their language, their color, and their poverty. It was, they said, the psychological uncertainty resulting from the limbo which Puerto Rico's commonwealth status had turned out to be. To the average Puerto Rican, the argument goes, commonwealth status means his or her being made a kept man or woman of the US" (Godsell 1980:13).

Puerto Ricans are perhaps most precisely to be considered "colonial emigrants" (or "[im]migrants" as Clara Rodríguez and Acosta-Belén [chap. 5] would have it) in the global metropolis, bearing closer congruences on an international scale with counterparts like Jamaicans in London, Martinicans in Paris, and Surinamese in Amsterdam.[9] In rebuffing Linda Chavez (1991), Serrano (1991) equates the psychological legacy of colonialism for Puerto Ricans with that of slavery for American Blacks, or at least relates them in the same breath as the unmentioned grounding for her shallow diagnosis of the "Puerto Rican exception." And indeed, it is in many ways their long, profound and complex relation to African Americans, even more than the outward marker of citizenship, that most clearly distinguishes the social position and interactions of Puerto Ricans from those of the other transnational Latino groups in New York. Throughout their century-long sojourn in New York, and especially since the late 1940s, New York Puerto Ricans have been at close living and working quarters with Blacks, perhaps closer than any other national group in the history of this country. In addition to unprecedented cultural fusions, most social indicators point consistently to Puerto Ricans bearing greater similarities to Blacks than to the other Latino groups or to the Latino aggregate (see Torres 1995). Needless to say, because of the gulf between sociodemographic and qualitative-theoretical analysis, little has been made thus far of those potent and demonstrable realities. And the foisting of a "Latino" construct onto the field of identity options has only further clouded the issue.

The colonial emigrants, different from transnational diasporic communities in general, are organically inserted into the racial divide and the cultural and class dynamic of the metropolitan society. Especially since the 1960s, the issue of Puerto Rican identity has been entwined with the social and cultural experience of African Americans, with the concomitant problems of blackness and "double consciousness"—indeed, more so than is likely even for that of the "blacker" Dominican community. Similarly, Puerto Ricans in the U. S. bear closer historical ties to the Chicano population than do their ancestral cultural kin from Central America, and even their Mixteco (Mexican) neighbors in El Barrio.

It is the directness of the colonial tie that thus places U. S. Puerto Ricans both inside and outside of U. S. domestic politics, with interests rooted equally in the struggles for justice and equality in the United States and in the struggles for sovereignty in the Caribbean and Latin America. The sense of ambivalence generally attributed to the limbo of commonwealth status has to do with this duality of political focus, this simultaneous grounding on two social fronts. But it is not just a "burden," as sympathetic fellow Latinos call it, nor does it necessarily spell dysfunction or identity crisis. Strategically, with an unprecedented half of the nationality living on either side, and with the "sides" constantly intermingling because of an unparalleled circular migration, there is no alternative to a multiple-identity position.

The adequacy of the embattled "Latino" or "Hispanic" concept hinges on its inclusiveness toward the full range of social experiences and identities. Specifically, use of the term Latino bridges the divergence within the contemporary configuration between recent "Latino immigrant" populations and the "resident minority" Chicano and Puerto Rican communities. In the context of the "New Nueva York," the toughest test of "Latinismo" is the need to negotiate the varied lines of solidarity and historically structured relations that inform Puerto Rican social identity: that is, for example, the links with other Francophone or Anglophone Caribbean communities; or with African Americans and Chicanos; or with other colonial migrants in "global cities"; or, of course, with other Puerto Ricans, "over there" on the Island, or "out there" in the diaspora. All of these crucial dimensions of New York Puerto Rican self-identification stretch the "pan-Hispanic" idea in different ways. They must be accounted for, however, or Puerto Ricans may once again, as reported in 1958, choose to "substitute [the terms 'Hispano' and 'Latino'] for that of 'Puerto Rican,' because the latter, in more ways than one, has become a 'bad public relations' ⸱⸱ᵻᵻᶜation for New York Puerto Ricans" (E. Padilla 1958:32). That is, unle⸍ ⸱⸱⸱ ⸱⸱ᵣast wide enough across and along language, racial, cla⸍ Puerto Rican component too readily equates with ⸍ cations of the label. As a result, Puerto Ricans are⸍ politics of Hispanic assimilation," in Linda Chave⸍

On the other hand, the influence is of cou⸍ the perspectives introduced by the new Latino g⸍ terms of a multigroup identity and social mov⸍ provisional and subject to reexamination, as ⸍ inter-Latino conditions in present-day Chicago⸍ ness" was first committed to sociological stuc⸍

1995, there are Latino groups calling for a dismantling of the congressional district they had once fought so hard to create. The reason given was that Mexicans and Puerto Ricans are, in their words, "racially different and have little in common beyond their language" (Oclander 1995:22-23). (The president of Chicago's Latino Firefighters Association Charles Vázquez pointedly responded to the quote, "To those who say we are 'racially different,' what's the difference between a poor Mexican making minimum wage and a poor Puerto Rican making minimum wage?" [Vázquez 1995:30]). Tales of such contention among Latino groups abound, of course, in Los Angeles, Miami and New York. They put to rest any too facile, wistful, or ominous image of Latinos as a seamlessly knitted tribe or horde. Yet practical disjunctures do not necessarily invalidate the strategic prospects and formative process of Latino unity. Rather, they emphasize the need for an eminently flexible, inclusive concept based on a clear understanding of historical differences and particularities.

With such a concept in view, one can only agree with Oboler when she argues that "differences in the ways that race and class are understood by more recently arrived Latin American immigrants are important to consider in assessing the issues that contribute toward or hinder the fostering of...a 'Latino Culture' in the U. S. context" (Oboler 1995:16). The lessons and experiences from Latin America and the Caribbean stand to enrich and broaden the cultural and political horizons of Latinos, notably Mexican Americans and Puerto Ricans, with a longer standing in U. S. barrios and workplaces. They offer grounds for hope that the idea and study of "Latino" might transcend—and transgress—the domestic confines of U. S. public discourse on politics and cultural identity, and engage (or re-engage) it to the global processes of which it is a part. This hope is very much alive in the "New Nueva York," as Puerto Ricans—U. S. citizens and increasingly English-speaking—are impelled in the name of Latino solidarity to reassert their commitment to immigrant and language rights, and to embrace the trans-Latino vision of nuestra América.[10]

NOTES

1. See for example the influential book by Sassen (1991). The idea of New York as a "global city" was also an integral part of the mayoral campaign and administration Ed Koch; see also Fitch (1993).

That report concludes: "The Commission's overall conclusion is that main- to Ricans generally continue mired in the poverty facing first generations of t or migrant groups. Expectations were that succeeding generations of o Ricans would have achieved upward mobility. One generation later, f poverty remains little changed. Indeed, the economic situation of Ricans has worsened over the last decade. The United States has never before had a large migration of citizens from offshore, distinct in culture and language and also facing the problem of color prejudice. After thirty years of significant migration, contrary to conventional wisdom that once Puerto Ricans learned the language the second generation would move into the mainstream of American society, the future of this distinct community in the United States is still to be determined" U. S. Commission of Civil Rights 1976:145).

3. For a discussion of pan-ethnic Latino organizations and activities in New York during the early decades, see Glasser (1995) and Vega (1984).

4. On the question of terminology ("Hispanic" or/vs. "Latino"), see Hayes Bautista and Chapa (1987), Treviño (1987), Shorris (1992), and Stavans (1995:24-27).

5. See López and Espiritu (1990), Espiritu (1992), and Winant (1994).

6. Misguided pomposity and downright errors abound in Stavans' book. They are evident in his use of wordings such as like "Latino metabolism," "a five-hundred-year-old fiesta of miscegenation," "Latino assimilation into the melting pot," "our aim is to assimilate Anglos slowly to ourselves," "society is beginning to embrace Latinos, from rejects to fashion setters, from outcasts to insider traders," "yesterday's victim and tomorrow's conquistadors, we Hispanics," etc.

7. See especially Calderón (1992) and Forbes (1992).

8. The term "transnational sociocultural system" was used in a study of Caribbeans in New York (Sutton 1987).

9. The specification of Puerto Ricans as "colonial (im)migrants" and their parallel position to colonial or post-colonial immigrants in other parts of the world is noted but scarcely elaborated by Rodríguez (1989). For a fuller discussion see Grosfoguel and Georas (1996) and Grosfoguel (1997).

10. For a discussion of the relation of Puerto Ricans to the issue of immigration, see Velázquez (1995). A valuable assessment of Latino politics in New York City may be found in Fuentes (1992).

REFERENCES CITED

Calderón, José
1992   Hispanic or Latino: The Viability of Categories for Panethnic Unity. *Latin American Perspectives* 19(4):37-44.
Chavez, Linda
1991   *Out of the Barrio: Toward a New Politics of Hispanic Assimilation.* Basic Books, New York.
Duany, Jorge
1994   *Quisqueya on the Hudson: The Transnational Identity of Dominicans in Washington Heights.* CUNY Dominican Studies Institute, New York.
Espiritu, Yen Le
1992   *Asian American Panethnicity: Building Institutions and Identities.* Temple University Press, Philadelphia.
Fernández, Enrique
1988   Estilo Latino: Buscando Nueva York [sic]. *Village Voice* 9 August:19.

Fitch, Robert
1993   *The Assassination of New York.* Verso, London.
Foner, Nancy
1987   *New Immigrants in New York.* Columbia University Press, New York.
Forbes, Jack D.
1992   The Hispanic Spin: Party Politics and Governmental Manipulation of Ethnic Identity. *Latin American Perspectives* 19(4):59-78.
Fuentes, Annette
1992   New York: Elusive Unity in La Gran Manzana. *NACLA Report on the Americas* 26(2).
Giménez, Martha
1992   U. S. Ethnic Politics: Implications for Latin Americans. *Latin American Perspectives* 19(4):7-17.
Glasser, Ruth
1995   *My Music is my Flag: Puerto Rican Musicians and Their New York Communities.* University of California Press, Berkeley.
Godsell, Geoffrey
1980   The Puerto Ricans. *The Christian Science Monitor* 1 May 1:13.
Grosfoguel, Ramón
1997   Colonial Caribbean Migrations to France, the Netherlands, Great Britain and the United States. In *Caribe 2000: Definiciones, identidades y culturas regionales y/o nacionales,* edited by Lowel Fiet, and Janette Becerra, pp. 58-80. Universidad de Puerto Rico, Rio Piedras.
Grosfoguel, Ramón, and Chloé Georas
1996   The Racialization of Latino Caribbean Migrants in the New York Metropolitan Area. *Centro Journal* 8(1/2):190-201.
Handlin, Oscar
1959   *The Newcomers: Negroes and Puerto Ricans in a Changing Metropolis.* Harvard University Press, Cambridge.
Haslip-Viera, Gabriel
1996   The Evolution of the Latino Community in the New York Metropolitan Area, 1810 to the Present. In *Latinos in New York: Communities in Transition,* edited by Gabriel Haslip-Viera, and Sherrie Baver, pp. 3-29. Notre Dame University Press, Notre Dame, Indiana.
Hayes Bautista, David E., and Jorge Chapa
1987   Latino Terminology: Conceptual Basis for Standardized Terminology. *American Journal of Public Health* 77:61-68.
Hernández, Ramona, Francisco Rivera-Batiz, and Roberto Agodini
1995   *Dominican New Yorkers: A Socioeconomic Profile.* CUNY Dominican Studies Institute, New York.
Hernández, Ramona, and Silvio Torres-Saillant
1996   Dominicans in New York: Men, Women, and Prospects. In *Latinos in New York: Communities in Transition,* edited by Gabriel Haslip-Viera, and Sherrie Baver, pp. 30-56. Notre Dame University Press, Notre Dame, Indiana.
Latin American Perspectives
1992   Special Issue: The Politics of Ethnic Construction. 19(4).

López, David, and Yen Espiritu
1990   Panethnicity in the United States: A Theoretical Framework. *Ethnic and Racial Studies* 13:198-224.
Mann, Evelyn S., and Joseph J. Salvo
1984   *Characteristics of New Hispanic Immigrants to New York City: A Comparison of Puerto Rican and Non-Puerto Rican Hispanics.* Department of City Planning, New York.
Millman, Joel
1992   New Mex City. *New York Times* 7 September:37-43.
Morales, Rebecca, and Frank Bonilla (editors)
1993   *Latinos in a Changing U. S. Economy: Comparative Perspectives on Growing Inequality.* Sage Series on Race and Ethnic Relations, vol. 7. Sage Publications, Newbury Park, California.
Novas, Himilce
1994   *Everything You Need to Know about Latino History.* Plume, New York.
Oboler, Suzanne
1995   *Ethnic Labels, Latino Lives: Identity and the Politics of (Re) Presentation in the United States.* University of Minnesota Press, Mineapolis.
Oclander, Jorge
1995   Latinos Split Over Keeping Their House District. *Chicago Sun Times* 13 December:22-23.
Padilla, Elena
1958   *Up from Puerto Rico.* Columbia University Press, New York.
Padilla, Félix
1985a   *Latino Consciousness: The Case of Mexican Americans and Puerto Ricans in Chicago.* Notre Dame University Press, Notre Dame, Indiana.
1985b   On the Nature of Latino Ethnicity. In *The Mexican American Experience: An Interdisciplinary Anthology,* edited by Rodolfo de la Garza, pp. 332-345. University of Texas Press, Austin.
1990   Latin America: The Historical Base of Latino Unity. *Latino Studies Journal* 1:7-27.
Robinson, William I.
1992   The Global Economy and the Latino Populations in the United States: A World Systems Approach. *Critical Sociology* 19(2):29-59.
Rodríguez, Clara E.
1989   *Puerto Ricans: Born in the U. S.A.* Unwin Hyman, Boston.
Sassen, Saskia
1991   *The Global City: New York, London, and Tokyo.* Princeton University Press, Princeton.
Serrano, José
1991   Taking Exception with Chavez. *New York Newsday* 23 October:83, 86.
Shorris, Earl
1992   *Latinos: Biography of a People.* Norton, New York.
Smith, Robert
1992   Mixteca in New York: New York in Mixteca. *NACLA Report on the Americas* 26(1):39-41.

Stavans, Ilan
1995 *The Hispanic Condition: Reflections on Culture and Identity in America.* Harper Collins, New York.
Sutton, Constance R.
1987 The Caribbeanization of New York and the Emergence of a Transnational Sociocultural System. In *Caribbean Life in New York City: Sociocultural Dimensions*, edited by Constance Sutton, and Elsa M. Cahney, pp. 15-30. Center for Migration Studies, New York.
Torres, Andrés
1995 *Between Melting Pot and Mosaic: African Americans and Puerto Ricans in the New York Political Economy.* Temple University Press, Philadelphia.
Torres, Andrés, and Frank Bonilla
1993 Decline Within Decline: The New York Perspective. In *Latinos in a Changing U. S. Economy*, edited by Rebecca Morales and Frank Bonilla, pp. 98-99. Sage Publications, Newbury Park, California.
Treviño, Fernando M.
1987 Standardized Terminology for Standardized Populations. *American Journal of Public Health* 77:69-72.
Understanding Socioeconomic Differences: A Comparative Analysis of Puerto Ricans and Recent Latino Immigrants in New York City
1996 Manuscript in author's possession.
U. S. Commission of Civil Rights
1976 *Puerto Ricans in the Continental United States: An Uncertain Future.* Washington D. C.
Vázquez, Charles
1995 Hispanics Must Forget Politics, Focus on Unity. *Chicago Sun Times.* 27 December:30.
Vega, Bernardo
1984 *Memoirs of Bernardo Vega: A Contribution to the History of the Puerto Rican Community in New York.* Monthly Review, New York.
Velázquez, Franklin
1995 Puerto Ricans and Immigrants: La Misma Lucha. *Critica 9.* 1 February:5-6.
Winant, Howard
1994 *Racial Conditions: Politics, Theory, Comparisons.* University of Minnesota Press, Minneapolis.

II

Cases of Identity Formation

7

Identities in the Diaspora

Mayan Culture and Community Today

Allan F. Burns

The identities of Mayan people in the diaspora reflect a fluidity and a distinction between essential Mayaness and the labels that have to be adopted depending on personal, community, legal, and work contexts. The assurance and confidence of Mayan people with their essential identity as members of communities and cultures from Guatemala gives Mayan people in the United States a self-confidence that sometimes seems at odds with the uncertainty they often face because of their immigration status, employment opportunities, and poverty.

The way that Mayas talk about their identity as essential to their very bodies has made many social scientists uncomfortable, especially since essentialism is only a step away from racism, and essentialism among Mayan intellectuals is counter to an ethic of cultural pluralism that many of us in anthropology carry with us (Warren 1992). So when Mayan people talk about their culture as embodied in their physical as well as social lives, it can sound like racism on their part.

Essentialism in Mayan identity is talked about in many ways. One Mayan refugee in Florida spoke to me once about the numbers of Guatemalan Mayan children who had been adopted by foreigners, often North Americans. He was concerned that many children were abducted and put up for adoption even though they had family members who could take care of them. The large number of orphans in Guatemala because of the violence of the 1980s had increased the numbers of adoption intermediaries, some of whom were less ethical than others. He related several cases he knew about where the children had mental breakdowns when they reached adulthood. He said it was because these children were Mayan, and socialization into a family from the United States could not undo that fact.

Mayan people have certainly experienced racism, both in Guatemala where the violence of the 1980s approached the killings associated with caste wars and ethnic cleansing, and in the United States. The discrimination of Guatemalan Mayan people by non-Mayas in places like Indiantown, Florida, is replete with references to them as "little Indians" (*Inditos*), "those little people," and a derogatory term school children use, "Watermelons" (taken from the Spanish pronunciation of Guatemaltecos). Bogin and Loucky (1997) have shown that the small stature of Guatemalan Mayan people is based much more on nutrition than genetics, but in a country where physical traits are taken as the first feature of identity, racial categorization of the Guatemalan Mayas as part of a different race continues.

Essentialism is not the only component of Mayan identity in the diaspora. On top of what is normally a personal and unspoken essential identity, Mayan immigrants to the United States have several layers of situational identities that can easily over shadow essential identities (Burns 1989). Even an identity of Mayan is not only found at the essential level but also found in the situational identity options available in the diaspora. A case I discuss later illustrates this well: Even Guatemalans who are not indigenous at times find it useful to adopt an Indian identity, something that would be next to impossible to do in Guatemala.

The Mayan diaspora from Guatemala began in the 1980s and spread throughout Mexico and the United States (Burns 1993b). Today there are over 200,000 Guatemalans in the United States, and many more in Canada and Mexico. Within this large diaspora community, Indiantown, Florida stands out as one of the key centers—ceremonial, social, and economic—for Guatemalan Mayas. In this essay, I discuss identity in a series of cases taken from over ten years of research in the community (Burns 1993b). I take a case approach because it seems to be the way best suited to capture the fluidity, the self-reflection, and the ironies of adding layers of identity to Mayan lives.

One of the features of Mayan experiences in the diaspora is transnationalism or the quick movement between different communities in different countries and the concurrent strategies of adapting behaviors appropriate to each. Since the signing of the peace accords in Guatemala at the end of 1996, this movement between places, like Florida and Guatemala, is even easier and safer. But instead of repatriation of Guatemalans from Mexico and the United States, a more common approach has been to add Guatemala, whether it be Guatemala City or a rural birthplace, to the possible places to move to for work, sentiment, or political advantage. The transnational identity of Mayan people provides them with what Appadurai (1991) calls a global ethnoscape in place of the more local one that anthropologists, geographers, and tourists are more accustomed to seeing.

Transnational identities are not that new for Mayan people. Since the division of Mesoamerica into different countries, Mayan families have adapted to life on national frontiers, living a borderlands existence (Rosaldo 1996). The borders of the Mayan world are the national boundaries between Guatemala and Mexico, Belize, Honduras, and El Salvador. Since the division of these lands into separate countries, many Mayan people have lived in families that reside on both sides of these borders. What is different today is that this traditional borderland existence has been enriched by the addition of several more countries, such as the United States and Canada. The ease of transportation between these countries has also facilitated movements of peoples. The transnationalism of today is certainly related to older patterns of binationality and migration in Guatemala. But it also is qualitatively different because of the historic circumstances of the Guatemalan violence and the establishment of many Guatemalan Mayan neighborhoods and communities that are available as stopping-off points for Mayan people in the diaspora.

One inspiration for writing about transnational identities in the way I present them here comes from the work of Oliver Sacks, a neurologist who often refers to himself as a neuroanthropologist (Sacks 1994, 1997). Sacks takes as his point of departure the social worlds of people with neurological conditions and then goes on to portray how these conditions can force creative and innovative social and cultural solutions. Similarly, disruption, distance from natal communities, poverty, and discrimination often are combined to paint a portrait of refugees, like the Maya, as victims who lack the cultural expressions found in their native communities. Indeed, several anthropologists who have worked previously in Guatemala have told me how hard it is to work with Mayan immigrants in the United States. Their difficulties point to the changes and new strategies that the Maya have developed in the diaspora. These strategies, coupled with a strong sense of who they are, make Mayan people who are outside of Guatemala more difficult to approach and work with than they are when in their more traditional villages.

I use a particularistic approach, as does Sacks, by relating five different events, or case studies of transnationalism and identity among Guatemalan Mayan people who have lived in South Florida. Transnational identities are not just an adaptation to refugee status and structural adjustment in Central America, but are rather creative, active interactions with what anthropologist Hannerz (1992) and others call the cultural complexities of local and global processes. The cases presented here explore different features of identity in the diaspora communities of Guatemalan Mayan people. I conclude with some reflections on how these cases suggest a new agenda of scholarship—one that is optimistic—that contrasts with the dismay many anthropologists have had when they find that the people they have studied in the past no longer wish to talk to anthropologists. About twenty years ago, Vine Deloria (1969) wrote *Custer Died for your Sins* with a chapter that basically told the anthropologists to leave native peoples alone. As a result, one of the phrases anthropologists heard from native people was, "don't bother me." Today the transnational identities of the diaspora suggest that a better slogan might be "don't other me." One way to make anthropological research better is to resist the temptations of exoticizing other people by putting them in the category of "the other" (Featherstone 1995: 99).

In addition to a case study approach, another insight that Sacks provides is to look at how people maintain their individuality and personal identity in the face of the overwhelming degradation and dehumanization forced on them by large institutions. It is easy to paint portraits of people who have been done in by "the system," whether that system is the repression in Guatemala, the nationalism of Mexico, or the discrimination of the United States Immigration and Naturalization Service. It is more insightful to focus on how the diaspora of Guatemalan Mayan people provides new options and new alternatives of identity and survival. The harvest of violence that was so eloquently described by Carmack (1988) has given away to a different social formation—the ever-increasing dispersion and return of Mayan people. One political science colleague (McCoy, personal communication 1996) recently wrote that the civil wars of Central America now sound to us like ancient history, so fast is the hemisphere reshaping itself through commerce, labor reallocation, *maquiladoras* (offshore industries), and regional integration. The communities of origin for Mayan people—the closed corporate and open communities that we anthropologists have so embraced (Wolf 1956) and, later, all but abandoned (Gossen 1986)—are now only one part of a larger chain of locations and activities that have created communities of sojourners and migrant workers, communities of Machine Age Maya (Nash 1967), Frozen Food Maya (Goldin 1996) and Maquila Maya (Peterson 1992), communities of bi- and tri-national families who move between places like Cancun, Mexico and Los Angeles, between Totonicapán and Houston (Hagan 1994), between highland Chiapas and lowland Florida (Burns 1993b). Along with this fluidity of movement has come a fluidity of identity so that pan-Mayanism is seriously talked about by scholars such as Victor Montejo (1993) as well as by the press.

It is easy to trace the penetration of capitalism to communities in Guatemala as Carol Smith (1990) did in order to show how labor migration develops as the only option for people who live in marginal lands with few resources. I take the view, however, that the kind of movement that is present today in Mayan communities harkens back to preconquest times, when trade routes, *pochteca* (Aztec merchant-diplomats) commercial networks, and travel in general in the Mayan world were not as controlled as they became through what Lovell (1992) calls the three conquests of Guatemala: the conquest of the contact period, the conquest of capitalism, and the conquest of state terror. In other words, it is important to uncouple the initial causes of the Mayan diaspora from the results of that diaspora. Certainly, the initial cause of state terror has left its mark on Mayan identity, but that mark is not a mark that overwhelms other features of the new Mayan identity. As one person told me when I first started working in Indiantown, South Florida, "We have babies here because we respond to tragedy with life, and what is more life-giving than having babies!"

INDIANTOWN, FLORIDA

Indiantown, Florida is the most recognizable town of Mayan people in the state. It is a small agricultural town, neither a refugee center nor a town of American Indians. The name refers to a label given to the area when the railroad came through in the early part of the century. The county seat for the Indiantown area is Stuart, located on the Atlantic coast. Historically, Indiantown has not received very many benefits from the county because of its inland location and the contrast between the new Florida of the coastal areas and the old Florida of inland agricultural areas like Indiantown. The town is on the edge of Lake Okeechobee, and, in the past, the lake and the remains of a native settlement were the area's most remarkable features. Today, the canal that connects the Atlantic Ocean to the lake and the lake to the Gulf of Mexico passes alongside the town. Indiantown is a service community and longtime residents worked in agriculture, ranching, and commerce that served the surrounding areas. These longtime residents of Indiantown, Florida did not invite the Guatemalans into their midst, and many resented the Catholic Church and the priest who first brought them there. Indiantown was a small agricultural community of just over 3,000 people in the early 1980s. By the 1990s the population had more than doubled, with most of the increase coming from Guatemalan Mayan people and other farmworkers attracted to the boom in winter vegetables, citrus, and, later, golf course construction in the area. This dramatic rise in population stretched the capacity of the town's services to the limits. Indiantown is located approximately 30 miles inland from the southeast coast of Florida. The land in the immediate vicinity of Indiantown includes thousands of acres of rich citrus groves, and at one time was the major lemon-producing area in the United States. The town is at the southern end of the large Florida cattle lands and also includes immense winter vegetable fields.

Agriculture, however, is only one important part of the attraction of Indiantown for people looking to survive in the U. S labor market. The community also is on the edge of the construction boom area of coastal Florida. The construction of professional golf course communities and the ever-increasing spread of planned communities of the coast create a need for many unskilled laborers. Day labor, construction jobs, and industries that support construction are all areas where the Maya can seek employment in the Indiantown area. But much of the work that the Maya find is temporary, seasonal, and often without benefits. High temporary unemployment and underemployment, and the seasonality of agricultural work, force the Maya into the migrant stream, providing a strong economic basis to their transnational identities.

Indiantown is unincorporated, and within it are several neighborhoods that are often thought of as different communities. Among them are several migrant labor camps. Some of the camps are apartment buildings, and others are areas of small dwellings. One of the most famous is Blue Camp, a large apartment building that has the look of a run-down motel. In the early 1980s, Yellow Camp, another apartment complex, became known as "the roach motel" owing to the conditions there. The nickname was effective in bringing attention to the poor housing in Indiantown, and the building itself was torn down. Booker Park, an area where migrant workers live, counts Haitian, African American, Guatemalan, and Mexican people among its residents. Blue camp is located in Booker Park, as is more recently built, government-sponsored migrant housing. Most of the older, nonmigrant population live in Indiantown proper, where they have modest homes and access to the stores, churches, schools, and post office of the community. In the early 1980s, a modest retirement community, "Indianwood," was built between Indiantown and Booker Park. It is an alternative retirement community for people unable to live in up-scale Florida retirement communities closer to the coast. Housing in Indianwood is made up of manufactured homes.

When the Guatemalan Mayan immigration began in the early 1980s, many residents felt threatened by an invasion of people who spoke unfamiliar languages, lived in poverty, and arrived with little more than what they could easily carry. Two features of the community lessened resentment to the arrival of the Maya in Indiantown. First, as a town that adapted well to different economic possibilities in the area, townspeople had an ethos of welcoming newcomers. Second, the town had a group of teachers, health workers, church members, and others who had developed a concern for the migrant workers who came through the area each year. This helping community, as they called themselves, learned of the plight of the Maya in Guatemala and developed ways to assist them in Indiantown. The town had one of the only migrant elementary schools in the state, which was run by a group of Catholic nuns. One of the nuns developed a textile cooperative for the new Mayan immigrants, hoping to provide year-long employment for women who had come from an area with a rich heritage of textile art. The school hired several Guatemalan Mayan immigrants as aids and assistants. One of them started a garden project behind the school, which made it possible for Mayan people to grow *chipilin* and other Guatemalan plants.

Other members of the helping community encouraged the Maya to re-enact the yearly patronal festival on the day of San Miguel [St. Michael], the patron saint of the community of origin for many of the first arrivals to Indiantown. The festival was held on the grounds of the Catholic church and later was moved to the fairgrounds. Members of the helping community made the festival successful by incorporating local features into the more traditional events of the festival. For example, one year a local barber and his wife demonstrated U. S. style popular dancing during the cultural night of the festival after demonstrations of traditional dances by Guatemalan, Mexican and Puerto Rican migrant workers.

But even given the goodwill of the helping community, Indiantown has not been able to provide for the health, educational, social, and emotional needs of the Maya. Indeed, residents of Indiantown never imagined that their town would become the destination of so many people from Guatemala. But the availability of agricultural labor, the small town atmosphere, and the hospitality offered by the Catholic Church have put Indiantown into the migration network of the Mayan diaspora.

In Indiantown, the Maya have had to adapt to a multiethnic, migrant worker community. In Guatemala, in the department of Huehuetenango, distinctions between different *aldeas* or towns are important, as are distinctions between Maya and *Ladinos* (Nash 1989). Even when the Maya go to the coastal plantations of Guatemala to do seasonal work, they tend to stay with friends and townspeople from their own language and community groups. They therefore have had little experience with the multiracial and multiethnic diversity of a U. S. small town. In the years since late 1982, when the Maya began to arrive in Indiantown, their social world has widened to include groups found in U. S. migrant work: African Americans, Whites, Haitians and other Caribbean peoples, Mexicans and Mexican Americans, as well as other Central Americans.

As in many small towns in the United States, low-paid work such as that found on farms and in citrus groves has attracted a multiethnic workforce. Over time, different groups have gravitated towards different employment sectors. In Indiantown, this has meant a tendency for Mexicans and Mexican Americans to work in the citrus industry, while African Americans tend to work in construction or in the pre-grown lawn industry. The Maya began working in the citrus industry, but many quickly moved into vegetable farm labor, the nursery industry, and unskilled construction. Guatemalan Mayan men found success in the golf course construction industry. Their careful attention to the delicate grasses and layout of golf courses, and their willingness to work long and hard, made them sought after employees.

The Mayan diaspora is made up of individuals and families who are creating transnational strategies in order to successfully adapt to their lives in new social arenas. The following five cases illustrate how Mayan identity has become more fluent in the community as a result of experiences of the diaspora.

José and Antonia's Kitchen

This first case of new identities in the diaspora community was brought to my attention one evening when I was in Indiantown for the one year anniversary of the death of several young men. The men had driven off the road into a canal while returning home from work on the other side of Lake Okeechobee. The accident was tragic and was caused by their exhaustion and the long, return drive from the agricultural fields to Indiantown. On the anniversary, there had been a service in the Catholic church, and afterwards some of the people at the service came back to the house of José and Antonia. The couple had successfully received a loan from a local bank and were proud of the home they had purchased. José and Antonia had known the young men who had died. About eight of us sat around the table eating tamales and talking about work, travel, and culture. José and Antonia were part of the first generation of pioneers from the Northwestern Highlands to Indiantown. As such, they had legal residency status and, over the years, had saved enough to buy their own home. Indeed, it was José who convinced the local bank to begin making loans to Guatemalans when there was a flight of long-term residents out of the community at the end of the 1980s. He was one of the first Guatemalans to purchase a home through the new loan program.

Among those sitting at the table were several young men in their early twenties who had only recently arrived in Indiantown. As usual, they were curious about me: What was I doing there? Where had I learned Spanish? What was my nationality? I told them about living in Yucatan and learning Yucatec Mayan when I was younger, and one of them asked if I had been to Cancun. I said I had, and he related how he had worked construction there for several months. The talk turned to immigration control and border crossing. One of the young men asked what passport I carry when I cross the border. I found the question odd, as I only have one passport. I replied that I carry a U. S. passport. He laughed and said, "I carry Mexican papers!" At first I thought that maybe he was a Q'anjob'al who had grown up in the refugee camps or perhaps had lived on the Guatemalan/Chiapas border. He said he was from San Miguel Acatán, Guatemala, but that he had purchased a Mexican birth certificate and other papers because, as he said, it is much easier to cross the border if you are Mexican. Once in the United States, he explained, he hid his Mexican papers and used his Guatemalan papers since here it is much easier to be a Guatemalan than a Mexican. In the United States, Guatemalan identity is helpful because it is easier for a Guatemalan to claim refugee status and, therefore, to have legal status while awaiting an asylum hearing. The young man knew full well that a hearing could take years to schedule. The talk around the table continued with more anecdotes about the comparative advantages of crossing the border with Mexican or Guatemalan identity papers. I was told that I, too, could be Mexican, if I so desired, as the papers could be purchased for sixty-five dollars in California. Passports and identity papers are of course the most visible and legal part of identity, and when anthropologists talk about identity, they seldom think of something as concrete as legal documents as a basis of identity. But I would argue that this is one of the features of the Mayan community in diaspora: the ease with which people slip in and out of different ethnic and national identities as circumstances demand. Another important aspect of this case is the way that identity is talked about. Around José and Antonia's kitchen table the talk was about transnational identity just like it is at anthropology meetings. The difference was that around that table there was the laughter of irony at the circumstances that led Mayan people to make strategic choices between being Guatemalan and being Mexican so that they could be American.

Marimba Mariachi

The second case of identities in the diaspora reflects how the diaspora cuts across class and ethnic boundaries. There is a long-standing tradition in anthropology of talking about how indigenous people assimilate to European categories such as mestizo or ladino. But assimilation in other directions also occurs. Several years ago, a friend and I went to pick up a couple of Guatemalans whom we were going to help with immigration papers. We drove through Miami and ended up at a gas station, where we met two men in a pick-up truck. They followed us back to a home in Indiantown that had a marimba (wooden xylophone). One of the two started playing the marimba. It was obvious that he was a professional marimba player, trained in music. He played parts of classical pieces, and his obvious joy at playing the instrument contrasted with the expression-less style that Mayan marimba players take on when they play. He also was quite adept at playing by himself, whereas Mayan marimba players prefer to play with several people at the same marimba. But most of all I was impressed with his skill. I asked him where he had learned to play so well, and he replied that he had learned in the national symphony in Guatemala City. When I asked him what he was doing in Florida, he said that he was working at a tourist restaurant. But then he laughed and said he was working as a Mexican. He said he had come to the states illegally the year before and had worked many jobs, but now he had found this very good job as part of a Mexican entertainment group that played mariachi and other Mexican music in the Miami area. And there is another Guatemalan in the group, he said. He explained that Guatemalan music was not as popular as Mexican music, so he had adapted his style to play better known Mexican songs. At work, he wore a traditional Mexican mariachi costume, even though Mexican mariachi bands do not include marimbas. Without legal papers, he was in danger of losing the job. He had come to see a Guatemalan who worked with political asylum cases, to advise him and his friend on applying for asylum. Both of the men were from Guatemala City and had obviously never been too far away from the metropolitan area. As we talked, I heard one of them ask the question, "Now Huehuetenango, is that a language?" "No," the political asylum worker replied, "Huehuetenango is a department. The language there is Akatec." "So Jacaltenango is a language?" the musician asked. "No, Jacaltenango is another city."

What was happening here was the acquisition of new identities, this time as Guatemalan Mayas, by these two individuals whom most would call Ladinos. As in the case of José and Antonia's kitchen, this event shows, once again, the force of the diaspora in the redefinition of identity as a pragmatic strategy for surviving and even flourishing in a transnational world. The kind of prejudice and discrimination against Mayan people that seems so pervasive in Guatemala is set aside when being indigenous might mean the difference in being able to continue playing with a Mexican mariachi marimba band.

Juana's Choice

From Indiantown to a powwow in North Carolina, Juana came along to demonstrate traditional Mayan dancing. At that time, she was living with one of the marimba players. During the long ride up from Florida to North Carolina, she spent hours sitting next to me, keeping me awake by telling me her life story. It was a complicated story, one that stressed the series of families that she had belonged to during the early 1980s. She had taken up with the guerrilla movement and lived in the mountains in early 1980. She had had a common-law husband and had two children by him. But by 1982, the movement was in retreat, and she was becoming disillusioned with the prospects of ever doing more than entering small towns, giving speeches, and then leaving quickly before the army came. She left the Guerrilla Army of the Poor and made her way to Guatemala City, where she lived for several years. But she wanted to go back to the highlands where she was from. She met a minor army officer and, through him, was able to return to her hometown. They had lived together for almost a year, when she decided that she wanted to leave Guatemala and come to the United States. She made arrangements with a Guatemalan coyote to transport her and seven other people to Arizona in 1984. One of the men in the group became her next common-law husband, and when they arrived in Indiantown, she had his child. But, she said, he abused her and was drunk so much that she left him. Now she was living with one of the marimba players from the band with whom we were traveling. Their union had lasted for several years, but a year after our appearance at the powwow, they were no longer together.

Juana's choices are another aspect of diaspora identities. Political affiliation and commitment are something that seem to most of us to be both natural and almost sacred; to Juana, however, they are something to be tried on and then cast off if they are not useful. The same is true of her relationships with men. Although she most certainly made strong commitments to men, these commitments were subject to change as the circumstances of her movements through Guatemala, Mexico, and the United States changed. Juana portrays another feature of diaspora identities—the ability to live with ambiguity and seemingly opposite values and ideals. This ability to successfully adapt through ambiguity was apparent in another event in which I participated. My wife and I were patrons to a Kanjobal wedding in Indiantown. We knew the young man who was to be married, but not the bride. She was quiet and from Los Angeles. The wedding was remarkable for the large number of men and women who came in traditional clothes, and I felt that we were in a truly indigenous event. After their wedding, the couple moved to Los Angeles to work. Several years later, the woman came up to me and reintroduced herself. She thanked me and my wife for standing in at her wedding. She said she had been especially nervous around all of the Guatemalan Mayan people of Indiantown because she had been raised in Los Angeles and didn't speak Kanjobal.

Oscar's Anger

The ambiguity of life in diaspora communities means that conflict and hostility also are subject to management in ways that can appear to be at odds with what is normal to many of us. Conflicts that go back generations in Guatemala remain important in factional splits in a community like Indiantown. There are circumstances, however, when these conflicts are suddenly and inexplicably dropped. On one occasion, I was the target of hostility that quickly dissipated (Burns 1993a). I had been out of the country for a year, and when I came back, I heard that one of the leaders of the community in Indiantown was saying that the people were sick and tired of being photographed and videotaped by myself and my students. This was surprising to me because I considered the person who was saying this to be a friend of some years. I was in Gainesville, and he was in Indiantown. I decided to wait and see what would happen rather than confront him on the issue. The time for the annual fiesta of San Miguel drew near, and this person was in charge of it that year. One afternoon I got a call from him, asking if I could videotape the festival. "But Oscar," I said, "I heard that you are telling people that you don't want me to bring any students down or videotape any more!" "Oh that," he responded, "that wasn't anything. You know how it is here, Allan, everybody is always talking about everybody else. No, I really want you to come down and videotape. Maybe you could teach Francisco how to run the camera so that he can videotape things when you're not here."

Had this conflict between Oscar and myself been an isolated event, I might have interpreted it as arising from the intrusiveness of anthropology or from some other conflict between the two of us. But when viewed through the lens of ambiguity that is a characteristic of the diaspora, the conflict takes on a new light. As Oscar suggests, conflict, envy, and talk about other people are endemic to the community, and I am not immune to the social glue of ambiguous conflict that characterizes so many relationships in Indiantown.

Francisco's Videorecorder

The fifth case is about videorecording and Kentucky Fried chickens blessed by shamans. One of the ways that I have worked with Indiantown's Mayan diaspora community has been through making videos for them. My colleagues and I have made four different videos with the community, ranging in subject from the fiesta of San Miguel Acatán to prenatal care. After my ambiguous conflict with Oscar, I decided that Francisco Lux, a young Maya originally from Totonicapán, would be an excellent local person to learn videography. I worked with him in the community, teaching him camera work, and then invited him up to Gainesville to stay with me and my family for a couple of weeks while he learned to edit. He was an enthusiastic and energetic student, especially at the beginning. But as the editing grew tedious, he finally said, "Why don't you do all of this, Allan, instead of asking me where I think each cut should be?" He had a point. At the rate we were going, the editing was going to take several months, and he had plans to work in a chicken-processing plant in South Carolina. One weekend he drove up with two friends to stay a couple of days at the house before heading north. While in Gainesville, he asked if I would help him to select a good videocamera. I asked what he wanted to videotape, and he said that he wanted to make a video about the United States that he could show in Guatemala as a way to convince people not to migrate. "They think it is so good up here and that there is lots of work," he said. "But there isn't. I want to show them how hungry you get waiting for work. I want to show them the kind of houses we live in. I want to show them how much everything here costs. Then if they want to come, fine. But they should know that everything isn't so great here."

Francisco bought his video camera and headed north. Eventually he made it to the chicken-processing factory in Morgonton, South Carolina. A few months later, he stopped by on his way back to Miami, where he planned to leave his car and fly to Guatemala with the money he had made. I asked if he had done any videotaping, but he said he hadn't. He had decided to use his videocamera in Guatemala, not in the United States, because he had had something of a religious conversion (he was an evangelical Christian) back to traditional Mayan religious belief. A year later, he returned with a tape he had made for me of different traditional rituals in Totonicapán. He said that he was instigating a new policy regarding traditional *costumbre,* or Mayan religion, in Totonicapán. Francisco explained, "Before, people didn't know much about *costumbre* and so everyone thought it was bad or something to be destroyed. Now, I'm working with a group of shamans to bring the ceremonies out into the open so that people know what they are so they won't be afraid of them. Maybe that's the way to stop repression of our religion."

One day, while Francisco was in Gainesville on his way to Guatemala, we were in a restaurant, talking about his experiences and plans. My father was visiting, and he was enjoying listening to Francisco tell of his experiences in the poultry factory. My father had grown up in Chicago, in the stockyards in the 1920s, and he knew what meat processing was like. So he asked Francisco if butchering the chickens was dangerous. "Yes," Francisco replied, "a lot of people cut themselves and get infections. You have to kill and dress about five chickens a minute at that factory." I asked him if he ever cut his hands. "No," he said, "I don't." When I asked him why not, he pulled out a photograph to give to me. "Here I am, doing a ceremony asking forgiveness of all of the chickens I am going to kill that week." The photograph showed Francisco and a friend in a small apartment in South Carolina, with forty or fifty candles on the floor, all burning. "That's why my hands don't get cut up," he said. "After I do this ceremony every week, the chickens protect me."

Francisco's case shows another aspect of the identities of the diaspora. He is quick to combine *costumbre* with video, evangelism with religious tolerance. He uses the skills he is learning as an apprentice shaman to make his employment in the chicken factory safer than is the rule.

CONCLUSIONS

Francisco's evolving role as a culture broker for Mayas who are in Guatemala but plan, someday, to come to the United States is not an identity that has clear characteristics, responsibilities, or imagery. It is a mix of the essential Mayan identity, that includes an absolute certainty of the efficacy of a traditional religious activity, coupled with the identities of a poultry worker, a student of videography, a convert to Protestantism, and a student preparing to become a traditional shaman. Sometimes the incomplete and changing nature of these activities and the identities that come with them make someone like Francisco appear eclectic or superficial. But that assessment denies the creative and innovative nature of forming identities in the diaspora.

The facility that Francisco has in passing between the poultry factory and the religious shaman's ceremony is much like the ease that the young Guatemalan

Maya men have switching between being Mexican and Guatemalan as they pass through the frontier between Mexico and California. That facility sometimes appears to be a calculated, almost cynical, approach to the experiences of migration. But it is a facility that is enlaced with humor and inventiveness of the kind that should be celebrated rather than rejected. Recognizing this humor and inventiveness is one way to recognize that the Guatemalan Maya in the diaspora are not so different from other people who are drawn into transnational contexts.

A difficulty of studying transnational identities is that there is always a temptation to attribute identity to the individual rather than to attribute it to a group of people. It would be wrong to see the case of the marimba players or that of Francisco and his videocamera as simply illustrations of personal choices and strategies. These strategies take place on an individual level, but they take place within the context of the opportunities and pressures of migration within the Mayan diaspora.

Identity has often been studied as either a shield that creates boundaries between groups of people or as an emblem that is shared within a group (Devos and Romanucci Ross 1982). But in the diaspora, the emblematic feature of identity has been reduced to a conviction that there is an essential Mayan culture that is tied to birth and blood. The shield of identity as a way of separating groups has been transformed in the diaspora to a more porous membrane that allows the adoption of sometimes radically different identities to suit pressing needs. The adoption of an indigenous identity by the professional marimba player so that he could continue playing music under the guise of being a Mexican mariachi player is an example of that porousness.

The cases of Mayan identity in the diaspora that I have recounted here present new challenges and tasks for the social sciences, especially anthropology. The first and, perhaps, most difficult task is to work with and to study the identity of people who are migrating across the geographic boundaries of several countries. Migration studies have a long history in anthropology, but they have been focused more on sending or receiving communities and not on the processes of moving between several sending and receiving communities. Even the research reported on here reflects a point of view of only a few of the many communities of the diaspora that add to the identity of the Maya.

A second task for understanding the Mayan diaspora is to reconcile the essential Mayan identity with the situational identities that serve specific purposes such as crossing the border or obtaining employment. At the outset of this chapter, I discussed the unease that is caused by the position that Mayan identity is essential to biology rather than socialization and enculturation. This seems especially problematic when other features of identity seem to be adopted or borrowed so quickly, as in the case of the musicians who learned to be indigenous. There is no easy formula for reconciling essentialist and socialization/acculturation perspectives on identity. The situational identity is more in line with Devos and Romanucci Ross's (1982) concept of identity as an emblem that is shown to others, whereas the essentialist identity of Mayan people is more of a shield that is the last refuge from the history of loss of resources and intellectual property of the Maya.

A third task is the need to find ways to work with the new plans for applying anthropology that many Mayan scholars have put forth. Victor Montejo (personal communication) has been working to build libraries and to fill them with materials written by and about Mayan people in the Northwestern Highlands of Guatemala. Publishing houses and other linguistic products have been developed by Francisco Peñalosa and Yaxte Press of Los Angeles as well as by the Academia de Idiomas Mayas in Guatemala City and other organizations. Pan-Mayan organizations and pan-indigenous organizations are also working more and more with Mayan people, as they become part of the North American Indian population in the United States and Canada. For example, whenever I talk with American Indian Movement members in the Plains, they ask me how their Mayan brothers and sisters are doing. Pan-Indianism in the United States is sometimes alluded to by references to "Indian Country," or to the many and distant places where American Indians are found—reservations, cities, government organizations, and so forth. The Maya are more and more finding themselves in Indian Country, and Indian Country is becoming another part of the culture and community of the Mayan diaspora.

REFERENCES CITED

Appadurai, Arjun
    1991   Global Ethnoscapes: Notes and Queries for a Transnational Anthropology. In *Recapturing Anthropology: Working in the Present*, edited by Richard G. Fox, pp. 336-342. School of American Research Press, Santa Fe, New Mexico.
Bogin, Barry, and James Loucky
    1997   Plasticity, Political Economy, and Physical Growth Status of Guatemala Maya Children Living in the United States. *American Journal of Physical Anthropology* 102:17.
Burns, Allan F.
    1989   Internal and External Identity Among Kanjobal Refugees in Florida. In *Conflict, Migration, and the Expression of Ethnicity*, edited by Nancy Gonzalez, and Carolyn McCommon, pp. 46-59. Westview Press, Boulder
    1993a Everybody's a Critic: Video Production and Applied Anthropology with Guatemalan Refugees. In *Anthropological Film and Video in the 1990s,* edited by Jack Rollwagen, pp. 105-129. Dual Printing, Brockport, New York.
    1993b *Maya in Exile: Guatemalans in Florida.* Temple University Press, Philadelphia.
Carmack, Robert (editor)
    1988   *Harvest of Violence: The Mayan Indians and the Guatemalan Crisis.* University of Oklahoma Press, Norman.

Deloria, Vine
    1969 *Custer Died for your Sins: An Indian Manifesto.* Macmillan, New York.
Devos, George, and Lola Romanucci Ross
    1982 *Ethnic Identity: Cultural Continuities and Change.* University of Chicago
    Press, Chicago.
Featherstone, Mike
    1995 *Undoing Culture: Globalization, Postmodernism and Identity.* Sage Publica-
    tions, Thousand Oaks, California.
Goldin, Liliana
    1996 Economic Mobility Strategies among Guatemalan Peasants: Prospects and
    Limits of Non-traditional Vegetable Cash Crops. *Human Organization* 55:99-107.
Gossen, Gary
    1986 *Symbol and Meaning Beyond the Closed Community: Essays in Mesoamerican
    Ideas.* Institute for Mesoamerican Studies, Albany, New York.
Hagan, Jacqueline Maria
    1994 *Deciding to be Legal: A Maya Community in Houston.* Temple University
    Press, Philadelphia.
Hannerz, Ulf
    1992 *Cultural Complexity: Studies in the Social Organization of Meaning.* Colum-
    bia University Press, New York.
Loucky, James, and Robert Carlsen
    1991 Massacre in Santiago Atitlan. *Cultural Survival Quarterly* 15(3):65-70.
Montejo, Victor
    1993 Tying up the Bundle and the Katuns of Dishonor: Maya Worldview and Poli-
    tics. *American Indian Culture and Research Journal* 17:103.
Nash, Manning
    1989 *The Cauldron of Ethnicity in the Modern World.* University of Chicago Press, Chicago.
    1967 *Machine Age Maya: Industrialization of a Guatemalan Community.* University of
    Chicago Press, Chicago.
Petersen, Kurt
    1992 *The Maquiladora Revolution in Guatemala.* Occasional Paper Series, 2. Orville
    H. Schell, Jr., Center for International Human Rights at Yale Law School, New Haven.
Rosaldo, Renato
    1996 Foreword: Surveying Law and Borders. *Stanford Law Review* 48:1037-1045.
Sacks, Oliver
    1997 *The Island of the Colorblind and Cycad Island.* Alfred A. Knopf, New York.
    1994 *An Anthropologist on Mars.* Alfred A. Knopf, New York.
Smith, Carol
    1990 *Guatemalan Indians and the State: 1540 to 1988.* University of Texas Press, Austin.
Warren, Kay
    1992 Transforming Memories and Histories: The Meaning of Ethnic Resurgence
    for Mayan Indians. In *Americas: New Interpretive Essays*, edited by Alfred Stepan,
    pp. 189-218. Oxford University Press, New York.
Wolf, Eric R.
    1956 Closed Corporate Peasant Communities in Mesoamerica and Central Java.
    Southwestern Journal of Anthropology 13:1-18.

8

Identities in the (Maquila) Making

Guatemalan Mayas in the World Economy

Liliana R. Goldin

They sit side by side in the production line. They sew, clean, press, or cut items of clothing. Most of them are young men and women, ranging from sixteen to twenty years old, with some older workers among them and several illegal minors. When they can talk, they often speak Spanish, unless they talk to friends from the same town; then they speak a Mayan language. These are Mayas and non-Mayas working in the assembly/*maquila* industries located in the central highlands of Guatemala, in the surroundings of the capital city and in the departments of Sacatepéquez and Chimaltenango. Wages depend on quotas, overtime, overall performance, task, and seniority. In most cases they make the minimum wage of approximately three U. S. dollars a day (sixteen quetzales as of October, 1994). The scene differs from others in Honduras, El Salvador, Malaysia or the Philippines in terms of the nature of the workers: who they are; how they see themselves; what kinds of people are working in the industry; and how people change their definition and presentation of self as they assume new labor practices.

Maquiladoras are factories that specialize in the finishing stages of production of diverse merchandise such as garments and electronic parts. These final stages are often labor intensive and require low-level training and skills. They include the assembly of previously designed and cut parts, and the packing of the finished product. The more sophisticated stages, requiring higher technologies and skills, take place in developed countries such as the United States,

Japan, or Korea. The finished products are returned to the originating countries without payment of export fees. Mexico, El Salvador, Costa Rica, Colombia, the Philippines, and Guatemala, among others, offer investors tariff-free zones with an abundant labor force willing to work for extremely low wages, in conditions that would often be unacceptable or illegal for the workers of developed countries (cf. Avancsco 1994; Fernández-Kelly 1983; Goldin 1996b; Nash 1983; Ong 1987; Petersen 1992; Safa 1983; Sklair 1989; Tiano 1994).

In 1992 there were more than two hundred seventy-five maquila factories in Guatemala, employing more than fifty thousand workers. Recent estimates (*Prensa Libre* 1995) suggest closer to seventy-five thousand workers employed in maquila. The growth of this industry is changing the lives of thousands of families in urban and rural communities. In the 1980s, when Guatemala joined several other Latin American and Asian countries as a new site for maquiladora industries, it formally established a link between its workers and the world economy. The link had existed informally since the European invasion. Productive changes and new strategies had been practiced since early colonial years, as production turned from cochineal and indigo to sugar, cotton, coffee and fruits. Maquila factories, however, add a striking degree of homogenization, which contributes to the globalization of production and, possibly, culture. In the factories, young men and women produce products for invisible consumers—the invisible mouths of the global market. The market articulates through international capital the efforts of the lower economic sectors of societies throughout the world, often comprising the poor, and their most marginal members. In the case of Guatemala, they are composed of mostly women and native peoples. The workers at these sites share similar labor processes, similar relations of production, and similar constraints. They also experience what they perceive to be positive benefits. In the world of the production line, a collective experience is valued and learned, as opposed to what is considered the lonely life of agriculture. In these shared struggles and joys, maquila workers of the world, with their 'worlds of difference,' become more of the same.

Globalization, a central concept to understanding the conditions generated by the internationalization of labor, is a process whereby workers are placed in common positions and exposed to shared experiences due to their insertion into the world economy (see Robertson 1990). However, a world culture is not necessarily characterized by uniformity but by the organization of diversity. Do the new workers of the international factory share a sense of self and identity? Is there a flow of meanings as well as goods in the definition of self (Hannerz 1990)? Are they borrowing or adopting meanings that evolve in the context of work? When internationalization of production reaches each corner of the world, the results of processes of change do not necessarily fit within homogenization, heterogenization patterns, nor do they always correspond to a center/periphery model. Rather, they tend to become indigenized: "The new global economy has to be understood as a complex overlapping disjunctive order which can no longer be understood in terms of the existing center periphery models" (Appadurai 1990:296). There is a need to examine different kinds of disjunctures in global cultures, ranging from ideological to technical, financial, and ethnic. Cultural perspectives need to be combined with historical, linguistic and political "situatedness" of the different actors with respect to nation-state, multinationals/ border communities, national groupings and movements as well as neighborhoods and families. All of these come together to construct new landscapes in the world economy. Disjunctions between production fetishism and consumption fetishism are more obviously expressed in the types of industries and labor processes that are discussed here in the context of transnational production. This type of production brings about a form of alienation twice intensified: the total separation of the producer from the product; the use of alien materials, sources, and styles; and even unawareness about the final destination of the product. In this context producers and consumers are truly worlds apart.

The experiences of Maya Indians in traditional attires and with culturally specific world views, roles, and expectations take a new decontextualized (Appadurai 1986) meaning in the context of the factory. Workers are immersed in new labor processes, expectations, behaviors, schedules, and new layers of power and status. The new forms of production also bring new styles of consumption (but almost always excluding the products workers produce in the factory). New needs, styles and assumptions about priorities of consumption are developed. New goods provide the 'building blocks of life work' as constituents of selfhood and identity (Friedman 1994a, 1994b).

The new economic opportunities allow men and women to contribute to the household and to complement the income derived from agriculture. The definition of a new lifestyle through habits/practice (Bourdieu 1977) brings about a new way of understanding and new forms of self maintenance and perception. Workers see themselves reflected in relations of domination and subordination. They not only redefine themselves in terms of the new practice, but they also see themselves in the new images that are imposed upon them by the dominant elements and it is in that context of domination that they reconstruct their images. But this process is never passive and uniform. The reconstruction of self takes place in conjunction with varied expressions of resistance (see Ong 1987; Scott 1990). In so doing, however, workers' identities develop across practices, not in compartmentalized units of practice. As they cross fields of action and engage in a variety of forms of capital (Bourdieu 1994), the need to move away from unidimensional notions of class becomes salient (Pakulski and Waters 1996).

In this paper, I examine new styles, preferences and social arrangements that, when combined, generate new ways of being, behaving and perceiving the self. The reformulation of identity in the context of practice is presented here within the following domains: new production styles and processes; identities in the context of ethnicity, nation and gender dynamics; and resistance as an expression of identity definition. I also examine the concepts of new and multiple identities as analytical devices that often are in contradiction with the classic concept of class.

METHODS AND COMMUNITY CONTEXT

From January through October of 1995, I conducted research in Santa María Cauqué, department of Sacatepéquez, and in the department of Chimaltenango, Guatemala with the assistance of several field assistants. We conducted focus groups with young men and women who work in the three area factories owned by Korean capital. We later visited several households and interviewed family members of maquila workers, in particular several sets of parents. We interviewed, separately, men and women who work in different factories and who hold different positions, from *operarios/as* (people involved in the simplest and lowest paid aspects of production) to supervisors and administrative personnel. We talked to both Mayas and non-Mayas, some of whom were native to the area and others who had migrated from other Guatemalan towns or regions. We also conducted interviews with several town and departmental authorities in both departments. Informal municipal and departmental records indicate that, in the last fifteen years, there has been extensive migration to the Guatemala City and the surrounding areas that harbor maquiladora industries. Departmental records report that the populations of the departments of Chimaltenango and Sacatepéquez have increased significantly in the last few years: in 1980, there were 350,000 inhabitants in both departments combined and 27,000 in the city of Chimaltenango; in 1990, there were 495,000 in both departments combined and 45,000 in the city of Chimaltenango (Censo Estadístico 1981, 1994).

When asked what people from the town do, the answer is often similar to the following: "People from here grow vegetables—beets, Chinese peas, tomato. They sell them in the markets or stores. Or they grow lettuce, and they harvest zucchini and a whole lot of other vegetables." When asked about the women's jobs in Santa María Cauqué, the answer has been as follows: "Young women go to the hill to work. They help in the kitchen. They sweep the patio. They wash clothes. They wash dishes. They take lunch to the fields." We know, however, that a large percentage of the young women work in the factories. Forty percent of households in a random sample of households in Santa María had one or more members working in the factories (Goldin 1996b). An informant says, "The factories need many people now. Many young women go to work there. Very few work in the fields or stay at home to help their mothers."

Indeed, when asked what people *in general* do, the response has to do with the traditional chores and expectations of men and women. When asked what *particular* people do, factory work becomes salient to all. What defines young women are the traditional chores they say they do, but this clashes with what many of them are actually doing.

Many communities in Sacatepéquez and Chimaltenango, and particularly along the Pan-American highway, are involved in the production of nontraditional agricultural crops and in the maquiladora factories. Most of the people interviewed live in Santa María Cauqué, a hamlet of Santiago Sacatepéquez—a village which traditionally has provided the capital city with vegetables and which was one of the first communities to engage in the production of nontraditionals for export. Toward the late 1980s, young men and women started to work in the factories. Approximately half the households of the communities are somehow involved in maquila production (Asturias de Barrios 1996:6). For generations, the people of the region identified themselves as agriculturalists and saw themselves fitting within systems of ideas and action that made sense in the context of agricultural life. But things changed quite fast. In the words of a woman from the hamlet, "Primero vino la religión, vinieron las fábricas, vino el terremoto, vino la agricultura de brócoli y arveja, y vino el gobierno tratando de echar a los Chinos [Koreans]." [First came the religion. The factories came; the earthquake; the agriculture of broccoli and peas; and then came the government trying to push the Asians away.][1]

IDENTITY IN PRACTICE

Identity is formulated, in part, in the process of production. It is also formulated in the re-evaluation of one's ideology, the understanding of the world around us. As we change our practice, we simultaneously revise through our own practice who we are. New moral standards evaluate what is fair or unfair, what is good or bad for the individual, the household, and the community. Men and women indicate that elements that used to be frowned upon are now identified as being 'good for you,' such as competition, accumulation, individualism, and other essential capitalist values. Most of these divergent values correspond to practices associated with industrial work in opposition to the ideology of agriculture.

The main distinction between working in the fields versus working in the factory has to do with individual versus social activities. "In the field you work alone. You don't work with friends. Only in the factory you meet friends; there are more people that you can talk to [in the factory]." This is an important area of definition of self. More people are working side by side with others sharing the same experience rather than working alone in the field or in the household. A non-Indian woman who moved to Santa María said that people in the town used to be too quiet and now "there is more life; they talk more." Even when there are many more controls in the factory than in the fields, and little freedom to talk during the day, women appreciate the shared experience in the factory. As a result, now men go out in groups of sometimes ten or more and women go out in groups of three or more. There is a new social experience, oriented towards larger group interactions and organized around coworkers in the factory. "They go and learn things in the *maras* [groups of workers working in the same production line and often associated with violence or disruptions]. They are not home on Sundays. The way of being has changed 'la forma de ser' because they go and bring new experiences, sometimes good, but mostly bad."

Wages are often understood as a measure of people's value and an extension of their abilities. While many complain about the salaries, others claim that people get paid 'what they deserve.' For example, a twenty-one-year-old man—recently married and a member of an agricultural family—who works as a supervisor in one industry, told us that "unlike in agricultural work, in the factory you get paid what you deserve." When comparing maquila work and agricultural work, he finds wages in the two contexts to be about the same. In the countryside, wages depend on the price of the product, just as in the maquila. In the factory, however, wages also are dependant on how one behaves. Personal behavior is perceived by workers to be a factor in the determination of wages in the factory. Being submissive, obeying, doing what you are expected to do can cause you to "improve yourself," "to progress." In contrast to the factory code of compliance, obedience, and listening, it is hard work that is thought to predict success in agriculture. The perception is that in the factory people earn what they deserve, as opposed to the already predetermined range of salaries (i.e., minimum salary) for a given type of work. "You have to sew very exactly. If you go beyond one centimeter or even a few millimeters, you have to do it again. If you do it wrong, they will not give you an incentive," says the same young man. The worker feels responsible for what he will be paid.

In agriculture, however, a good harvest or a good agricultural year—and therefore a good income—depend both on hard work and on external forces such as weather conditions, amount of precipitation, or the availability of laborers. Often, failure in agricultural work is neither expressed nor perceived as a result of personal failure or lack of personal effort. In fact, most agriculturalists feel they work very hard, and they are proud of it, but factors such as 'bad luck' rather than personal behavior or effort can contribute to bad outcomes. In the factory, there is a sense of control, and there is also a framework for understanding bad outcomes. Workers are taught that *they* are to blame for the bad treatment or the low wages. A woman working in one of the factories indicates that Korean managers are good to the people who behave well and bad to the people who behave badly, again pointing to the sense of the individual worker's personal responsibility for the treatment he or she receives. The notion that "if you behave badly, they treat you badly; and if you behave well, they treat you well" is quite widespread: "El trabajador se busca las regañadas, porque no hace bien el trabajo o no se porta bien. No vi cuando los regañaban pero si los regañaban era porque se portaban mal o se tardaban mucho en el baño."[2]

The factory has provided independence to many young men and women. Operarias who came from the Pacific Coast indicate that they prefer the move to Chimaltenango because of the weather and the people. They like not to be known by everyone as they are in the Coast. In the highlands people do not know them and do not prejudge: "They see me as who I am [tal como soy], and I don't hear comments from anybody." There is more anonymity in Chimaltenango while working in the factory and operarias appreciate this new state of being. One of the operarias noted that her sister used to be able to buy clothes because of factory work, and now she can do the same. Her parents would buy her what she needed, but she enjoys the newly acquired independence that factory work provides. The women from the Coast do not use traditional *corte* [dress] anymore. Although women in the highlands "dress very differently," coastal women indicate that dress would not be a reason to treat them differently; that is, "eso no quiere decir que yo le haga de menos." The women emphasize that they have many Indian friends and that they all get along well.

When a woman is asked how she has changed since she started working in the factory, she responds that she does not think she has changed but that she is now more responsible; she helps her mother economically and shares her income with her. The term in Kakchiquel that they use is *chuka'*, which translates as strength, and independence. This particularly applies to married women who can feel less dependent on their spouses. In all these cases, the self is re-created in the context of practice, it is defined in relation to other workers, to the value of one's work, and to a sense of empowerment and autonomy.

IS IDENTITY DEFINED IN TERMS OF CLASS?

The question of whether new class relations are formed in the context of the factory must be viewed from the perspectives of Guatemalan families who participate in the practice of 'householding.' Householding implies the pooling of different economic activities and sources of income into the household and the combination of capitalist and noncapitalist processes (Halperin 1994; see Goldin 1996b). In Guatemala, householding implies the combination of factory work, production of nontraditionals, sale in markets, day labor, artisan production, unpaid family labor, and other sources of income. It is in this context that a new definition of self and identity and a redefinition of group belonging are shaped. The transnational communities that we are describing, involved in house-holding strategies, are very difficult to understand in terms of class—groups narrowly defined by their relation to the means of production.[3] People find themselves involved in multiple relations and at multiple levels of self-identification. Cook and Binford (1990:228) observed this when they discussed the nature of differentiation and the complexity of economic relations that are present in Oaxaca, which they refer to as "ambiguous" (cited in Kearney 1996:96). How can we focus on the notion of class when we have multiple activities, multiple identities and truly multiple relations of production? Some people own some land but in turn work as day laborers for others, work in factories, rent land, and occasionally hire workers themselves. Their activites include wage labor, petty commodity production, trade and subsistence production. It is very difficult in Guatemala, and probably elsewhere in the world, to identify rural sectors of the population that are clearly extracting surplus from the labor of others (Goldin 1996a; Goldin and Saenz de Tejada 1993; Smith 1990). We find individuals in households that are positioned at both ends of the economic spectrum, as exploited and as exploiters, or rather at multiple points in the economy. By being in those complex positions, they do not choose to identify in terms of class affiliation. They use other elements of identification such as their preferred occupation, their identification with the land and its strong cultural and symbolic connotations, gender identity, their connection with a religious group, or their main source of employment (i.e., the factory). The new communities transcend the 'peasant/proletarian/bourgeois' categories. New categories placed in the borders of social and economic positions need to be defined. The disappearance of the use of some of these categories "demonstrates not the nonexistence of class but the impotence of class, as a basic dimension of identity, to inform subject identity" (Kearney 1996:146), and the need to find tools that will provide us with the power to understand 'the rules of motion' of society—what class analysis first setout to do so as to be able to change and improve it (Pakulski and Waters 1996:147).

In a state that is today "transnational, postdevelopmental, and global," emerges a "postpeasant" subject who defines transnational identity (Kearney 1996:43; chap. 4 this volume). Men and women in the maquiladora industries offer the foremost example of these new subjects developing new identities. The notion of transnational identity is not only relevant in the context of transnational migration, where people from underdeveloped countries move to developed countries. Internal migration is present within Guatemala and in the areas that house the maquiladora industries. Mostly, transnational identities are formed within new spaces that provide new styles of being and new understandings about the nature of things. It is not the nation-state that defines and inform identities (Glick Schiller 1992; Kearney 1996). New landscapes and new sets of people working and living together contribute to the creation of self and new survival strategies. Innumerable messages are communicated through these new, complex spaces. It is this participation in different modes and relations of production that generates the new conceptions of self. However, it is not a case of replacing one mode of production by another, one element of value by another, such as land over capital. It is a question of *multiplicity*. Land continues to be an element of prestige, if not economic viability. In times of limited access to land, individuals participate in units of multiple activities. As indicated above, diverse strategies are combined in rural households. Changes in world view do not imply any form of syncretism or replacement of one ideology by another. Alternative and often contradictory sets of assumptions coexist.

As people move between and within social and economic spaces—for example, in Santa Maria, the movement of people within their own communities, from the field to the factory, from the factory to the market or to the household hearth—they generate new understandings of self. In a conversation involving courting practices inside the factory and changes in women's dress and general style of clothing and adornment, a young man indicates that things are different in the factory than in the town.

> Down there [in the factory] it is a job, and if a women wants to wear skirts or makeup, if she wants to break away [from traditional practice] she does ["si le da la gana de safarse, se safa"]. You can do things one way here [in the town], but when you are down there in the factory, you have to do things in a particular way; and if I don't do things the way the Koreans want, then, I have to come back and work in the fields. Down there women can wear makeup or wear skirts, but up here *they have to go back to what they were before.* (Emphasis added)

People consciously express that you can be one person in one place and another in a different place. In the factory, the worker can adopt one way of being, one way of behaving that fits with the idea the worker has of who she or he is, or should be, in that context. There are distinct ways of being, dressing, working, speaking, addressing others, and relating to men and women, to Indians and non-Indians, and to nationals and foreigners that pertain to different social spaces: "When you are back in the town, or in the fields, things are different." These ways include the use of language and participation in formal education. The identification with the Kakchiquel language seems to be related to power positions; lower level workers tend to speak Kakchiquel to one another, but those in intermediate or managerial positions speak Spanish to each other. The same is the case with officers of the cooperative, who reportedly turn to speaking only Spanish as they move up in the cooperative's hierarchy. Language is an important element of identification of power relations. Language and labor go together in defining a sense of identity in the workplace. Several informants regret that many do not know how to speak Kakchiquel anymore. Important in the construction of identity are the access to and influence of any form of formal education. Many have left school to work in the factories and do not plan to return as long as there are jobs available to them.

Some people have been able to move up economically thanks to the factory. A young woman talks about buying a color television for her family and about sending her younger sister to study in Guatemala City. A couple has been saving money to buy their house; they expect to make a lot of money and save some in the bank. These are new values and expectations. Eventually, it is conceivable that young couples may move away from the complex, multi-activity household setting and restrict themselves to one source of income, such as that provided by industrial work. A proletarian identity and class affiliation may perhaps develop. But at the moment, the transnational landscape seems to elude the lineal conceptions of class.

CLASS, ETHNICITY AND NATIONALITY

It is quite apparent that in these multiple subjects *ethnicity* seems dissipated, as people are defining themselves in broader terms that seem to intentionally forgo ethnicity (as in Indian or *Natural* versus non-Indian or *Ladino*). The distinctions that appear again and again in Santa María Cauqué are those of Guatemalans versus Koreans: "We, the Guatemalans."

Here Mayas and Ladinos work side by side in the factories. In the case of Korean-owned factories, workers' discussions present ethnicity or ethnic divisions in terms of national divisions rather than internal ethnic distinctions. In this context, national boundaries overlap with class boundaries. For example, many of the higher rank administrators in the factories are Guatemalans, but workers complain that, whenever there is a dispute, "they favor the Koreans, rather than the Guatemalans." "If one goes to complain to the *licenciado*, who is from here, from Guatemala, he favors the Koreans and against the Guatemalans, that is, when one goes to the office. But when the Koreans become too excessive, then all the people go on strike." Here the issue is presented in terms of class affiliation, Guatemalan management allies with Korean management, along class lines rather than national boundaries.

Occasionally Guatemalan men are sent to train in Korea: "When they come back here [a young worker said], they hire them as Koreans." [Ellos allá se van a estudiar en filas y entonces cuando regresan acá, los toman como Coreanos.] This is a commentary of ethnicity as practice: If you act like a Korean, you are very close to being one. A "Korean" here is a synonym for Manager or Supervisor; it is an expression of class. The opposition between management as the Koreans and the local people as 'Guatemalans' is important. The common identity as 'Guatemalans' reinforces the new apparent solidarity generated in the factory in the context of work. The distinction between Koreans and Guatemalans is also presented in terms of different pay schedules: Koreans indicate (in response to a man who asks why is he not paid in dollars, like Koreans are) that the reason for the differential salaries people get is that this is Guatemala and not Korea, and that the two are two different things. Again, differential pay scales are justified in terms of nationality, which here translates into class.

People are classified as "those who have" or as "those who do not have" [hay gente que tiene y gente que no]. "Those who do not have, need to work for those who have. If you have land, says one man, you need someone to help. If you do not have land, you work for someone who does. When working for others does not give you enough, then you work in the factories."

Ladinos are not presented as a main concern; instead, the government is viewed as the enemy and other Ladinos as potential coworkers: "Most outsiders that come in are Ladinos. There is good relation with Ladinos. It is the government that we have bad relations with because they want to close the factories!" And the "North Americans" are also in the picture: "In the factory, they need a lot of production because the North Americans come and they tell the Koreans, 'we need this style or that style for that date because we are late.' Then they make us stay for extra hours."

Never before had Mayas and non-Mayas had in their daily lives abstract images of the needs and requirements of the world economy, where the North Americans (in general) replace the individual "gringos" they used to sell to in the market. Now the "Koreans" (in general) also referred to as "the Chinese" take a new place in the local people's ethnic/national landscape. Class, ethnicity, and nationality are woven together in the conceptual blend that describes transnational identity.

GENDERED WORK:

THIS TYPE OF WORK IS NOT WHO I AM, IT IS WOMEN'S WORK!

The wife of a factory worker tells us that her husband stopped working at the factory because he did not always want to be among women. He thought the work he did was women's work, and he did not want to take the abuse women take. He felt like a slave. He thought the factory was not "who he was." He was a fieldworker, and he was hoping for better conditions. He liked to take his hoe and go to the fields. That is how he defined himself. He did not want to be mistreated or insulted. As another worker said, "Even the way they talk to you is insulting. They give you orders!" In other words, they do not use the polite, gentle expressions that are used in Kakchiquel, which translate into "please do me the act of kindness" or, in Spanish, "hágame el favor." It is not just an issue of gender, men say, "the young people are putting up with a lot." By deciding to go back to agriculture, the man in his thirties is asserting his identity, and, in the process, he is also executing an act of resistance towards the new practice. Others, however, consider agriculture to be a thing of the past or, in their own words, "our parents' jobs"; they do not consider it to be a viable alternative. Most young men have not even learned the skills required to work in the fields.

In spite of men and women in the factory working side by side, men still view gender relations as stratified relations of domination/subordination. For example, young male factory workers indicate that the traditional residency rules, which require a woman to livê where the man sets his residence and often temporarily with the husband's family, make sense because residency patterns contribute to determining who is in charge: "If she has bad temper, she can treat me badly in her house or her parents' house. The man is the head of the household, and he has to command over the woman. They both have the same role, but the one who has more power is the man." Equal pay and equal access to work have not changed the attitudes about gender roles and people's positions in the household.

IDENTITY CAN BE DEFINED IN TERMS OF RESISTANCE

Resistance is a form of self assertion. Expressions of resistance are not scarce in the Guatemalan factories, sometimes taking the forms of "leaving the job," physically or verbally fighting back, and participating in or contributing to the organization of strikes. Participation in a strike is an event that contributes to the construction of a personal history. Being on strike and loyalty to friends and coworkers are signs of identity at the group and individual levels. The strike is the ultimate form of resistance or self-assertion. Strikes take place against bad treatment and, sometimes, against low salaries. A worker indicated how one strike was organized: The workers passed a small piece of paper along the lines, telling others not to return after lunch.

If some returned, the *maras* threatened and intimidated them. "They told me to work but I told them I couldn't because my friends would be mad at me. They [the Koreans] were mad at me. The salary is too low. You work. You go on strike, and everybody gets something." This woman was fired for not working. She says she cried not for her job, but for her friends. She felt great ambivalence about housework, factory work, going back with her family, and missing her friends. Among workers there is great ambivalence about the right thing to do.

When workers go to the office to complain, they are in turn reprimanded for doing so. As one man says, "They will not even let you complain because one has rights to go and claim for his salary. ...And the *licenciado* says, 'This is the salary. If you want it, fine! If you don't, then leave! This is your problem. It is not the factory's problem. Then leave and let's see where you get another job'." The discussion of whether one has or does not have any rights is a discussion about definitions of self and identity. It is about self-worth and self-esteem, and it is more explicitly expressed in the context of wage labor, where self-worth is not a metaphor for identity but the literal and reified measure of who one is, expressed in a wage.

In a discussion with a Korean supervisor, a worker was told to leave. In response, the worker said, "If you want me to leave, you come with me and we both go outside" [suggesting they should go out and fight]. However, the Korean did not go outside to fight. The worker then indicated, "They say they know how to fight, but it is only one that knows how to fight. He would not go." Here the worker asserts his superiority in the context of defending his rights, in spite of having lost his job. He was later hired by another factory.

A woman saw a Korean manager hit a young woman:

> They just want you to work and work and not get up. The Korean woman went to talk to her, and she started to shout to the young woman. The young woman did not listen and continued sewing. The Korean woman pulled the young woman's head back by grabbing her hair. When the worker realized what the Korean woman had done, she slapped the Korean woman in her face. Then they fought, and they took her to the office. There they told the young woman not to complain if she did not want to have any more problems. So they convinced her that she hadn't seen anything, as if nothing had happened...and she kept working.

Identity is also about power, and acts of resistance are used to establish or confirm power hierarchies. They remind workers and management where each one individually and collectively stands.

DISCUSSION AND CONCLUSIONS

Significant changes in the rural communities and households of Guatemala have been taking place in recent years. They include new migration networks and actors in everyday life, new forms of access to and distribution of income, and new leisure activities. There are noticeable changes in the domestic economy, including relations between parents and children, access to luxury items, and the bygone possibility of learning traditional crafts and activities such as weaving, or even making tortillas [tortear], an activity that takes skill and practice. The relationship that women establish as they spend hours cooking, and specifically *torteando,* is probably different from the one established within the factory (Goldin 1996b). In the context of these complex changes, new aesthetic preferences, images of women and men, of appropriate behaviors and styles serve to construct new understandings and presentations of self. A young woman, for example, thought that when she worked in the factory, she looked different, she looked 'better'.

With the factory, the image of young people has changed. Men can now aspire to move up, maybe to become a supervisor or to go to Korea to learn other jobs. There is talk of "improvement" [superación] that the company offers in Guatemala, particularly among young men. It is said that "women give themselves too fast to men" [se regalan rápido a los hombres], suggesting sexual promiscuity. There is talk about the changing sexual standards and the young women who become pregnant before marriage. Concepts of work and leisure have also changed. Some women now associate the concept of leisure with the outdoors or outside the household. In that context, they perceive men to have more access to fun and play than they do. Women get 'bored' with being indoors. Factory work does not take place in the household, and it offers the opportunity of 'going out' or reaching beyond the household walls. Overall, young people feel more independent. Young men see the maquila as a way of reaching a lifestyle that only people in the capital city may obtain, but without having to 'become' Ladinos. Young women express that having money to give to their families, and also to cover their own expenses, allows them to be more independent.

The new landscape of the maquila age looks more and more urbanized as factories attract people from diverse rural and urban backgrounds. The urban-like nature of the new towns holds diverse complex populations that have been brought up in the midst of agricultural cultures and calendars. The new actors see themselves as better, improved, and 'lucky' to participate in the age of modernity. The association with the factory—even within the abundant criticisms and complaints about conditions, salaries, and treatment—seems to enhance the lives of the workers by producing the monthly or biweekly wage. Capital, although very limited, brings access to goods. Goods bring in more than prestige and convenience. Goods bring in new ways of being and acting. The new identities in the making are subtle expressions of globalization and not so subtle examples of the contradictory positions in which workers, producers and consumers of global wares are located in the new capitalist realities. As the Kakchiquel-speaking woman holds the tailored garment that she is about to press, suffering from the heat and tired legs, does she wonder who and where the user will be? Is she curious about the identity of the consumer as she molds her own identity in the process of production and in the hopes for consumption? Are the links of domination, subordination and resistance as severed as they seem? Can globalization have some mitigating purpose in the plight of the oppressed by bringing into depressed areas of the world images of difference?

ACKNOWLEDGMENTS

This research was possible thanks to a Faculty Development Research Award, Office for Research, SUNY Albany. A modified Spanish version of this article was presented in the Congreso de Estudios Mayas II, August 6-8, 1997, Guatemala and in English at the meetings of the American Anthropological Association, Washington D. C., November 1997.

NOTES

1. In the last few years some factories have closed and moved to other countries such as Honduras or Mexico, where they find better conditions (tax breaks and even lower salaries). The perception of some people in the communities is that the government wants to push the factories away. Some say the military wants them out, probably confusing the ongoing civil war and role of the military with their perceived impact on the factories. In fact, the government is eager to keep the factories in Guatemala. The quote also refers to religious change and conversions to Protestant religions which have increased significantly in the last twenty years, and to the impact of the devastating earthquake of 1976, which brought European planners who encouraged agriculturalists to engage in the production of nontraditional crops.
2. "The worker looks for trouble, because he/she either does not perform the job well or does not behave well. I did not see when they were being reprimanded, but if they were being reprimanded, it is because they were misbehaving, or they were taking too long in the bathroom."
3. See Michael Kearney's (1996) discussion of class and identity and also chapter 4 of this volume.

REFERENCES CITED

Appadurai, Arjun
1986   *The Social Life of Things.* Cambridge University Press, Cambridge.
1990   Disjuncture and Difference in the Global Cultural Economy. In *Global Culture: Nationalism, Globalization and Modernity,* edited by Mike Featherstone, pp. 295-310. Sage Publications, London.

Asturias de Barrios, Linda (Coordinator)
1996   *Producción agrícola en Santa María Cauqué.* Asociación de Investigación y Estudios Sociales (ASIES). Guatemala City.

AVANCSO
1994   *El Significado de la Maquila en Guatemala.* Asociación para el avance de las ciencias sociales en Guatemala. Cuadernos de Investigación No.10, Guatemala City.

Bourdieu, Pierre
1977   *Outline of a Theory of Practice.* Cambridge University Press, Cambridge.
1994   *Language and Symbolic Power.* Polity Press, Cambridge.

Censos Estadísticos
1981   *Censo Nacional de Población y Habitación.* Instituto Nacional de Estadística, Guatemala City.
1994   *Censo Nacional de Población X.* Instituto Nacional de Estadística, Guatemala City.

Cook, Scott, and Leigh Binford
1990   *Obliging Need: Rural Petty Industry in Mexican Capitalism.* University of Texas Press, Austin.

Fernández-Kelly, María Patricia
1983   Mexican Border Industrialization, Female Labor Force Participation and Migration. In *Women, Men and the International Division of Labor,* edited by June Nash, and María Patricia Fernández-Kelly, pp. 205-223. State University of New York Press, Albany.

Friedman, Jonathan
1994   *Cultural Identity and Global Process.* Sage Publications, London.
1994   *Consumption and Identity.* Hardwood Academic Publishers, Chur, Switzerland.

Glick Schiller, Nina, Linda Basch, and Cristina Blanc-Szanton
1992   Towards a Transnational Perspective on Migration: Race, Class, Ethnicity, and Nationalism Reconsidered. *Annals of the New York Academy of Sciences,* p. 645.

Goldin, Liliana
1996a   Economic Mobility Strategies Among Guatemalan Peasants: Prospects and Limits of Nontraditional Vegetable Cash Crops. *Human Organization* 55:99-107.
1996b   Maquila Age Maya: The Changing Nature of "Community" in Rural Guatemala. Manuscript on file at the Department of Anthropology, State University of New York, Albany.

Goldin, Liliana, and María Eugenia Saenz de Tejada
1993   Uneven Development in Western Guatemala. *Ethnology* 24:237-251.

Halperin, Rhoda
1994   *Cultural Economies: Past and Present.* University of Texas Press, Austin.

Hannerz, Ulf
1990   Cosmopolitans and Locals in World Culture. In *Global Culture: National-ism, Globalization and Modernity,* edited by Mike Featherstone, pp.237-252. Sage Publications, London.

Kearney, Michael
1996   *Reconceptualizing the Peasantry. Anthropology in Global Perspective.* Westview Press, Boulder.

Nash, June
1983   The Impact of the Changing International Division of Labor on Different Sectors of the Labor Force. In *Women, Men and the International Division of Labor,* edited by June Nash, and María Patricia Fernández-Kelly, pp. 3-38. State University of New York Press, Albany.

Nash, June, and María Patricia Fernández-Kelly (editors)
1983   *Women, Men and the International Division of Labor.* State University of New York Press, Albany.

Ong, Aihwa
1987   *Spirits of Resistance and Capitalist Discipline: Factory Women in Malaysia.* State University of New York Press, Albany.

Pakulski, Jan, and Malcolm Waters
1996   *The Death of Class.* Sage Publications, London.

Petersen, Kurt
1992   *The Maquiladora Revolution in Guatemala.* Occasional Paper Series, 2. Orville H. Schell, Jr., Center for International Human Rights at Yale Law School, New Haven.

Prensa Libre
1995   "Despegue y consolidación de la maquila en Guatemala." Revista Dinero, March 22, Guatemala City.

Robertson, Roland
1990   Mapping the Global Condition: Globalization as the Central Concept. In *Global Culture: Nationalism, Globalization and Modernity,* edited by Mike Featherstone, pp.15-30. Sage Publications, London.

Safa, Helen
1983   Women, Production and Reproduction in Industrial Capitalism: A Compari-son of Brazilian and U. S. Factory Workers. In *Women, Men and the International Division of Labor,* edited by June Nash, and María Patricia Fernández-Kelly, pp. 95-116. State University of New York Press, Albany.

Scott, James C.
1990   *Domination and the Arts of Resistance.* Yale University Press, New Haven.

Sklair, Leslie
1989   *Assembling for Development. The Maquila Industry in Mexico and the United States.* Unwin Hayman, Boston.

Smith, Carol
1990   *Guatemalan Indians and the State, 1540 to 1988.* University of Texas Press, Austin.

Tiano, Susan
1994   *Patriarchy on the Line: Labor, Gender and Ideology in the Mexican Maquila Industry.* Temple University Press, Philadelphia.

9

The Borderless Borderlands

Texas's Colonias as Displaced Settlements

Duncan Earle

MARGINAL BORDERLANDS

It is a well-worn idea in understandings of U. S. history that the frontier expresses something essential about the nation that is less apparent in the more staid and conventional center. While the major metropolis envisions the periphery as marginal, wild and uncultivated, it has another historic role: to frame the future. This notion has renewed vigor in the juxtaposing of the marginal borderlands and the paradigmatic center of the nation. Cultural geographer Rob Shields (1991:276) recently noted, "margins become signifiers of everything 'centres' deny or repress; margins as 'the Other', become the condition of possibility of all social and cultural entities."

Anthropologists are expert at seeking out the Other in the far margins of the world, but here I want to focus upon the marginal southern borderlands and specifically the border between Mexico and the state of Texas. I see this little studied area as one that places the nations that meet here in a different perspective—one that is contradictory and at the same time revealing of the "condition of possibility" for the future of a region and a hemisphere embarking on the long journey towards closer relations based on trade. The border is a line made into a region, a marginal place in the mainstream of history, a frontier that has much to say about the center, and a place characterized by the settled migrant, the mobile transnational making a local home.

This is not the same perspective one gathers from national media about The Border (never Canada): an out-of-control place of drugs, prostitutes and illegal immigration. Most of the derision aimed at borders are really about binational problems that are confused with border issues. Migrants mostly pass through borders. Borders are not their destination. From the border perspective, it is a strange irony that the national media focus on immigration as a border issue, when most are heading for some interior destination. We do not attack a door when people we don't like come through it, unless we are displacing our avoidance of them. It seems that the center is in denial, and the border is easy to blame.

Yet this border area has been seriously affected by migrational patterns from the very onset of the current political segregation, and often even before then. The El Paso/Juarez region, for example, is largely made up of immigrants from other places, both north and south, old movements and new ones, with each new wave serving as a demographic benchmark for serious shifts in the relative conditions of the two nations. The Mexican Revolution, the U. S. Depression, the Bracero Program, the Border Industrialization Program *(maquilas)*, and NAFTA are all events that differentially impacted the two nations and resulted in movements of people from one side to the other. Many of these border jumpers have remained on the border. In that sense, the history of border crossing and displacement undergirds the history and identity of the two nations' borderlands.

BORDERS AND MIGRATION

What distinguishes border migration from other forms of international population dislocation can be seen in the communities it creates and the kinds of adaptational patterns, coping strategies, and social arrangements that arise. Moreover, many of the distinctions made by both passing through migrants and interior nonmigrants about who is who and why, become grey, blurred, indistinct, and even contradictory, in the borderlands. Identity, order, authority, and social community are all more contested spaces in a place where none has a good grasp of the hegemonic mantle, and all cultural practices are contingent and subject to (re)negotiation: Will I kiss the cheek, shake hands, say "howdy"? What should I bring to the *quinceañera*? Is chili allowed on ribs? Is code-switching a sign of insider solidarity or linguistic incivility? These and a thousand other questions arise daily in a social and cultural environment that is variably indeterminate. All cultural canons are problematically deployed; Goffman's (1981) social theater has competing directors wrestling just off stage, with the actors left to manage as best they can. In so far as we derive some aspect of our identity from the total social context, all identity is contingent, partial, in flux, and under constant renegotiation.

This odd state of affairs, a multiculturalism in like-it-or-not daily practice, has created on the border a kind of social laboratory, much in keeping with the historians' idea of frontiers-as-future. The historically given forced march into Anglo-Latino habitual cultural encounters serves as a foreshadowing of the implications of a social science of hemispheric integration. If for Anglo-America the trajectory of globalization is predominantly to the south, it will be places that have already lived this integration that can provide the richest insights into that process. These U. S.-Mexico borderlands are such a laboratory—one with much to say about the national interiors. Nations that reactively want to assign borders to the role of differentiating edges rather than that of unifying regions have trouble with the idea that the borders are signs of things to come, not of the past. The centers have much invested in their misunderstandings of the border.

The theme of this essay is how the margin defines or critiques the center; how border regions, as marginal spaces, give rise to social forms that deconstruct the categories and distinctions that are normally maintained without question in the nonborder, the center, what we call, "the interior." It is a discussion about migration as impact as well as a process, a condition as much as an event. The specific anthropological border subjects employed to exemplify these issues of bordering are the residents, the mostly Mexican heritage households, that make up what have been called *colonias*. A borrowed term from the Spanish for residential subdivisions, the term now has been transformed on the border into a moniker for the nearly 1500 shanty suburbs that dot the border landscape. They house as many as one-half million of Texas's Mexican-heritage, low-income population. Many of these people are either immigrants from Mexico or points farther south, out-migrants from border cities in the wake of declining public housing, or historic agricultural migrants who have incrementally settled down with the shifting labor opportunities in that sector. In very different ways, nearly all colonia adult residents are "migrants" and as such experience the impact of displacement. The idea of settled migrants and displaced placemakers gives us a taste of some of this contradictory social landscape called borderlands.

COLONIAS AS NONORDINARY SPACE

Colonias are not just marginal settlements but ones that assault numerous categories of spatial segregation by their very "border" position in relation to the normal categorizations that make up the settlement divisions in U. S. discourse about housing. They also call into question our concepts of community development, nationhood, and civic membership. In a sense, colonias are a space of social deconstruction constantly under construction (Earle and Huang 1996). They are a constantly growing form of settlement that allows households to successfully adapt to the changing conditions of global capitalism along the only geographical boundary between the so-called Third World and the First. Their marginal position, the newness and instability of their settlements (a mature colonia is twenty-five years old), and their inverted and contradictory social logic makes them volatile. It is suggestive that almost no social science research has been conducted on them, even though some have been around for over two decades (for exceptions see Briody 1986; Vila 1994), and they constitute the poorest discrete social sector in the entire country. They escape neat social definition, places of the liminal and the interstitial, not just ambiguous but conceptually contradictory, categorically messy. Not really rural, nor suburban, nor urban, not really acculturated but not Mexican either, and with very ambiguous notions of national identity, they are neither here nor there.

How one defines groups leads inevitably to how one understands them and acts towards them. Anderson's (1983) imagined nation and the more reduced imagined community provide cognitive landscapes of the intelligible, where all things can be placed in categories familiar to the imagined social whole. The problem of defining borders arises when a border is no longer a boundary in a two-dimensional sense, but an area with full spatial and social characteristics impossible to cleave apart with parsimony to its respective sides. This betwixt and between place seems to call out for some form of order-giving encounter, through a position of silencing or rejecting as alien the dissonant elements, or alternatively through their incorporation in an encompassing and familiar discourse, a normalization of the aberrant, the regularization of the unruly. This might well capture the essence of how Texas has approached this unique sociospatial phenomenon called colonias: rejection and regularization, ignoring the social problems of the colonias and, at the same time, trying to "fix" them with top-down, high-priced infrastructure projects. Neither strategy brings the colonias closer to any category of the normalized, even when their physical conditions are improved.

Contradiction and Colonias

Colonias were, for years, completely outside of the awareness of most Texans. They were a form of semi-illegal land development that politically connected developers profited from unscrupulously. They turned the vast, unserved demand for low-income border housing into profits on investment in a patch of remote real estate, beyond the jurisdiction of the closest city. In Texas's counties, until 1989, there was no regulation of housing, so a former onion field or a worthless stretch of desert could, with a few passes of a tractor, become a dirt street with no services—a parodic version of a normal subdivision. With a plot secured, people would begin the process of incrementally constructing a home and obtaining such services as they could afford. In the majority of cases, they lacked (and still lack) what would be considered minimum services—public water, paved streets, sewage and drainage systems, deed-based home ownership, fire and police services—yet the homes offered the hope of permanence and control of one's residential space. Moreover, most colonias in Texas appear well appointed compared with their low-end *"colonia popular"* counterparts on the other side of the border. While conceived of as a terrible planning and housing disaster by state and federal officials, the residents generally have perceived the colonias as a step up from their past. Residents do recognize many drawbacks to colonias, but they also see them as a resource, an opportunity, a chance at the "American dream." Based on other experiences with housing, they also have an expectation that regularized services will eventually reach them, as they so often do in Mexico. So colonias are terrible errors or a needed resource, depending on the perspective applied.

Made up of incrementally self-built homes, colonias in Texas represent the single greatest example of successful self-help, low-income housing efforts in the United States. They constitute both a disaster and a dynamic, participatory, grassroots solution to the serious lack of low-income housing. The contradictions continue. They are illegal forms of land development, yet most of the development of these settlements lies within the law or just beyond its reach. The legal status of the residents is heterodox. As many as half of the residents may be recent, undocumented migrants, former, seasonal migrants with tenuous or unprovable claims to citizenship, or part of a household in which some member or members are undocumented. A sizable number of the residents are Mexican Americans who were in the region before the border was even drawn— ex-urban out-migrants possessing historically prior rights: "We did not cross the border, the border crossed our ancestors." The documentation of high numbers of legal colonia residents contrasts with most public representations of colonia residents as recent and undocumented (Jorge Chapa, personal communication). Colonias house the earliest and most recent residents of the Texas Borderlands, and many more in between.

As a settlement form, colonias escape simple classification. These settlements are urban in the sense they represent migration to urban settings for many immigrants and migrants, and the houses themselves are densely crowded. They are suburban in that the settlement pattern has low building density, with one-fourth to one-half acre plots laid out in grid street patterns, located a stiff drive beyond the jurisdiction of cities, with residents relying on cars and highways to reach places of employment. They are rural in that, like the rural ranchos, they often have clusters of residences on one lot, often with animals or some other use of the space for productive purposes beyond residence. Chickens, horses and goats are all popular, as are food-bearing gardens and trees (Earle and Huang 1996).

Culturally they appear quite homogeneous, being mostly made up of people of Mexican origins, yet they are highly fragmented socially between those from diverse points on the border, those various streams of seasonally migrating laborers, and those who have come from various parts of the interior of Mexico, many of whom preserve a regional identity. This creates a general ambiance of low social cohesion, one that has parallels in refugee and resettlement camps I have studied (Earle 1988, 1994).

Since most colonias are relatively new (10 years is common), and people buy plots on a first-come, first-served basis, most people share little history or prior social linkages. Some are fairly acculturated to the border region—itself a hybrid region—while others are not at all acculturated, reflecting their place of origin. There are also social divisions based on time of arrival (Vila 1994). In contrast to the land invasions that characterize many Mexican low-income settlements, U. S. colonias have no prior social order, and the random nature of lot purchases works against clustering of connected households, be they kin, *compadres*, or people from the same region. In a sense, the randomizing impact of unimproved land markets serves to divide people who have historically maintained cohesive communities.

Origins: Contrasts in Time and Space

Historically, the formation of colonias is a confluence of at least three major trends, apart from the high local demographic growth. Step migration from interior Mexico, drawn to the border by the *maquiladora* industry and over it by better wage and educational opportunities, represents one highly diverse pattern. The break with the revolutionary, agrarian social contract represented by the "structural adjustments" of the last two Mexican regimes, has helped to abet an exodus likened to the flow of refugees from a war-torn zone, but worse, in that it leaves many ex-peasants with a sense of both betrayal and of profound insecurity. The peso devaluation is but the latest wave of this economic abuse of the poor, in the context of dramatic restructuring of the national economy in a far more globalized econosphere. For this sector, unlike that of the middle-class immigrant, there is little to inspire a sense of exclusive Mexican nationalism, a concept weak to begin with for those in remote regions or of indigenous descent (Verrillo and Earle 1993). Many colonia residents celebrate the public festivals of both nations, seamlessly and without apparent contradiction. National identity is a nonissue, the border a nuisance.

A second trend, older than the first but hard sometimes to distinguish from it, derives from a century-long pattern of seasonal agricultural migration, one that was sanctioned formally during the Bracero Program but which continues largely illegally today. Colonias represent for migrants a jumping-off place that is neither a return to the capital-starved place of origin nor to the overly regulated interior regions of the United States, where work is seasonal and settling difficult, expensive, and in an unfamiliar sociopolitical landscape. A compromise is the border, where Mexico is accessible, deportation is but a mild inconvenience, and housing is affordable and situated among a large group of culturally similar people. With the rise of the low-wage manufacturing, textile, and service industries along the Texas border—part of the decentralization of industry that characterizes late capitalism—economically viable alternatives to migration become feasible, especially if housing costs are low and a public and private social service net exists to buffer the periods of unemployment (Briody 1986).

A third trend is the movement out of U. S. cities (on the border and elsewhere), especially out of Latino barrios, into the colonias by people tired of renting when they can own their own piece of land and control their living space, in a less strife-torn location and with more hopes for bettering their family. This movement is also a response to the urban renewal process in many downtown sections of cities like El Paso, where major sections of the barrio close to the river were destroyed for city development without construction of new low-income housing. Low-end rental costs are unusually high in many border cities, as compared with the general economy, and this tends to fuel an exodus into the colonias (Towers 1991). There are some colonia residents who have come from as far away as Chicago, paralleling the Anglo "winter Texan" phenomenon of climatic migration, one that often leads to permanent retirement in the borderlands. This sector feels disenfranchised as they have felt the brunt of the collapse of affordable, low-income housing in the last two decades. These conditions helped stimulate the colonias' boom.

Liminal Labor, Marginal Industry

Immigration, migration and out-migration are distinct threads of origin, all drawn together by the opportunity to make a new life on the border, providing cheap labor to the booming industrial sectors. These industrial sectors are also liminal, in that they flee from the U. S. interior because of wage costs, unions, and other requirements that have become more difficult to support in the face of global competition. Yet many of these companies will not cross into Mexico, or enter the Third World in general, owing to concerns about infrastructure, political and fiscal stability, and a myriad of other problems that cannot be controlled from abroad. The border serves as a compromise: the cheapest deal for a nonunionized, dependent, hyperabundant labor force in the United States (and border Mexico); labor that builds its own housing and does not complain; and a population that lives far away from everybody and tolerates it.

This situation gives rise to another contradiction: At one and the same time, conditions of labor are exploitative in the extreme from a U. S. perspective and comparatively lucrative for workers from a Mexico standpoint, given Mexico's ravaged economy. Like that of the colonia developers—who both provide a much-needed service that no one else will offer and are horrendously exploitative of the colonia residents, with their high interest rates, suspect contracts, and inflated land prices—the labor situation harbors great social contradictions. The superabundance of labor that unemployed colonia residents represent is perceived by many as leading to lower wages for everyone in the region. For this reason, many people on the border dislike the colonias, and the term has taken on pariah status in much of the Texas border. Yet this perception is often not tempered with one that notes the value to the entire region of the low-cost labor that has led to an industrial boom in low-end manufacturing and services on both sides of the border. The cost of labor is carefully examined, in this era of relative wage decline, but not so much attention is given to the profitability of this group as an "on-call" labor pool. Likewise the taxes contributed by the residents of colonias are not taken into consideration.

Developer ambivalence becomes much enhanced, in a form reminiscent of the hacienda patron (owner). On the one hand, developers have control over the land so long as the contract is not completely paid off. They use this control to intimidate and to manipulate people, even into a form of debt-peonage (where interest compounding for late payments makes it nearly impossible to ever pay off the lot). On the other hand, if a resident should be forced into bankruptcy, the land would be taken over by creditors, and all the years of improvements, all the equity the resident has in the home, would be lost. Recently a colonia in El Paso County fell into the hands of the Internal Revenue Service, and people there are having to fight eviction, their years of improvements imperiled. Residents find themselves hoping their exploiter is a financial success so that they themselves are protected from ruin. Many colonia families find themselves in personalistic relations of dependency with charismatic developers who they know both cheat and serve them. Land tenure is so insecure that some houses have been built on stilts, to facilitate getting a flat-bed truck under the house in case of eviction.

COLONIA IDENTITIES AND NATIONAL IDENTITY

Given the context described above, it is not surprising to see colonia residents manifesting forms of identity that are not bounded by typical categories. As Michael Kearney (1991) noted for the Mixtecs on the California border, the transnational and postnational nature of the border region undermines the notion of national boundaries. People in the colonias celebrate U. S. and Mexican national holidays, often going to Mexico for the latter. The goal of learning English is to become bilingual (like the dominant Latino sector, which uses code-switching as an identity boundary marker) not to exchange or replace one language for another, nor to acculturate. There remains a lot of mobility across the border and between the two nations regardless of the vagaries of immigration policy. In fact, for many low-income borderlanders, border-crossing is an absolutely essential dimension of their adaptation. Their economizing activities take advantage of the differences in wages, purchase prices and service costs. The presence of both sides makes life possible.

While the more established middle-class Mexican Americans tend to bifurcate between hypernationalism towards the United States and the staunch retention of Mexican national identity (Vila 1994), colonia residents seem to embrace both nations without much conflict. Colonia identity, I believe, dissolves the boundary between the nations, being at the same time smaller (focused on the development of a sense of local community or colonia identity) and larger, as a kind of hemispheric transnational identity. In this way, colonias are postnational in their approach to identity.

The mobility characteristic of the poor, as labor adjusts to the spatial distributions of work opportunity, provides a network of information and continual social contact that erodes the segregating boundary function of the border, making it more a transnational, cosmopolitan zone than one where this nation stops and another starts. This is in marked contrast to European immigration of the modern era. Immigrants in colonias are tethered to transnational networks that contradict the norm of melting-pot immigration and again create a contradiction between acculturation and enclave maintenance, assimilation and colonization. Entering the new does not mean necessarily leaving the old behind.

The heart of the U. S. assimilationist project has always been to equate citizenship with acculturation, and nowhere is this more true than in the current congressional debates about social services for legal immigrants. Clearly, as Kearney (1991) argues, the state is on the defensive in terms of national identity maintenance. This ideological armature, in search of classificatory clarity as a part of its efforts at hegemonic control, finds resistance less in those who wish to keep their foreign passports and affiliations than it does in those for whom a nation is but a part of a larger and the edge of a smaller socioeconomic landscape, and for whom appeals to national identity are never exclusionary. In fact, the discourse of exclusion, for this group, is the ideational enemy since the more binational one becomes the more successful one is at the transnational adaptation that migration, immigration to the border region, and out-migration to colonias represent. Sociocultural affiliation to one side or the other exclusively represents an adaptational deficit to be overcome. Colonia residents represent the undoing of nationalism in the borderlands. For them it does not make common sense. Nation is no longer coherent as a means of cognitive or social segregation, as it is for most of the rest of the globe.

THE BORDER OF ILLEGALITY AND IDENTITY

What are the implications of a dissolved border and a collapsed dichotomy of distinction upon which nationalism must normally rest? At the level of political discourse, the impact of Proposition 187[1] is clearly not in being effective in arresting immigration, but of making it more difficult for the evocatively termed "illegal alien" to take advantage of social services, education and normalized employment. In turn, this maintains an underclass that will be even more easily exploited, more financially precarious, less healthy, and less likely to resist abuses or claim civil rights. It participates in a new wave of criminalizing or "illegalizing" the Other. Michael Kearney (1991:58) comments on this ambiguous zone of law on the border:

> A Latino reconquest of much of the northern side has already taken place. But this Latino cultural and demographic ascendancy is not congruent with jural territorial realities which are still shaped by continued unitedstatesian police power. This incongruity of cultural and political spaces makes of the 'border area'...an ambiguous zone. It is in the border that identities are assigned and taken, withheld and rejected. The state seeks a monopoly on the power to assign identities to those who enter this space. ...But every day thousands of 'undocumented' persons successfully defy the state's power to control their movement into and through this space and in doing so contest not only space, but also control of their identity.

Colonias provide a place of refuge from illegality since the laws are mostly not enforced, even as colonias are themselves illegal. The proximity to the border undermines the efficaciousness of civil authorities and warps the sociolegal landscape because all authority must weigh the potential costs and risks when the border allows easy escape from any crime short of terrorism. Even cop-shooting may not be sufficient reason for an international incident, and that fact is noticed by all who live in the Borderlands. Colonias exist in a twilight of law and authority.

Illegalization is not just in terms of immigration status. Colonias are by definition far from the cities they serve, and public transportation is rare and unreliable. This means most colonia residents need to maintain a functioning vehicle. Vehicle insurance costs are prohibitive, so most residents purchase only a month of coverage per year, allowing them to get the necessary stickers. The rest of the year they live in violation of state law. Many other forms of illegal-ization also arise in the space of poverty, and these conspire to constrain civic development. Colonia residents, like their mobile migrant cousins, live in a space of illegalization. This has a very negative impact on the development of leadership and a sense of belonging to the larger nation. Rejected as "pochos" or sell-outs by Mexico, illegalized by the United States, the colonias' residents live in a third space, again reinforcing their postnational posture.

The federal government and the state of Texas have tried to stop colonia formation, with the Texas Attorney General waging over sixty lawsuits against developers. Yet colonia development continues—especially where there are grandfathered lots not subject to new laws—with no entity making a concerted effort to create a better alternative, and the border population continues to swell. The suggestion here is that state control of the border serves not to keep people out but rather, as Kearney (1991, following Foucault) notes , to discipline people, teaching them they have no civil rights, that they are situational criminals with no right to exercise a civic persona: a semi-person. For colonia residents, like migrants, this is a message contradictory to the one of becoming a citizen and participating. For community development concerns, the suppression of supra-familial organization inhibits the ability of colonias to help themselves collectively, to vote strategically, or to seek resources available to them.

THE EDGE AS CENTRAL

In terms of anthropology, we must not turn away from this kind of liminal so-cial landscape in favor of the (supposed) discrete "Other" communities of the old days, but look to the borders between the historically colonized and the colonizers, and give special attention to where these processes involve inver-sions, contradictions, and ironic appropriations. We must look at the colonias as places that themselves deconstruct our neat and discrete categories. Colonias do this for us because they are in part immigrant colonies reacting to financial and industrial recolonization of Mexico. Capital goes south in search of invest-ment return, people come north in search of better labor value. The colonizers are colonized in the colonias—parodic faux suburbs that undo everything that makes suburbs familiar. Residences vary from $300 shacks to $50,000 houses, challenging the hypersegregation characteristic of unitedstatesian subdivisions. Colonias break all the housing codes by blending in a single home both Mexi-can and United States building forms and residential arrangements of lawns and goats, playscapes and dismembered vehicles, spacious house plots and densely occupied huts, rolled trailers, lush gardens, and derelict RVs. Nations are places on the shopping list, not sanctified boundaries of self and Otherness. The cultural order of settlement, so naturalized for us, is rendered problematical by people who are not easily glossed nor contained in the notion of nation. Colonias make grey what otherwise we tend to see in black and white. In so many ways they reside in the Borderlands—a place neither here nor there.

CONCLUSION:
CONTRADICTIONS, COLONIAS AND THE BORDERS

Borders seem to be places where contradictory tendencies operate. On the one hand is the extreme, even caricatured effort to conform to the trends of the nation, to express the essence of the national position often in a manner more direct or dramatic than the interior. Paradoxically, there are efforts that form of counteraction to the acculturative and socializing forces of the state, a special variety of resistance to Americanization that is less reactive than inactive, less opposed than indifferent. In this way, for much of the Latino population—whether recent arrivals, historic residents or somewhere in between—the border is both glorified and erased, made both sharp and very fuzzy. An extreme of this contradiction resides in the low-income, underserved, and sociogeographically isolated colonias.

Colonias represent in great part the latest epoch in a three-century history of periodic immigration into the United States and are tied to a near century-long pattern of labor immigration from Mexico. Not only do colonia residents seek normalized integration into the socioeconomic landscape, but their homesteading efforts also have launched the largest self-built, spontaneous, grassroots affordable housing effort the century has known. They have sought their integration ticket by "making it" within the colonias. But the sheer numbers of culturally Mexican residents, isolated from the Americanized populous and crowded into settlements, tend to create cultural colonies of Mexico that only adopt a few American traits, often negative ones (such as gangs). At the same time, there is motivation to learn English and to get an education for children and even for adults, for the most part, in order to participate more dynamically in the labor market, and to understand and work "the system". Many people make almost no progress in assimilation efforts, and remain "neither here nor there."

The word community suggests a coherent, articulating social body, with a history, ramified social networks, and common cultural idiom. "Resident" suggests a free individual working for personal self-improvement and advancement. But colonias are in fact a social form where the household serves a more central role in the economic and sociocultural adaptations that these "post-peasants" and ex-urban homesteaders use to survive. While it is not unique of colonias—but it is a strong element of much of the Latino Southwest (Velez-Ibáñez 1993) in the context of social, physical, legal and "national identity" isolation—households become the only coherent social units. Community-building is arrested. Colonias also differ from more historically stable cases because of the absence of a common specific social history, since they are made up of people from extremely different circumstances within the general cultural milieu, randomized in their settlement locations by the housing market. These settlements house a highly heterodox population. There is next to nothing that has joined these people together socially, beyond the fact of proximity itself and the common sharing of the adversity of living in chronically underserved, infrastructurally inferior settlements. They remind this researcher very much of camps of refugees from Central America—families radically displaced from a field of violence to a world that clashed and still clashes with the cultural traditions of their native communities.

Many colonia residents are driven from Mexico by the structural violence of Mexico's political continuity and the economic change that removes the subsidy safety net for those unable to enter into commerce or labor and show a profit. The U.S.-born citizens are similarly displaced in the public housing vacuum that has arisen in border cities. The "everybody out of the nest" neoliberal thinking, so popular now in Washington, crashes against the reality of the wildly galloping economic system, booming and crashing in the extreme, while people still need to eat. The social contract to tide people over with cheap corn and basics (a kind of systemic social security) is now replaced with "everyone hustle to eat." It is survival labor, in a fragile environment, where mistakes, sickness, and bad luck mean migration or economic ruin.

Colonias these days are seesawing on the edge, between rising up as ever more normalized communities and subdivisions, and falling down into cycles of more desperate impoverishment (in every sense) and institutional dependency, just as we begin the removal of some or all of the social safety net. Which way they will go is in part a question of how the colonias are perceived and interacted with to the end of the century and beyond. It also depends upon how well colonias can learn and participate in the larger system, overcome their isolation, and find some avenue of effective integration.

One cannot help but wonder if this is not a sign of things to come in the interior also, as the divisions between wealthy and poor grow, and the contradictions of democracy and the free market make themselves felt within not only the United States and Mexico, but also across the hemisphere and the world. The postnational, permanently displaced colonias may foreshadow the fate of the masses as we head for "hemispheric integration" in the "globalized" interamerican free trade zone. The borderless borderlands just might travel beyond the edge toward the interior.

NOTES

1. Proposition 187, passed into law in 1996 in the state of California, places severe restriction on the kind of medical attention, educational opportunities, and other public services available to undocumented migrants, and represents a new trend towards restriction of public services to the unauthorized needy.

REFERENCES CITED

Anderson, Bennedict
1983 *Imagined Communities: Reflections on the Origins and Spread of Nationalism.* Verso, London.

Briody, Elizabeth K.
1986 *Household Labor Patterns Among Mexican Americans in South Texas: Buscando Trabajo Seguro.* AMS Press, New York.

Carmack, Robert
1988 *Harvest of Violence: The Mayan Indians and the Guatemalan Crisis.* University of Oklahoma Press, Norman.

Earle, Duncan
1994 Constructions of Refugee Ethnic Identity: Guatemalan Mayas in Mexico and South Florida. In *Reconstructing Lives, Recapturing Meaning: Refuge Identity, Gender, and Culture Change*, edited by Linda A. Camino, and Ruth M. Krulfeld, pp. 207-234. Gordon and Breach, Basel, Australia.

Earle, Duncan, and Chang-Shan Huang
1996 Building Identity on the Border: Texas Colonias as Cultural Texts. In *Permeable Boundaries and the Construction of Place*, edited by Nezar AlSayyad, Traditional Dwellings and Settlements Working Papers Series, vol. 77. University of California, Berkeley.

Goffman, Irving
1981 *Forms of Talk.* University of Pennsylvania Press, Philadelphia.

Kearney, Michael
1991 Borders and Boundaries of State and Self at the End of Empire. *Journal of Historical Sociology* 4:52-74.

Shields, Rob
1991 *Places on the Margin.* Routledge, New York.

Texas Water Development Board
1987 *A Reconnaissance Level Study of Water Supply and Wastewater Disposal Needs of the Colonias of the Lower Rio Grande Valley.* Austin, Texas.

Towers, George
1991 *Colonia Formation and Economic Restructuring in El Paso, Texas.* Unpublished Ph.D. dissertation, Department of Geography, University of Arizona, Tucson.

Velez Ibáñez, Carlos
1993 U. S. Mexicans in the Borderlands: Being Poor without the Underclass. In

The Barrios Latinos and the Underclass Debate, edited by Joan Moore, and Raquel Pinderhughes, pp. 195-220. Russell Sage Foundation, Albany, New York.

Verrillo, Erica, and Duncan Earle
1993   The Guatemalan Refugee Crafts Project: Artisan Production in Times of Crisis. In *Crafts in the World Market: The Impact of Global Exchange on Middle American Artisans*, edited by June Nash, pp. 225-245. State University of New York Press, Albany.

Vila, Pablo Sergio
1994   *Everyday Life, Culture and Identity on the Mexican-American Border: The Ciudad Juarez-El Paso Case.* Unpublished Ph.D. dissertation, Department of Sociology, University of Texas, Austin.

10

Tied to the Land

Maya Migration, Exile, and Transnationalism

Victor D. Montejo

ANECDOTE

The massive migration of indigenous people from Guatemala to the United States is a recent phenomenon. Prior to the 1960s, travel to distant places was an extreme challenge for the indigenous people of western Guatemala, and those who managed to visit places such as Guatemala City or Mexico City were considered great adventurers. It was common for these individuals to brag about these unmatched challenges and to exaggerate in their accounts. They were easily recognized in the communities because people tended to attach to a person's regular name the name of the place he or she claimed to have visited. For example, a man called Maltixh (Baltazar) among the Jakalteks always bragged about his adventures in Mexico City in the early 1950s, so he became known as Don Maltixh Mejiko. During the first half of the twentieth century, it was difficult to travel across Central America (Stephens 1949), especially since most Mayas traveled by foot, mainly towards Guatemala City. If travelling to Guatemala was difficult, to travel north towards Mexico was even worse. A few travelers who crossed the Guatemalan-Mexican border in search of work in Mexico's southern Pacific coast have told horrible stories of fights and near death escapes from bandits and thieves. Thus, to travel north was considered dangerous because of Mexican bandits and because *El Norte*, or the land of the Rinkos, was a conceptually distant place.

The United States was considered to be at the edges of the world, and language was the major obstacle to even dreaming of visiting such a place. Mayas' only glimpse of the United States was from the Christian missionaries who came to the indigenous communities, showing slides of the great cities there. Everybody thought that, in the United States, there were no more forests but only cities after cities. It happened that one of these missionaries took a Q'anjob'al man to the North, and this man stayed in the United States for a few years. When he returned to his homeland, his presence and his accounts about the United States attracted people, who were amazed to listen to his stories. My father told me about this case while we were watching the traditional dances in San Marcos, a neighboring Jakaltek town. It is a tradition that during the festival of the patron Saint Mark hundreds of Q'anjob'al people come down from the highlands to enjoy the festivity and the marimba music. The man of this story was said to carry a lot of money, and he paid a marimba band to play for him so he could dance and drink in the streets, as he desired. After every marimba song, he went inside the house where he was staying and changed his shirt. Then, he came out with a new shirt every time. While he danced and jumped, he enjoyed throwing his hat high up into the air while shouting. "¡Yo soy hombre! Conozco Los Angeles Kalipornia." [I am a man, I have been to Los Angeles, California.] Then more loudly he shouted, "¡Que viva Los Angeles Kalipornia, Chingado!" That was a great spectacle according to the poor peasants, who were marveled to see the many shirts this man exhibited. I remember that, in these poor Mayan communities, people could buy only one shirt a year during the festivity of the patron saint. For a Maya, it was extraordinary to have many shirts.

INTRODUCTION

Since World War II, exile and mass migration has increased dramatically, and the new category of social identity called "refugee" has become a universal phenomenon. At present, there is constant migration and dislocation of entire communities worldwide as a result of ethnic conflict and the failure of the states to impose their hegemonic and nationalist ideologies on their minority populations. In the case of the Americas, there is an increase of transnational migration, especially toward the United States. Migrants are pouring north, not only from the cities (with Ladino populations) but also from rural and indigenous communities. There are several reasons, or "push" factors, for these massive migrations. The most pervasive in Latin America (for example, in Guatemala, El Salvador, and southern Mexico) is the political violence that has affected these countries as a result of governmental violence and guerrilla warfare.[1] Of course, indigenous transnationalism, as we observe it at the present, is part of the globalization process of the world economy, communications, and geopolitics. In other words, "territorial space of indigenous communities is now globalized as a result of communication technology, migration, return, bifocality and multifocality of life of those who migrate cyclically, and who are immersed existentially in one, two, or multiple cultural spaces" (Varese 1996:19).

Prior to the 1980s, indigenous people in Guatemala endured violence in their communities. Now, by changing their strategies as workers and altering the flow of the labor force to the coastal coffee plantations, they have found a way to temporarily leave the country, instead of enduring violence in their natal communities. They have done so by migrating to industrialized places such as Cancun in Mexico or to the United States. As a consequence of this shift in the locus of their labor, the traditional patron/laborer relationship has also been altered in Guatemala. In other words, over the last twenty years, migration of Mayas to the coffee plantations in Guatemala has decreased.

This transnationalization of labor has led to the development of large differences in the economic status of the local workers as compared with that of migrant workers. Those who have continued to go to the coffee plantations remain the same (poor peasants), while those who have gone to *El Norte* for a few years have greatly improved their economic status. In either place, their unskilled labor is the only thing that they can sell, but in the United States, at least they are paid by the hour and with dollars. After, with great difficulty, saving some money, migrant workers return home to build stucco houses in rural areas, to own 4-wheel drive pick-up trucks, or to buy pieces of land on which to plant coffee and corn. This creates the great economic difference that pushes people to migrate to the North in search of better opportunities, while escaping violence in their homeland.

In this essay I discuss briefly the theoretical underpinning of migration and exile from the perspective of the sending community. Thus, while the individual or group ventures far away from the community, in distant and dangerous worlds, the community too remains in a state of liminality, awaiting the return of absent members to the town. In order to understand the Mayas' strong attachment to the land and the danger of being removed from one's own homeland, I focus on the concept of place and displacement from the community's perspective. Three different kinds of separation from the community are discussed: first, the individualistic venturing to far away places, known by the Jakaltek Maya as *"porisal"* *(irse al carajo);* second, an individual or group's seasonal migration or travel to distant places for business or in search of work, called *"yinh smeb'ail,"* which literally means "absence by necessity"; and third, the *"elilal,"* a forced dislocation and exile of a great part of a community as a result of repression (i.e., massacres). The *elilal* denotes the situation of refugees and exiles who migrate massively to other places in search of peace and security for their families. This is the case for the Guatemalan Mayan exiles and recent migrant workers to the United States to whom I refer in this study.

THE HISTORICAL CONTEXT OF MAYAN MIGRATION AND EXILE

While current studies of exile, migration, and transnationalism are focusing on the struggles of refugees and migrant workers to accommodate themselves within the cultures where they arrive (host country), little attention has been given to the cultural aspects of exile itself. From an anthropological perspective, it is necessary to document the reactions of the community from where the individuals have been removed (voluntarily or forcibly), and how the families, or the community as a whole, deal with the long absences of refugees, exiles and migrant workers. In this context, the concept of place (community and sacred geography) and identity (to have a primordial link to that community) become essential. For the Mayas, the abandonment of the homeland implies the rupture of the sacred link with the protective power that circumscribes the community, which is considered to be at the sacred center or navel of the universe. In this way the sacred geography (mountains, volcanoes, rivers, etc.) are strongly remembered as the individual removes himself/herself from the community. There always has been the tendency or desire to go back home after the situation that has forced exile is alleviated, or after fulfillment of one's desire to wander around in search of opportunities (work) for the betterment of one's economic condition.

For the indigenous people of Guatemala, the desire to remain tied to the land despite violence against their lives is emphasized by their ancestors, who have said that their people will never be scattered and that their destiny will triumph over the difficult days they face now and in the future. In other words, they will always be secure in the land where they are now living (Roys 1933). Unfortunately, the security of living in one's own homeland has become more difficult as the "ill-fated days" mentioned above have become too unbearable in modern times. Massive migration and exile have characterized the life of present-day Mayas, and some seem to have finally severed their ties to the land, as is the case of the Q'anjob'al refugees in the United States. In the context of transnationalism, the Q'anjob'al have developed other strategies for the maintenance of their Mayanness in exile. In order to feel "at home," they have had to invent new Mayan communities with social relationships far more complex and dangerous than they imagined. In Florida and California, they have come into contact with diverse ethnic communities (e.g., Mexican migrant workers,

Native Americans, Jamaicans, Asians, Chicanos, and White Americans) with whom they interact or whom they try to avoid. It is interesting to note that the concept of exile is not new to the Mayas. From ethnohistorical documents such as the *Popol Vuh*, the *Annals of the Kaqchikels*, and the *Chilam Balams*,[2] we already have the complaints of those who have been uprooted from their homelands in prehispanic times. In the *Popol Vuh*, the tribes who abandoned their traditional homeland—which they called Tulan—were looking for a place to establish themselves among the people already indigenous to the area we today call the Guatemalan highlands. From Tedlock's translation, we have the K'iches reflection on their wandering and self-imposed exile: "'What have we done? We all had one identity, one mountain, but we sent ourselves into exile,' they said when they talked among themselves" (Tedlock 1996:159). Then, during the Spanish Conquest, the indigenous people were persecuted and violently dislocated from their communities. Bartolomé de Las Casas states that, after the K'iche' Lords were burned alive by Pedro de Alvarado, "the people abandoned their city and hid themselves in the mountains" (Las Casas 1989:116).

In other cases, indigenous leaders who were knowledgeable of their culture (e.g., calendrics and divination) were considered witches and punished harshly. For example, their belief in the *tonalli* (an alter ego or soul bearer) was considered an evil practice (i.e., witchcraft) by the colonial missionaries, so the Indians were punished and removed from their lands in order to uproot this practice. "Perhaps the most famous case is that of Martin Ocelotl, accused of idolatry and witchcraft by the Holy Office in 1536 and sentenced to life imprisonment in Seville, where his alleged supernatural powers and anti-Christian acts could have no further influence on the Mexican Indians" (Musgrave-Portilla 1982:25). This is a horrible case of exile in which the individual was banished and sent as a captive to the invaders' home for his supposed crime of being a witch—a blatant attack against people who maintained and practiced their traditions and struggled to keep their indigenous knowledge alive. During the Colonial period, Mayas were persecuted and many found refuge in less accessible Maya communities into which they integrated. With the creation of the international border between Guatemala and Mexico, refugees or exiles from repressive governments in Guatemala became permanent residents in bordering Mexican communities. This is the case of Guadalupe Victoria, a Jakaltek migrant community that settled in Mexico during the late 1880s. According to Juvenal Casaverde:

> An older informant in Guadalupe Victoria noted that her grandfather was an official of the *alcaldes rezadores* [prayermakers] of Jacaltenango during the late 1880's. At this time the *departamento* officials ordered the killing of a number of Jacaltecos, among them the informant's grandfather. She added that his body was cut into

> pieces and thrown over the cliff into the Azul River. Older people
> of Jacaltenango also have memory of these killings. As a conse-
> quence, she says, many people from Jacaltenango decided to move
> out to Guadalupe Victoria to escape from the easy reach of the feared
> *departamento* authorities. (Casaverde 1976:242)

When this diaspora became massive, the refugees created new towns in Mexico while continuing their cultural traditions and links with the mother towns in Guatemala. A common practice of Mayan refugees or permanent migrants to new settlements is to revive the cult of the saint who was the patron of their community of origin. Oliver La Farge, referring to San Jose Montenegro, now Guadalupe Victoria, says, "Until recently the Indians of San Jose came to Jacaltenango for the Year Bearer Ceremony, but now have their own church of Candelaria, the same patron as that of the parent town" (La Farge 1931:84).

There are many other settlements in Chiapas that developed at the same time as that of Guadalupe Victoria as a result of the repressive Liberal government in Guatemala during the 1870s. Historically, Mayas have migrated massively as a result of political or armed violence in Guatemala during the past century. More recently (1982), the presence of some forty-six thousand refugees in Mexico, of which several thousand have since migrated to the United States, confirms that in Guatemala there is yet no justice nor respect for the human rights of the indigenous population. During the past three years (1993-96), some refugees have returned to their homeland, where their placenta are buried. Others are struggling to return, while still others have made the painful choice not to return because they have become permanent residents of Mexico or the United States.

PLANTING OUR IDENTITY

In this section, I discuss the practical and symbolic forms of attachment to the land. I draw some examples from my own personal experience and knowledge of the Jakaltek and Q'anjob'al cultural traditions. I believe all human beings are ethnocentric, myself included. I am one of those who talk about their culture constantly, even in dreams. Since I became exiled in 1982, I have tried to understand my country and my people more carefully as I have enriched my experiences by learning about other cultures. I would like to mention then how Mayas view themselves (identity), while giving meaning to their existence and location on earth. I will refer briefly to the ritual of symbolically planting our

Mayan identity in the land of our ancestors, in an effort to understand exile from a Mayan feeling and experience.

Most Mayan linguistic communities, including the Jakaltek, believe they are placed in a privileged position at the navel of the earth. Because of their alleged links to the Classic period Mayan culture, they believe that not only are they placed at the navel of the earth, but also that they are linked to the navel of the universe (*smuxuk kanh*). That is why, when a child is born, the placenta is buried ceremonially, so that the individual is symbolically planted to the ground (the center of the universe), establishing the links between the individual, the earth, and the universe. Similarly, the house is a sacred place because it replicates the universe in the community. According to Mayan beliefs and rituals, the four corners of the house are sanctified, replicating the four *bacabs* who have been placed by God to sustain the four corners of earth. The identity of the individual then is complex since the individual does not live in isolation but as a member of the community and as an integral part of the universe. If you are going on a long trip, you must kneel at the center of your house and pray for a safe journey and a safe return home. The four corners of the house, or your micro-universe, must be the witnesses of your departure so that you will be protected until the day comes when you return home safe and healthy. But, as is usual in any given community, there are some individuals who do not fit into the general pattern of community life. We can place in this group those who venture to unknown places without any given destination. This brings to our attention the first type of Mayan exile or migration, which I call the *porisal*.

The Porisal

The porisal refers to the voluntary, individual decision to abandon one's community for the sake of adventure or to wander without a fixed goal or destination. This usually happens to lazy men who decide to disappear from the town or community where they are already known for their bad attitude. These individuals have traveled to distant places (most often Mexican cities) and stayed away from their hometown for long periods of time (10 to 12 years). According to the local folklore, the porisal is an exotic place full of challenges that no one actually knows and where no one in the community has ever been. When these individuals abandon the community, there are no major concerns for their well-being because they are considered antisocial and and are thought to have other vices as well (drunkenness, thievery, laziness). Sometimes when they return, they may have changed, and often they have a lot of stories to tell. Among the Jakaltek Maya there are many stories of *el porisal,* or *el carajo,* in which the rabbit, a trickster and adventurer, is the main character. These types of individuals are found mostly among Ladinoized Mayas and non-Mayas living in indigenous communities.

Yinh Smeb'ail

The second form of exile or banishment from the community is what the Jakaltek call *yinh smeb'ail*, literally meaning "absent because of being poor." These are groups of men who migrate to distant places as merchants or in search of work. They become the focus of community attention because their absence from town is due to a powerful reason, not for the sake of adventure. To travel faraway is to expose oneself to the dangers of the road and illnesses. In the past, few people took the risk of abandoning their community in order to travel to distant places for work or adventure. The elders ask in their prayers that these individuals who remove themselves from the center think of their parents, town, people, and culture so they may decide to return home where their placenta is planted. Traditionally, when villagers were absent from their communities, there was a common concern for their safety and well-being. For this purpose, the elders would organize kin members and send a commission to search for the absent "son" to bring him back to his community. Perhaps this insistence of being always united and caring for each other stems from a reminder in the *Popol Vuh*, "Let there not be one or two among us who remains behind" (Goetz and Morley 1983:200). It is then important to understand that the individual becomes a permanent member of the community at the moment of birth and that he or she is expected to pass on the norms and cultural traditions of the ethnic group to the new generations. The symbolic birth of the *tonal*—animal companion—of a newborn child reinforces this concept of being tied to the land and the community. When an individual is born, an animal companion also is born in the mountain, and both, the individual and the tonal, remain linked together until the moment of death. Their fate and their attachment to the land are sealed because they belong to the place—that is, the community and the environment.

When a person dies in a distant place, a group of prayermakers go with the relatives of the deceased to the place where he has died, in order to bring his spirit home so that he may rest in eternal peace. The elders do not want anybody to be forgotten and therefore lost in a distant place. Even the spirit of someone who has died far from the community must be helped to find its way home; if the body has already been buried, a committee of elders is organized to go to the place where the person has died and perform a ritual to rescue the "lost spirit" and bring it back home. In the ceremony, the elders ask the spirit to accompany them on their journey back to the community. A prayermaker is designated to lead the committee. He hits the ground thirteen times with a wiping-stick, calling the name of the dead person and exhorting him to rise from the ground and return to his community or cemetery of origin. The prayermaker constantly repeats the name of the deceased and insistant appeals to rise and return home with the group:

Ahanwanoj wuxtaj (Pel), machachkankanoj sat hune txo'tx' nahat yeloj yinh ha konhob' ti'. Okanh tzujnoj jinhan katko meltzo yul ko konhob', machach kankanoj yinh naq k'ayb'alk'uleal ti'. [Get up brother (Peter), don't keep wandering on this land distant from your homeland. Now follow us, and join us. Let's go back home. Don't remain lost, and confused in this strange place.]

The people believe that the spirit is with them on their journey back home, and the leader talks to the spirit along the way as if the real person is there following them. The other members of the committee remain silent and cannot talk to each other for fear that the spirit will get confused and remain behind the group. When the committee needs to rest and eat, they must plant a candle on the ground and the leader tells the spirit that it is time to rest: Waltinanh wuxtaj Pel, chonh xew ninoj. Nahatxa chonh b'elwitij. [Now brother Peter, we must rest for a little while, we have already walked a long distance.]

When they arrive in their community, they go directly to the cemetery where the spirit is presented to the other spirits, who must receive it as their new member. The ceremony concludes in the cemetery with the integration of the dead person into the realm of the dead. Meanwhile, the living relatives are relieved from their grief by knowing that their loved one has now returned to the community's cemetery to rest in peace. If the spirit of the dead person is abandoned and forgotten by his relatives, it will continue to wander eternally without finding its way home or to a resting place. That is why Mayan families become very concerned when their loved ones do not return to the community after a few years' absence, and there has been no news of their whereabouts. There is concern for the health or well-being of the absent ones as well as fear that they may be totally assimilated into an alien culture and thus abandon their roots and the culture of their ancestors.

The Elilal

The third type of exile is called *elilal* in the Jakaltek Mayan language. Elilal is the massive, violent dislocation of entire communities as a result of violence and warfare. It is a spontaneous mobilization of people in order to escape imminent death and persecution. A good example is the massive migration of Mayas into the Mexican territory from 1981 to 1982, when the Guatemalan army bombed and massacred entire communities. As a result, some forty villages were razed to the ground, twenty thousand people killed, and one million became displaced as internal and external refugees. In this context of violence, the ceremonies for petitioning the return of refugees and exiles could not be performed; the number of people exiled was too great, as was the danger of making a return home in the middle of an armed conflict.[3] The elilal then is the event of escaping from death and destruction and the act of becoming a refugee or exile in a strange land distant from one's homeland. Recently, when I went back to my country, an elder said that it was difficult to continue with this communal practice of burning candles to petition the return of the exiles since young people no longer believe in these ceremonies. Also, since there are thousands of refugees and exiles, their return becomes more complex and involves political issues that are beyond the reach of the elders.

ON THE CONCEPT OF EXILE: PLACE AND IDENTITY

The concept of exile has become, in this century, a source for inspiration, literary production, and a search for ethnic and cultural identity. For example, "it has become fashionable recently for educated Americans to search nostalgically for 'roots' from which they were severed long ago. Some write books in which, traveling like visitors encased in a time machine, they visit the people and places of their supposed ancestors" (Kaufman 1984:5-6). There is a tendency to romanticize exile; for example, some bourgeois intellectuals, having migrated to more prosperous countries to fulfill their dreams of success, call their voluntary migration "exile" (Martin 1992). I am not much concerned about this variety of pleasurable exile, but rather the forced exile of those whose human rights have been grotesquely abused. In the case of the Guatemalan refugees, the government/army has continued to insist that refugees (forced exiles) are bad or dangerous individuals who threaten the harmony of the nation-state. The existence, however, of thousands of refugees from countries such as Guatemala, demonstrates that "it is not they (exiles) who require cleansing, but rather the societies that banished them in the first place" (Dahlie 1986:3).

As a result of forced exile and the constant questioning of one's future and that of one's homeland, the history of one's home nation-state becomes more relevant and transparent, as the exiled individual begins to understand the nation-state's colonial or neocolonial foundations. This is only possible by the constant telescoping of time in exile, in which one constantly bring one's distant homeland into closer view and reflects on its past, present, and future. A political identity is developed as a result of exile that is ideologically less radical and parochial because the individual is enriched with the understanding of other cultural traditions. The Argentinean writer Julio Cortázar has stated that we should not see exile only in its negative connotation—bitterness, and desolation—but we must also recognize that "exile enriches the individual who has his eyes open and his guards always ready" (Cortázar 1985:136). This political transformation, which is enriched and nurtured by the bitterness of exile and the hopes of the individual for a return, is what makes the exiled person's struggle more powerful. According to Cortázar, "if exile has to become something significant, it will not be by its given negative connotation, with its baggage of suffering and nostalgia, but from an inversion of these views which gives the feared power of the boomerang, the power of the return" (Cortázar 1985:135). Perhaps this hope for a powerful return is what helps the individual in exile to struggle against the forces of assimilation and despair. Obviously, to be distant from one's own cultural context can produce different kinds of effects on the person who lives in this liminal state. It can move the individual to be absorbed or assimilated into the mainstream of the culture where he or she subsists. In other cases, it can strengthen and reaffirm the ethnic identity that ties the person to his or her distant community and cultural background. Nevertheless, it is evident that a syncretic identity arises as a result of "the understanding of one's self, culture, and society through the lens of other persons, cultures and societies" (Weiss 1992:5).

For those who are merely concerned with the romantic or pleasurable feeling of exile, it becomes difficult to understand why indigenous people feel tied to the land of their birth and remain at the same space during their adulthood, or even ask to be buried in the same community after death. In this regard, the concept of place and identity are interrelated in a dynamic way that can be expressed or represented literally and metaphorically. This connection between people and place—between life or death, and land—is explained in terms of both past and recent migrations of the Mayas from their homelands in Guatemala.

RECENT MIGRATION, EXILE AND TRANSNATIONALISM

The concepts of migration and exile (elilal) have changed through time because the Mayan communities are now more open to external influences. For centuries, political, military, and social forces have been transforming community life and the concept of community itself; thus, the concept of the "closed corporate community" (Wolf 1956) is becoming a romantic image of what Mayan communities were in the past. A great number of Mayas now migrate to distant places to fulfill their illusions of improving their life economically. The media has brought flashing images of great cities such as Miami, Los Angeles, San Francisco, Chicago, New York, and Washington D. C., which are attracting migrants from all over the world. The idea of Mayan identity is becoming more complex as modern Mayas venture into the heart of the capitalist world. More and more Mayas are migrating to developed countries (the United States) to make money and then returning to their communities to buy land and to build better houses. Those who have been successful have moved across municipal and ethnic boundaries in Guatemala and bought houses in the cities or land in other *municipios*. For example, the Q'anjob'al Maya have used the power of the dollar to buy houses in more Ladinoized communities such as Nenton, San Antonio Huista, or in the city of Huehuetenango. Some have bought land in other municipios such as Jacaltenango, thus creating conflict and antagonism with the local inhabitants. But, since these intruders are used to life in the United States, they find people to rent their houses or they simply close them up and return to their jobs in the United States.

Adding to the situation, rural western Guatemala has become the major route for migrants from the rest of Latin America, who cross into Mexico on their way north. After years of watching so many migrants pass by (including women and children) the Mayan *campesinos* started to ask themselves, Why not follow those people who are heading north? According to the Jakaltek, "If the pregnant women can venture into a long trip heading toward the U. S., then, why not try such adventure for ourselves?" This has been the strategy of the Q'anjob'al Maya, who bring their newly born children on their back and journey north until they reach the land of Uncle Sam, or the land of the Rinkos[4] (Saq Xil). They establish themselves, not in New York City, but in Intamtam (Indiantown), or Pamilixh (Farm Worker's Village), Florida or in Los Angeles, California, where they make efforts to replicate the political and religious structures and organizations of their previous communities. Allan Burns (1993; chap. 7, this volume) has documented their festivities; for example, the coronation of the Indian Queen; the celebration of the day of the patron saint, San Miguel; and the multiplication of marimba groups. Another important feature in the development of their new communities is their concern for the ecology of the house. Despite the vegetables that are abundant in Florida where they work, they continue to plant corn, chipilin, and chili pepper in their backyards since they do not have other land on which to cultivate these products that are very important in their traditional diet.

Indiantown, Florida derives its name from its association with the Seminole Indians, but, since the arrival of the San Migueleños in 1980, it has become a major center for Guatemalan refugees and Q'anjob'al migrants. Among its new residents, it has been renamed San Miguel Intamtam. The attachment to community life and the meaning of community itself are important for the survival of these refugees, who are thousands of miles away from their beloved San Miguel Acatán. In other words, the intertwined concepts of place, community, and identity are essential for the continuation of their Mayanness—that which sets them apart from the other migrant workers who live around them. In this way, the original community, now a remembered community, works as a support for the construction of the identity that Q'anjob'al Mayas are developing in Indiantown.

The new community, Intamtam, does not have ancient roots in this place, Indiantown, but the people have Mayanized the name of the town in order to feel that it is a Mayan community by the sound of the name. In other words, to be Mayas in Guatemala is different from being Mayan in Indiantown. In Indiantown, the Q'anjob'al Mayas are struggling to accommodate themselves in the middle of an already well-defined, occupied space. They have to make their world meaningful in order to plant their roots in the new land. This situation can be compared to the removal of Native Americans during the aggressive westward expansion of the United States in mid-1800s. For example, when in 1834 the Chikasaw Indians were removed from their homelands in Tennessee, they protested that no space was better than the place where they had grown up, where the graves of their ancestors were located, and where they hoped to die and to be buried. Their relocation and exile became inevitable, however, because the U. S. government needed the land for new white settlers; they became uncertain of their future and doubted that their roots and life would revive again in the unknown land (reservation) to which they were sent. Levi Colbert describes this sentiment involved in the uprooting of his Indian tribe, saying, "We never had a thought of exchanging our land for any other, as we think that we would not find a country that would suit us as well as this we now occupy, it being the land of our forefathers, if we should exchange our lands for any other, fearing the consequences may be similar to transplanting an old tree, which would wither and die away, and we are fearful we would come to the same"(Nabokov 1991:151).

The Mayan refugees in Florida are now facing the same problem. They have abandoned their communities in Guatemala, forcibly. Now they are defending themselves, not against the violence of guerrilla and army warfare, but from the threat of immigration authorities who are trying to send them back to their country of origin. Their roots (community) are constantly shaken since some of them have frequently changed their place of residence to avoid deportation. In order to deepen their roots, the refugees in Florida and in California have managed to organize themselves into various committees. The most important of these are the cultural committee, which focuses on the strategies for maintaining cultural traditions, and the emergency committee, which deals with various emergencies that arise in the migrant communities. The most immediate service that the emergency committee offers is to contribute to the repatriation of the body of any cowor dent or is killed by a drunk driver.

Thus, transnationalism for the Mayas has become stay at home and continue to maintain the traditional w nity, and thus remain poor; or to venture as a migrant bring the dollars home to build a modern house and t The prolonged absence from home is also considered period that each journey implies is different. Those who migrate to the regional coffee plantations usually spend from two to four months working and then return home. But migration to *El Norte* (U. S.) is more difficult and expensive, so the migrant worker must decide to stay away at least five to ten years before returning home. This latter group, which is composed mostly of young adults, have found life in the United States very difficult and dangerous. For example, they lack education about the dangers of being infected by the AIDS virus. In some cases, they take it home when they return; although most of those who have been infected by the disease do not want to go back home because of shame. Transnationalism has become then a double-edged situation, which recently has had a tremendous impact on Mayan communities.

Another major problem is that the adventure in search of "Clouwer City" or the mythical city in the North of the United States (Castañeda 1993), has become too expensive. It destroys the ties with the land. First, migrants have to pay great amounts of money to the "coyote"[5] in order to be taken to the land of opportunities. To find money, some borrow with high interest from wealthy villagers, or they sell their little piece of land in the hope that they will come back to town within a few years with sufficient funds to build a good house and buy back their land. Unfortunately, some of these migrant workers are captured by immigration authorities a few times before they actually cross the Mexican-U. S. border. Others are robbed by thieves during the long journey and must remain longer in Mexico while they earn money to pay another coyote. In this way, their absence may stretch five or six years before they actually make some money and can return home. Saving money is also difficult. Illegal immigrants do not have bank accounts, and some hide the money in their rented trailer homes. Thieves find these places very easy to rob. In Indiantown, the clash between Mayas and the black Jamaican community has been very dramatic. Most of the stories of violence that migrant workers tell to other villagers when they return to Guatemala state that in Florida the blacks (Jamaicans) are *"muy cabrones"* and a danger to the Guatemalan Mayan migrant community (Burns 1993; Carrescia 1994).

The Q'anjob'al refugees also endure discrimination in Florida and California. Most are illiterate peasants, and in the United States, they are discriminated against not only by the Guatemalan and Central American immigrants in the region, but also by Mexicans, Chicanos, Blacks and White Americans. The Q'anjob'al are placed in a very inferior status among the migrant workers themselves, and they have to endure this unequal social relationship in addition to their struggle with immigration authorities to hold their status as refugees and political exiles. As a form of resistance against this multifaceted oppression, have managed to live in large communities; thus, Indiantown is now their the United States their homeland. Most importantly, their children are and have become Americanized so that it will be almost impossible for them to return to their remembered community. "Though they may continue to talk of a place thousands of miles away as their real home, their actual home is a shared room or dormitory for the bachelors, a room in a run-down multi-occupancy building for the family. Whatever the needs of the system, then, whatever their original intentions, they have become changed people, with new aspirations and identities" (Worsley 1984:238).

CONCLUSION

I have focused on the ethnography of exile, with the intention of shedding some light on the concept of community solidarity and on the liminality of those who are left behind by the migrant workers and refugees. The traditional concept of attachment to the land and the ceremonies performed to bring the absent children home have changed dramatically in the past twenty years. The elders are not as respected now as they used to be, and their authority has eroded as a result of the militarization of the countryside. Similarly, the young people go to study abroad and become more Ladinoized, so they grow up ignorant and disrespectful of community traditions. Why should the elders bother to bring these cultural brokers back to the community? There are several barriers against the continuation of the traditional ceremonies of "calling the absentee to return home." First, the distance is too great; there is no possible way to walk there and to return home without disruption of the ceremony. Transportation by airplane would solve the problem of distance, but the elders are the poorest people in town. Who wants to spend his own savings to bring an adventurer home? Second, some of the migrant workers have been back home and then returned to the United States. There is no need to go convince these individuals to come home. They are travelling because they know that in the United States they can make more money than anywhere else. That some have started to build good houses and own vehicles in their hometown has created envy in the rest of the community; therefore, most villagers who cannot travel prefer that those who now have money not return. Yet another barrier is that some migrants seem to have forgotten that they have families back home and do not send money. They may live with other migrant women or go out with prostitutes, and sometimes they become infected with the AIDS virus. These individuals pose a health threat to their family and community if they go back. Furthermore, transnational migration will continue, and the type of exile called *porisal* is becoming stronger as a result of the global economy.

Meanwhile, in the United States, the anti-immigrant sentiment is increasing, and the refugees are paying the consequences. Hispanic migrants and refugees are seen as an ethnic problem for white hegemony (Brimelow 1995). The Mayan refugees in Florida are being discriminated against even by their own nationals and are called "Guatemalitas" by Ladino immigrants in Florida. In this context, and as Peter Worsley (1984:234) has stated, "The cumulative effect of all these congruent forms of segregation is the consolidation, over time, of a generalized culture of ethnic inequality, in which immigrants are perceived in stereotypical terms by the indigenous population, whatever their actual attributes, as race apart, as primitives."

Despite all of these changes and problems faced by migrants and the community, the ceremony for the death and the rescue of the lost spirit is still practiced. Recently, a young man was killed by a drunk driver in Los Angeles, California, and his body was sent in a coffin to Jacaltenango, his native community. People waited several days at his home, praying, until the body arrived. This is the kind of event that the older people relate to remind members of the community about the dangers of removing oneself beyond one's own cultural setting. In this case, the body of the deceased arrived by plane in Guatemala City, thanks to the contribution of the other migrant workers in Los Angeles. In this way the "emergency committee" has helped to shoulder some of the economic burdens that the families of deceased persons have to bear. To make their space less dangerous, the Jakaltek and Q'anjob'al migrants in Florida try to replicate their communities in their own settings by organizing committees that deal with culture as a way to maintain their ties to the land and to their distant communities thousands of miles away. In this context of dislocation and accommodation in a different geographical setting, "cultural continuities and cultural changes become evident with the passing of time and shifting of place and space" (Nolin Hanlon 1995:126).

Finally, I recognize that the condition of exile has been a theme that most poets and writers have used to express their feelings of frustration, and absence from their homelands. In *Men of Maize*, Miguel Angel Asturias (Nobel Prize Winner in Literature) writes the following passage, reflecting his own feelings of exile in an almost satirical way. "I knew a man who went off like that, half naked, with a beard and hair as long as a woman's. He ate salt like the cattle do, and was always starting from his sleep, because even when you're sleeping it must feel strange when the earth you're lying on isn't your own earth, and surely you can't rest easy like when you bed down in your land, where you can go off to sleep for good, stretched out for always on the earth where they'll bury you by-and-by" (Asturias 1975:30).

The proximity of my own life to these issues of human suffering and dislocation has pushed me to get involved in the discussion of refugee life as well as to document the insecurity of life in exile (Montejo 1993). Exile, which can be so negative in the fulfillment of the individual's dreams of liberating himself or herself from the dark memory of painful events, is also a condition that moves the person to struggle for life. So, if anyone talks of the pleasure of exile (Lamming 1992:24), it must be about the very fact of being alive. Exile has become the road to survival for thousands of indigenous people from Guatemala during the past decade.

NOTES

1. For example, in Guatemala the armed conflict has endured for more than 36 years and has claimed the lives of some 100,000 Guatemalans.
2. The *Popol Vuh* is an ethnohistorical document written in Mayan by a K'iche' Maya Indian, and translated into Spanish by the Friar Francisco Jiménez in 1700. The original manuscript remains in the Newberry Library of Chicago, Illinois. The *Annals of the Kaqchikels* is another ethnohistorical document written in Mayan by Kaqchikel Maya authors right after the Spanish Conquest in 1524. The *Chilam Balams* are prophetic books written by the Yukatek Mayas after the Spanish Conquest.
3. The armed conflict continued in Guatemala until the signing of the Peace Accord on December 29, 1996.
4. The white-skinned and blond-haired people.
5. The person who deals in the trafficking of illegals to the United States.

REFERENCES CITED

Asturias, Miguel Angel
  1975 *Men of Maize*. Translated by Gerald Martin. Delacorte Press-Seymour Lawrence, New York.
Brimelow, Peter
  1995 *Alien Nation: Common Sense About America's Immigration Disaster*. Random House, New York.
Burns, Allan
  1993 *Maya in Exile: Guatemalans in Florida*. Temple University Press, Philadelphia.
Carrescia, Olivia
  1994 *Mayan Voices, American Lives*. Icarus Film, New York. Videorecording.
Casaverde, Juvenal
  1976 *Jacaltec Social and Political Structure*. Ph.D. dissertation, Department of Anthropology, University of Rochester. University Microfilms, Ann Arbor.
Castañeda, Omar
  1993 *Remembering to Say 'Mouth' or 'Face'*. Fiction Collective Two. University of Colorado, Boulder.
Cortázar, Julio
  1985 *Textos Políticos*. Biblioteca Letras del Exilio, Plaza and Janes, Barcelona.
Dahlie, Hallvard
  1986 *Varieties of Exile: The Canadian Experience*. University of British Columbia Press, Vancouver.

Goetz, Delia, and Sylvanus Morley (translators)
1983 *Popol Vuh: The Sacred Book of the Ancient Quiche Maya*. University of
Oklahoma Press, Norman.

Kaufman, Wallace
1984 Introduction. In *El K'anil: The Man of Lightning*, by Victor Dionicio Montejo,
pp. 6-13. Signal Books, Carrboro, North Carolina.

Lamming, George
1992 *The Pleasure of Exile*. University of Michigan Press, Ann Arbor.

Las Casas, Bartolomé de
1989 *Brevísima relación testimonial de la destrucción de las Indias*. Ediciones
Cátedra, Madrid.

Martin, Stoddard
1992 *The Great Expatriate Writers*. St. Martin's Press, New York.

Montejo, Victor D.
1984 *El Kanil: The Man of Lightning*. Signal Books, Carrboro, North Carolina.
1993 *The Dynamics of Cultural Resistance and Transformations: Mayan Refugees
in Mexico*. Ph.D. dissertation, Department of Anthropology, University of Connecticut. Translated by Wallace V. Kaufman. University Microfilms, Ann Arbor.

Musgrave-Portilla, L. Marie
1982 The Nahualli or Transforming Wizard in Pre-and Postconquest Mesoamerica.
Journal of Latin American Lore 8:3-62.

Nabokov, Peter
1991 *Native American Testimony: A Chronicle of Indian-White Relations from
Prophecy to the Present, 1492-1992*. Penguin Books, New York.

Nolin Hanlon, Catherine L.
1995 *Flight, Exile, and Return: Place and Identity Among Guatemalan Maya Refugees*. Unpublished Master's thesis, Department of Geography, Queen's University,
Ontario.

Roys, Ralph L. (translator)
1933 *The Book of Chilam Balam of Chumayel*. Carnegie Institution of Washington
Publication 438. Carnegie Institution, Washington D. C.

Stephens, John L.
1949 *Incidents of Travel in Central America, Chiapas, and Yucatan*. Rutgers
University Press, New Brunswick, New Jersey.

Tedlock, Dennis (translator)
1996 *Popol Vuh: The Definitive Edition of the Maya Book of the Dawn of Life and
the Glories of Gods and Kings*. Simon and Schuster, New York.

Varese, Stefano
1996 Identidad y destierro: Los pueblos indígenas ante la globalización. *Revista de
Crítica Literaria Latinoamericana* 23(46):19-35.

Weiss, Timothy F.
1992 *On the Margins: The Art of Exile in V.S. Naipaul*. University of Massachusetts Press, Amherst.

Worsley, Peter
1984 *The Three Worlds: Culture and World Development*. University of Chicago
Press, Chicago.

11

Miracles on the Border

Retablos of Mexican Migrants to the United States

Jorge Durand and Douglas S. Massey

In recent decades the volume of migration between Mexico and the United States has risen dramatically, and a transnational movement has emerged as a major force binding the two countries. During the 1960s, legal Mexican immigration was at 430,000, and in the 1970s, this figure grew to more than 680,000 (U. S. Immigration and Naturalization Service 1992). During the 1980s, the flow became truly massive: more than three million Mexicans were admitted to the United States as legal immigrants, and another 800,000 arrived without legal documents (Woodrow and Passel 1990). Over the same period, more than twelve million Mexicans entered the United States as visitors (U. S. Immigration and Naturalization Service 1992), and more than 13 million people of Mexican origin now reside north of the border (U. S. Bureau of the Census 1991).

Although Mexican immigration has been the subject of many statistical and ethnographic studies, few have examined it from the viewpoint of the migrants themselves (for exceptions see Fernandez 1983; Gamio 1931; Herrera-Sobek 1979; Siems 1992). We seek to redress this gap by undertaking an analysis of migrants' *retablos*. Retablos are small votive paintings left at religious shrines to offer thanks to a divine image for a miracle or favor received. Typically they tell the story of a dangerous or threatening event from which the supplicant has been miraculously delivered through the intervention of a holy image. We consider the meaning these votive paintings hold for one group of people: Mexico-United States migrants.

Drawing upon texts and images from migrants' retablos, we attempt to construct a fuller picture of the complex process of Mexico-United States migration. In doing so, we depart from the usual mode of social-scientific analysis to follow a lead signaled two decades ago by Gloria Giffords, a leading scholar of retablo art (1974:124): "An examination of all the ex-votos [votives] in any one shrine or church would produce a fascinating record of the people's hopes and fears, their thoughts, lives, and experiences, a record more honest than the fullest statistical study."

MEXICAN RETABLO PAINTING

The word retablo comes from the Latin *retro-tabula*, or "behind the altar." Originally it referred to decorative or didactic paintings and sculpture placed behind the altar of Catholic churches in the early middle ages (Giffords 1974). Later it came to denote reliquary boxes placed at the rear of the altar (de la Maza 1950), and during the twelfth and thirteenth centuries it was generalized to refer to all painted altar panels and frontal pieces (Cousin 1982; Giffords 1991; Schroeder 1968). In a literal sense, therefore, retablos are religious paintings associated with the altar.

The practice of leaving objects to supplicate or thank a deity has very ancient roots (Egan 1991). Archaeological evidence reveals that the ancient Greeks, Romans, Etruscans, Iberians, and Gauls all possessed well-developed votive traditions (Decouflé 1964; Egan 1991). In these ancient cultures, it was common to acknowledge or pray for the restoration of health by leaving small figures of clay, wax, wood, or stone shaped like hands, eyes, arms, legs, feet, or vital organs. During the fifteenth century, however, these anatomical tokens gave way to a more elaborate display of gratitude: votive paintings.

The first such paintings appeared in Italy at the end of the 1400s. Growing out of the Italian Renaissance, this new votive practice spread rapidly throughout the Mediterranean and ultimately diffused to the rest of continental Europe and the New World (Cousin 1982; Egan 1991). Votive traditions were brought into Mexico by Spanish soldiers. Hernán Cortés himself, upon being bitten by a scorpion in Yautepec, Morelos, commended himself to the Virgin of Guadalupe and promised to prepare a votive if he survived his misfortune (Egan 1991). Cortez kept his promise and ordered the goldsmiths of Azcapotzalco to fashion a votive containing forty emeralds and two pearls set in gold box that housed the remnants of the poisonous creature that dared to attack the conqueror of Mexico (Valle Arizpe 1941).

In transplanting votive traditions to Mexican soil, of course, the Spanish did not encounter a cultural vacuum; votive practices were well known in

Mesoamerica before the conquest. According to one sixteenth-century chronicler, "the most important duty of the priest, and the Mexicans' principal religious ceremony, consisted in making offerings and sacrifices on certain occasions to obtain a favor from heaven or thanks for favors received" (cited in Montenegro 1950:11). Prehispanic votive objects have been found in a variety of Mexican archaeological sites (Sánchez Lara 1990; Solís 1991; Townsend 1992).

Despite the existence of a prehispanic votive tradition, the practice of votive painting never took hold among Mexico's indigenous populations after the Conquest. Although expressions of prehispanic religiosity were tolerated by Catholic missionaries, they were not encouraged, and priests instead sought to insert European practices into the native spiritual milieu (Lafaye 1976). In regions of Mexico dominated by Indian cultures, evangelization encouraged native traditions of dance, music, and crafts, but it discouraged practices that competed directly with Christian rituals.

As a result, votive painting first took root among American-born Spaniards, or *criollos* (Giffords 1974:119). As in Europe, the practice grew out of altar paintings of Biblical scenes commissioned for didactic purposes. Montenegro (1950:11) explains, "when transforming the old religion the missionaries followed a tradition adopted from time immemorial by the nobles of Europe: they commissioned from artists pictures of miracles and included themselves in the pictures standing beside the saint and giving him thanks. Such was the origin of these votive pictures."

Dating the beginnings of retablo painting in Mexico is difficult because the earliest works were executed on perishable media such as canvas or wood that have not survived. A series of engravings of the Virgin of Guadalupe done by the Belgian artist Stradanus between 1604 and 1622 suggest that retablos were present in Mexico by the early seventeenth century. One of these engravings shows four painted retablos hanging to either side of the Virgin's altar, each containing an explanatory text recounting a miraculous happening (Genaro Cuadriello 1989; Orendain 1984; Sánchez Lara 1990).

Votive painting ultimately became associated with Mexico's mestizos—people of both Spanish and Indian origin in whom prehispanic sentiments were united with European styles and techniques in a way that did not threaten the sensibilities of the Catholic Church. The introduction of tin plate in the nineteenth century provided a cheap and versatile medium that displaced canvas and wood and opened retablos to broader social participation (Giffords 1974, 1991). Over time, the racial origin of the supplicants shifted from criollo to mestizo, and the geographic center of retablo painting shifted away from the Valley of Mexico toward the heavily mestizo, west-central region of the country. By the 1920s, the production of votive art was concentrated in a few key western states, notably Guanajuato, Jalisco, San Luis Potosí, and Zacatecas.

Mexican retablo painting thus represents the application of Old World techniques to a New World medium in order to satisfy deeply human desires for supplication that are rooted in the ancient cultures of Europe and America. Although votive practices have diffused widely throughout the Catholic world, painted retablos achieved their fullest development and greatest expression in Mexico, and only there have they continued to be practiced as a living artistic tradition (Durand and Massey 1992).

MEXICAN PILGRIMAGE SITES

On any given day, scores of retablos are on display at popular pilgrimage sites throughout Mexico, to the extent that the new arrivals create real problems of disposal for priests who must somehow cope with the excess (Giffords 1991). Out of the hundreds of icons scattered in sanctuaries large and small, we focus on votive works associated with eight specific images: four of the crucified Christ, one of the child Jesus, and three of the Virgin Mary. These images were selected because their pilgrimage sites all lie within a few hour's drive of Mexico's leading migrant-sending communities, which are scattered throughout the states of Guanajuato, Jalisco, Michoacan, Nayarit, San Luis Potosí, and Zacatecas (fig. 11.1).

Together these states compose the most important migrant-sending region in Mexico (Dagodag 1975; Gamio 1930; North and Houston 1976; Ranney and Kossoudji 1983; Samora 1971), and the eight images together constitute the most important shrines in the area. Each site has a long history of votive supplication by U. S. migrants, so that by focusing on these eight images we ensure sufficient material for a detailed analysis of migrants' retablos.

The sanctuary of El Señor de Villaseca is located at Mineral de Cata, a silver mine situated on the outskirts of the modern city of Guanajuato, capital of the state of Guanajuato. According to legend, the image was brought from Spain in 1618 by the mine's proprietor, a wealthy hacienda owner named Don Alonso de Villaseca. Its materials and style of construction, however, point to a Mexican Indian origin sometime during the sixteenth century (Sánchez Lara 1990:58). Less is known about the origins of El Señor de la Conquista, located in the city of San Felipe Torres Mochas, also in Guanajuato. The icon was named for the "spiritual conquest" of the Indians during the sixteenth century. Although its exact date of creation is unknown, historical references suggest that it was installed in the sanctuary at San Felipe in 1585.

The image of El Señor del Saucito is of more recent origin. Its story begins in 1820 at a crossroads settlement located some four kilometers from the center of San Luis Potosí. In that year, a carpenter of modest means came upon a willow

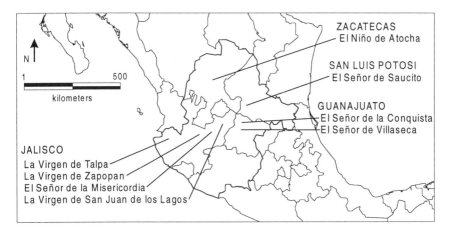

Fig. 11.1   The states of western Mexico and the locations of key shrines in Guanajuato, Jalisco, San Luis Potosí, and Zacatecas.

trunk with two branches that reminded him of a crucifix (the word *saucito* means "little willow"). He thereupon commissioned an Indian craftsman to carve an image of the crucified Christ from the trunk (Alvarez 1987). Within a few years, the image began to attract pilgrims from the city and surrounding countryside. In 1826, a professional sculptor, José María Aguado, was hired to rework the image and to smooth over its imperfections, giving the icon its present form.

El Señor de la Misericordia was likewise fashioned from a tree trunk early in the nineteenth century. The history of this image begins on September 6, 1839 in the rural town of Tepatitlán, Jalisco, when a poor farmer saw a strange light emanating from a gully near his home (Casillas 1989). Thinking that a neighbor was making charcoal, he approached the glow only to find an oak tree offering itself to him as a crucifix. Soon an itinerant wood carver mysteriously appeared in town and carved the crucifix (Casillas 1989). Little more is recorded about the miraculous image until 1852, when it was installed in its present sanctuary to accommodate the growing number of eager supplicants.

El Niño de Atocha provides a convenient transition to the three Marian images, since it is the only figure of the Christ child that we consider, and it is closely associated with a well-known image of the Virgin, Nuestra Señora de Atocha (see Giffords 1974:50). In Mexico, however, the child is separately venerated and has become "an overwhelming favorite among the representations of Christ in this folk tradition" (Giffords 1974:29).

The principal place of worship for El Niño is the small mining town of Plateros, near Fresnillo, Zacatecas. Although the origins of the image at this location are obscure, we know that by 1566 a small settlement had grown up around the mine and that, sometime during the eighteenth century, the Spanish owner commissioned a replica of Nuestra Señora de Atocha, an image he had venerated in his homeland, to display in the local sanctuary (Juárez Frías 1991).

During the Colonial period, homage was generally paid to the Virgin rather than the Child; but after the 1820s, patterns of veneration shifted, and El Niño acquired a separate identity and was given a special place in the Sanctuary above the main altar (López de Lara 1992). The image presently in use dates from 1886 (Giffords 1974:29).

Although images of Christ command devoted followings in many communities, the Virgin Mary is even more widely venerated throughout Mexico, and we have included three of the western region's most important images in our study. The first is the Virgin of Zapopan, whose story begins in 1541, when Fray Antonio de Segovia is said to have arrived in the village of Zapopan ("place of the zapote tree") just outside the present city of Guadalajara. With him was a small image of the Virgin of the Immaculate Conception (Alvarez 1987), which was probably sculpted by Indian craftsmen in the state of Michoacan sometime around 1531 (Juárez Frías 1991).

The origins of the Virgin of Talpa also go back to the early Colonial period. Like the Virgin of Zapopan, it was created in the late sixteenth century by artisans from Michoacan; but the statue is smaller, only about 15 inches tall, and its underlying identity is that of the Virgin of the Rosary rather than the Virgin of the Immaculate Conception (Carillo Dueñas 1986). The Catholic Church confirmed the Virgin's miraculous status in a document dated 1670, a copy of which (from 1832) survives in the parish archives. The present sanctuary was built in the second half of the eighteenth century, and the facade and towers were completed during the middle of the nineteenth century.

Although each of the foregoing images has attracted significant veneration by some inhabitants of western Mexico, by far the most important icon in the region is the Virgin of San Juan de los Lagos (Alvarez 1987; Olveda 1980). The town of San Juan is located in a region of Jalisco known as *los altos* (the highlands), aptly named for its high chaparral of windswept hills and dry pastures. Since early in the twentieth century, this area has been a center of migration to the United States (Cornelius 1976; Taylor 1933).

The legend of the Virgin of San Juan begins in 1542, when a small image of the Virgin of the Immaculate Conception was brought into town by a Spanish priest, Father Miguel de Bologna (Alvarez 1987). Little else is recorded of the image until 1623, when legend relates that the young daughter of two Indians fell gravely ill but was miraculously cured by the Virgin (Alvarez 1987). After the miracle, the image acquired a distinctly Mexican identity, separate from that of the Virgin of the Immaculate Conception, and since that time it has been known simply as the Virgin of San Juan (Alvarez 1987; Oblate Fathers 1990).

The Virgin of San Juan also was sculpted in the early sixteenth century by Indian artisans from Michoacan. Standing about 20 inches tall, the Virgin is usually depicted in full view with her hands clasped in front of her breast (Alvarez 1987), in keeping with fifteenth-century iconography (Giffords 1974:48-49). The first stone of the present church was laid November 30, 1732, and construction continued for 58 years, but the Virgin was installed on her present altar on November 30, 1769.

RETABLOS IN THEORY AND PRACTICE

Retablos are usually painted on pieces of tin that have been reduced down from larger sheets by a progressive cutting in half (Giffords 1991:37-38). Most are rectangular in shape, with the largest about 280 square inches (14 x 20 inches) and the smallest around 18 square inches (3.5 x 5 in.). The most common sizes are 140 square inches (10 x 14 in.) and 70 square inches (7 x 10 in.) (Giffords 1974, 1991; Orendain 1948).

Mexican retablos are composed of three basic elements: a holy image, a graphic rendering of a threatening occurrence or miraculous event, and a text explaining what happened (Giffords 1974, 1991). The holy image is usually depicted suspended in clouds and located to one side of the composition. Although the representation of the holy image must bear some relation to official iconography, the rules of interpretation are loose rather than rigid. In order to function effectively within the context of a votive, a holy image need only convey identity in general terms. A variety of colors, styles, shapes, props, and levels of detail may be used to depict a holy image, as long as overall recognition is achieved. Strict reproduction of a holy image is not important because the action itself is the focus of the work and its raison d'être. Moreover, since votive paintings are left at specific shrines, the identity of the image is usually obvious from the context in which it is placed (votives to the Virgin of Talpa are not deposited before the Virgin of San Juan de los Lagos, for example). Finally, any doubt about the identity of an image is often dispelled by the text, which mentions the image by name.

Textual material is generally found at the bottom of Mexican retablos. In addition to thanking the holy image, the text normally states the place of origin of the donor; the date, place, and circumstances of the event; and an account of the miraculous intervention by the holy image. Expressions of gratitude draw upon a standard vocabulary of faith and devotion that has evolved over scores of years and thousands of pilgrimages. Most begin with the words *"doy gracias"* ("I give thanks") and express a heartfelt need to *"hacer patente"* ("make known") the miraculous results of a divine intervention. In them, the supplicant states that at the moment of crisis, *"me encomendé a la Virgen"* ("I entrusted myself to the Virgin") and tells how *"me concedió el milagro"* ("she granted me the miracle"). Texts often end with the simple statement that *"por eso dedico el presente retablo"* ("for this I dedicate the present retablo").

The largest and most important part of the pictorial space is given over to depicting the miraculous event. In rendering the dangerous or threatening circumstances under which divine intervention occurred, there are no rigid rules and few strict protocols. According to one art historian, "the imagination of the artist has ample scope to express the supernatural and divine intervention that is superimposed on logical reality and only is acceptable in terms of a blind and irrational faith" (Moyssén 1965:26). The principal desideratum is that artistic devices used in the execution of the votive heighten the emotional intensity of the moment and emphasize the ongoing drama of events. Although the choice of materials, styles, and methods is open and flexible, several techniques have become conventional.

First, Mexican retablos rely on bold, bright colors to augment the emotional effect of the scene. In order to convey the power of extreme circumstances, retablo painters make full use of the color spectrum, yielding luminous and vibrant works. Luxurious reds, deep blues, shining golds, pale pastels, translucent greens, pure whites, and bright yellows abound in votive paintings. Although scenes of family members gathered around a sick bed may occasionally be rendered in subdued tones, the colors are rarely dark. Actions and dramatic events are almost always presented in vivid colors. Background detail is frequently painted using divergent hues to add emotional power to the composition, and the actors themselves are often rendered in contrasting tones.

Second, Mexican votive paintings undertake a deliberate and self-conscious manipulation of space in order to underscore the drama of the unfolding events. Scale and proportion are sacrificed to intensify emotion. Angles become sharper and perspective awkward in order to increase the dramatic power of a scene. The helplessness of mortals in the face of a dire situation is captured by juxtaposing tiny human figures with larger-than-life holy images (in real life, sacred images tend to be small). The bewildering nature of the moment is enhanced by a surreal placement of figures, props, and background constructions.

Third, Mexican votive painting systematically segments, deconstructs, and reorders time. Events that occurred sequentially are broken down into representative instants and shown simultaneously. Different stages in the pro-gress of a miraculous event are arranged within a common pictorial frame. Supplicants shown in the throes of a dire circumstance in one part of a retablo are pictured offering thanks to the image in another. Actions occurring before, during, and after the miracle are shuffled and recombined for maximum psychological effect.

Fourth, theater props and stage motifs are used from time to time to emphasize the drama of unfolding events. Action takes place on crude stages erected magically in the picture space. Curtains are pulled back to reveal figures in critical situations and lush and lustrous fabrics are draped over walls and furniture as if in a set. Actors appear to perform before audiences of horrified onlookers. Cinematic techniques such as the flashback and fast forward are employed to move about in time.

Finally, over the course of the twentieth century, Mexican retablos have incorporated new materials and techniques in their construction to create collages that blend traditional painting with modern media. Photographs of family members are affixed to lend verisimilitude to painted scenes. Photocopies of documents are appended as proof of the divine intercession. A commercially printed image of the Virgin is glued to a spot on the retablo specially prepared for the purpose. Unlike santos, therefore, Mexican votives have not been threatened with extinction because of the advent of cheap, industrially produced products. On the contrary, the range of techniques available to retablo artists has multiplied and the genre has continued to evolve.

These conventions are combined in manifold ways to create the form and substance of modern retablos. From an aesthetic point of view, the artistic power of Mexican retablo painting comes from an economy of execution and an innocent intensity of emotions. "The drawing is naively painstaking, the color choices are odd, the perspective is awkward, space is reduced to a rudimentary stage, and action is condensed to highlights. Adherence to appearances is less important than the dramatization of the ghastly event or the miraculous encounter between the victim and the resplendent holy image" (Herrera 1983:151).

Retablos thus condense the most extreme of human emotions—fear, sorrow, apprehension, gratitude, relief, horror—onto small sheets of tin painted in the most elemental of styles. Looking at people depicted in the throes of a circumstance that appears to have no earthly remedy, or facing an imminent personal loss so crushing and painful that all consolation seems hopeless, we not only share the intensity of the fear and sorrow, we also experience the relief of delivery and the unmitigated joy that follows an unbelievable stroke of good luck.

It is the rendering of such powerful and elemental human emotions in simple and unpretentious artistic terms that makes retablos so compelling as works of art. As the folklorist Frances Toor has noted, "*retablos* or votive offerings are the most important and popular aspect of folk painting at the present time. Many of these *retablos*—realistic pictures of super-realistic events—are painted with great sensitivity and profound recognition of a truth that makes a miracle of reality and of reality a miracle" (1947:67-68).

STUDYING MIGRANTS' RETABLOS

Our interest in migrants' retablos began in September of 1988, when we traveled to the church of San Juan de los Lagos to visit the Virgin and her famous paintings. As we admired the colorful pictures and dramatic texts, we noted several that dealt with experiences in the United States. As students of Mexico-United States migration, our interest was piqued, and we began to look for more of these paintings. Within an hour, we had located a dozen votives left by U. S. migrants. As we reflected on these works, it occurred to us that they might shed new light on a well-worn topic. Unlike other sources of information, retablos capture events as they were experienced by the migrants themselves. The pictures and texts provide a rich source of historical and sociological data on a subject that has been notoriously resistant to study. Because they depict salient events at the moment of their occurrence, moreover, they provide an immediate record of migrants' most pressing concerns. By scrutinizing these paintings, we can glimpse how U. S. migration felt and was understood by the people who experienced it.

During the period from September 1988 through December 1993, we sought out religious shrines known to support a votive tradition and scoured galleries and antique dealers looking for retablos that touched upon the subject of U. S. migration. In religious sanctuaries, we took photographs and transcribed texts whenever we came upon a retablo that dealt in any way with migration to the United States, and in private galleries, we purchased any such retablo that we encountered.

In all, we located 124 retablos painted or commissioned by U. S. migrants or their relatives. The scenes and texts contained in these votive works constitute the basic data for our study. In each case, we have a photograph of the painting and a transcription of the text, and in 64 cases we own the retablo itself. We include in our analysis any votive painting that we judged to have been left by a current or former migrant to the United States, or a member of his or her family.

All of the retablos were executed on a durable medium, in most cases tin. Of the 124 retablos we examined, 114 (92%) were painted on metal, five were on masonite, and three were on wood. Only two are executed on paper, and both are enclosed in a glass frame and mounted on durable backing. We chose to focus on durable media in order to control for the selective way that votive paintings survive. Although we can observe contemporary votive offerings on all sorts of perishable media, we can only observe past works that have survived. Thus, any view reconstructed from retablos of the past is likely to be more highly selective than a view pieced together from votive materials encountered in the present. In order to hold constant the degree of selection over time, we focused on retablos painted on tin, the most durable of materials.

Because votives sometimes address multiple icons, the 124 works contain 129 separate holy images, the distribution of which is shown in table 11.1. By far the most popular image is the Virgin of San Juan de los Lagos, which comprises roughly half the icons referenced. No other image comes close to the Virgin of San Juan in attracting the devotion of migrants to the United States.

Table 11.1
Distribution of retablos by image

Sacred Image	N	%
Images of the Virgin Mary		
Virgen de San Juan	64	49.6
Virgen Talpa	5	3.9
Virgen de Zapopan	4	3.1
Virgen de Guadalupe	4	3.1
Virgen de los Remedios	1	0.8
Images of Christ		
El Niño de Atocha	10	7.7
Señor de la Conquista	9	7.0
Señor de la Villaseca	8	6.2
Señor de la Misericordia	5	3.9
Señor del Saucito	5	3.9
Images of Saints		
San Miguel	7	5.4
San Martín de Porres	4	3.1
San Martín de Terreros	1	0.8
San Francisco de Asis	1	0.8
San Judas Tadeo	1	0.8
Total images mentioned	129	100.0

The next closest figure is El Niño de Atocha, which comprises about 8% of the images, followed by El Señor de la Conquista (7%) and El Señor de Villaseca (6%). Closely related to the image of El Señor de la Conquista is that of San Miguel (comprising about 5% of the sample). This minor icon is located in a small chapel in the sanctuary of San Felipe Torres Mochas. In practical terms, San Miguel and El Señor de la Conquista constitute a single pilgrimage site. The Virgin of Talpa, El Señor de la Misericordia, and El Señor del Saucito each add another 4% of the images to the sample, and the Virgins of Zapopan and Guadalupe comprise another 3%.

THE CONTENT OF MIGRANTS' RETABLOS

Although U. S. migrants share many of the same problems as others who bring votives before a sacred image, the experience of international imigration yields distinct circumstances that distinguish them from other supplicants. A typology of retablos developed for general use, such as that of Creux (1979) is therefore of limited utility in attempting to comprehend and classify the range of problems experienced by Mexican immigrants. Although illness, catastrophe, war, fire, falling, work, and animal problems (Creux's categories) may befall migrants, the meaning of these problems is very different in a foreign context. In addition, Mexico-United States migrants face the pain of separation, the hazards of moving north, the risks of crossing the border, the fear of falling sick in a strange land, the threat of arrest and deportation, and the thorny, ever-present issue of documentation.

In view of these distinctive concerns, we developed our own typology of retablos that builds on the earlier efforts of Creux and others, but which takes into account the unusual situation of U. S. migrants. The scheme contains six major headings and 16 detailed subcategories. The major headings follow the course of a migrant's journey to and from the United States. They include "Making the Trip," "Finding One's Way," "Legal Problems," "Medical Problems," "Getting by in the U. S.," and "Homecoming." Under these broad rubrics, we define a variety of subcategories that address particular topics.

In order to carry out a detailed content analysis of retablos, we classified each votive into one and only one of the 16 subcategories. In cases where more than one subcategory could have applied, we classified the retablo according to the subject that, in our judgment, was dominant. The results of this operation are shown in table 11.2. The first general heading is "Making the Trip," and it considers three salient issues involved in moving from Mexico to the United States. Difficulties encountered while travelling north fall into the first subcategory and those faced while crossing the border make up the second. The third subcategory focuses on the special problems that women face in going north. As table 11.2 indicates, nearly 15% of the retablos in our sample deal in some way with one of these themes.

Roughly 2% of the pictures fall into the subcategory "heading north." A good example under this rubric is the retablo left by a woman from León, Guanajuato, who was travelling north to the United States in October of 1946 when the roadway suddenly washed out and several of her companions were swept away. Fearing the worst, she called upon the Virgin of San Juan and entrusted them to her protection; later they miraculously turned up unharmed, a piece of good fortune the woman credited to the divine powers of the Virgin.

Another 3% of the retablos come under "women's issues." One such painting, dated November 19, 1989, was left by María del Carmen Parra, who gives "thanks to the Holiest Virgin of San Juan de los Lagos for having granted that [my] daughter could marry in the United States." For many women, marriage to a migrant, a Chicano, or an Anglo-American (from the retablo it is not exactly clear who her daughter married) provides a path of potential mobility to a better life, one free from the strictures of poverty and patriarchy in Mexico, and one to which mothers frequently aspire on behalf of their daughters (Goldring 1995; Hondagneu-Sotelo 1992; Reichert 1982). Whatever the case, the mother felt sufficient gratitude to commemorate the marriage with a retablo.

By far the most frequent subject mentioned under the general heading of "Making the Trip" is "crossing the border," a subject that concerns 9% of the retablos in the sample. As this relatively high frequency indicates, the risks of border-crossing loom large in the minds of Mexican migrants, who lack legal documents and must enter the United States surreptitiously. In addition to the risk of arrest and deportation (according to the latest estimates, the odds of getting caught are about 33% on any attempt—see Espenshade 1990; Kossoudji 1992; and Massey and Singer 1995), undocumented migrants also

Table 11.2
Distribution of retablos by subject
(Totals for categories shown in bold)

Subject	N	%
Making the Trip	**18**	**14.5**
Heading north	3	2.4
Crossing the border	11	8.9
Women's issues	4	3.2
Finding One's Way	**5**	**4.0**
Getting a job	2	1.6
Getting lost	3	2.4
Legal Problems	**18**	**14.6**
Arranging documents	8	6.5
Run-ins with the law	10	8.1
Medical Problems	**30**	**24.2**
Getting sick	22	17.7
Having an operation	8	6.5
Getting by in U.S.	**27**	**21.8**
War	7	5.7
Work accidents	5	4.0
Traffic accidents	12	9.7
Crime	1	0.8
Getting ahead	2	1.6
Homecoming	**22**	**17.7**
Grateful migrants	7	5.6
Thankful relatives	15	12.1
Unnamed Miracles	**4**	**3.2**
Total retablos	124	100.0

face the hazards of fraud, injury, robbery, thirst, hunger, and drowning. Those who make it through the gauntlet of border-crossing hazards naturally feel indebted to a holy image for watching over them, and for delivering them from danger.

Angelina García Solís, for example, left a votive addressed to El Señor del Saucito "for the miracle that he granted me in the year 1949. Finding myself drowning in the waters of the Rio Grande in el Norte in the company of other friends, in the most desperate moment I invoked his help after I had given up hope. I give him a thousand and one thanks, and also to God, that through his mediation He did me such an immense favor." Another anonymous votary thanked the Virgin of Talpa for saving "me from death on the twentieth of September of 1948. Upon wishing to cross the Rio Grande, two friends were killed but I was able to save myself."

After a migrant has entered the United States, new difficulties arise and these form the subject of the second heading, "Finding One's Way," which comprises 4% of the retablos in our sample. Getting lost in a strange setting is a problem treated in about 2% of the retablos. Frequently, this misfortune befalls migrants from small towns who arrive in large U. S. cities, but it also occurs in the countryside, often in arid parts of California, Texas, or Arizona, where migrants travel for work. Ponciano Guzmán did not give details on his retablo of September 4, 1951, he just gave "thanks to the Virgin of Zapopan for having gotten us out of this desert without harm."

A big part of finding one's way is getting a job, for without work migrants cannot repay the expenses of the trip, support themselves, or send money back home to family members in Mexico (Massey et al. 1987). About 2% of the retablos treat this theme. One of them was left by J. Melquides Murillo of Puerto de Loja, Guanajuato, who in 1961 gave "thanks to Holiest Mary of San Juan de los Lagos, because I prayed to Her that I might go and come across the border and that I might be hired."

The third major heading is "Legal Problems," the subject of roughly 15% of the retablos in our sample. First and foremost in this category is the problem of documentation since without a legal residence card, or some other form of legal documentation, a person's tenure in the United States is insecure and can end at a moment's notice. As a result, undocumented migrants are vulnerable to exploitation and are confined to an underground economy of unstable, poorly paid jobs.

Nearly 7% of the retablos we sampled concerned the issue of documentation. One of them was left by Luz Bravo Magaña, who on November 8, 1945, simply offered "thanks to the Virgin of San Juan de los Lagos for the miracle of having obtained without difficulty my passport from the American consulate." (Anyone who has ever waited in line to get a visa at a U. S. embassy can appreciate how "miraculous" this event seemed.) In 1989, another man left a retablo giving thanks to the Virgin of San Juan "for having acted on the petitions that I made to you for my brother to get his visa."

A second subcategory, comprising another 8% of the sample, focuses on encounters with law enforcement officials, the most feared of whom are immigration officers. Migrants occasionally run afoul of other authorities, however, and at times end up in jail. For such people, the usual problems of loneliness and fear are magnified; incarceration isolates them in a strange culture and prevents them from seeing loved ones who remain in Mexico. Thus, Juan Jaime Delgado addressed his retablo to the "Lord of Villaseca that is venerated in the Sanctuary of Mineral de Cata. I give infinite thanks for helping me get of jail in the United States and for arriving safely in the city of Guanajuato in the year 1986." In his retablo, José Gutiérrez likewise gave "thanks to the Lord Saint Michael for having saved me from a sentence of 20 years in a prison in Chicago, U.S.A., releasing me after only 8 months."

The fourth general heading, "Medical Problems," is the largest subject category in our sample. Getting sick is especially terrifying when one has no friends or family nearby, when one does not speak the language, and when one lacks money or insurance to pay doctors' bills. About 18% of the retablos we sampled mention sickness in the United States. The gratitude that María de Jesús Torres felt after her daughter got well was such that she traveled all the way to Jalisco from her home in National City, California to "offer infinite thanks to Our Lady of San Juan for having given health to my daughter, Teresa Torres, who suffered from asthma and epileptic attacks for several years." Facing an operation is also threatening when one cannot communicate effectively with the medical staff, or when one does not fully understand the medical system or its technology.

About 7% of the retablos in our collection explicitly give thanks to an image for the supplicant's survival of a surgical procedure performed in the United States. On January 3, 1962, in Santa Fe, New Mexico, for example, Concepción González Anderson underwent a surgical procedure in which "they did an examination to see if I had cancer. Thanks to the Holiest Virgin of San Juan, I was spared from this sickness for which I give infinite thanks for the miracle she gave me."

While living and working in the United States, Mexicans face a variety of additional issues related to well-being that are grouped under the fifth general heading, "Getting by in the U. S.," which comprises 22% of the retablos examined. Unlike Mexico, the United States is a global power with many foreign commitments, and entering its armed forces carries the very real risk of going to war in a far off place. Legal immigrants, as well as children of Mexicans born in the United States, are subject to the U. S. military draft (including the children of undocumented parents), and Mexican immigrants have fought in all major wars of the twentieth century, most recently in the Persian Gulf. Among the 124 retablos we assembled, 6% thanked an image for a safe return from war. The oldest such retablo in our sample was prepared by the uncle of Angel Turburán and deposited in the Sanctuary of El Señor de Villaseca on July 19, 1917. Referring to his nephew's service in World War I, the text states that "having been mortally wounded in the war, his uncle Roberto Rodriguez, from…New Mexico, commended him to the Holiest Lord of Villaseca that he should not die. … Having cured him from his sickness he makes public this miracle."

Aside from the extreme case of warfare, Mexican migrants face other risks while abroad. One is accidents at work. Migrants tend to be employed in agriculture, construction, the garment industry, and small-scale manufacturing, hazardous sectors where employers are under intense competitive pressure. In order to keep expenses low, companies invest little in safety devices or new equipment, thereby increasing the risk of work-related accidents. Some 4% of the retablos in our sample mention an accident at work. One such retablo was left by Manuel Reyes, who was picking cotton near Brawley, California during the fall of 1954 when he got his hand caught in some machinery. At this moment, he invoked the image of San Miguel, who intervened to free him, "losing a finger but saving my life, and in proof of gratitude I dedicate the present retablo." Another 10% of the retablos in the sample revolve around traffic accidents, a danger especially prevalent among migrants travelling to large urban areas in the United States. In 1954, one grateful migrant gave "thanks to the Virgin of San Juan de los Lagos for having saved me from an automobile accident in which four persons were left dead and four injured that occurred in San Francisco, California."

For Mexican migrants living in large U. S. cities, such as Los Angeles, crime constitutes another hazard of life, and one retablo in our collection deals with this issue. But getting by in the United States is not simply a matter of surviving negative experiences such as crime and car accidents. Ubiquitous among the votive objects left in Mexican sanctuaries are tokens of some foreign success: a driver's license, a report card, a high school diploma, a college degree. Although it is less common to find retablos commemorating these events, we did encounter two votive paintings that give thanks for a personal achievement in the United States. One offers thanks to the Virgin of Zapopan for "having been able to obtain a nursing certificate in the U.S.A." Another, from a migrant in Los Angeles, simply thanks this Virgin for "a miracle obtained in the artistic world some years ago."

The last phase of the migrant journey, Homecoming, involves the return of migrants to the warmth of their families and familiar soil of their birth. Given the many hazards and difficulties faced in the course of a U. S. trip, migrants and their families are often overcome with gratitude when a long separation finally comes to an end. The strength of this emotion is such that a votive of thanks is commissioned and left at a local shrine. Roughly 18% of the retablos in our sample fell under the general heading "Homecoming," with 12% expressing the gratitude of family members and 6% offering thanks from the migrants themselves.

Typical of the grateful migrants is Tereso López, of Rancho de la Palma, near Silao, Guanajuato, who contributed a retablo on the occasion of his return to Mexico from the United States. He "gives thanks to the Holiest Virgin of San Juan. Finding himself in the United States and commending himself to the Virgin he asked that upon arriving on his soil he would go to visit her." Another retablo illustrates the relief felt by family members left behind when a loved one returns. Candelaria Arreola of El Grullo, Jalisco, was praying for her son's return in 1955 when he miraculously arrived. As she explains, "I give thanks to the holiest Virgin of Talpa for having brought my son home from the United States, where he stayed for a long time. I began to pray your novena and I hadn't even finished when he returned. Thank you my mother!"

A systematic analysis of the content of migrants' retablos thus provides a glimpse into the special problems and difficulties faced by Mexican immigrants. If we simply list those subcategories with relative frequencies of 5% or more, we see that crossing the border, arranging documents, and avoiding encounters with legal authorities are principal preoccupations of U. S. migrants, and that getting sick, having an operation, getting drafted, and experiencing traffic accidents are major risks of life in the United States. When they manage to overcome these problems and return home safely, migrants and their family members are filled with gratitude.

Additional insight can be gained by classifying the subject of migrants' retablos according to the period in which the trip took place, a task that is carried out in table 11.3. This analysis employs five temporal categories: (1) from 1900 to 1939 represents the Early Years of Mexico-United States migration; (2) from 1940 to 1964 corresponds to the Bracero Era, when the U. S. government sponsored a temporary labor program that brought some 4.5 million Mexicans into the United States to work (see Craig 1971; Samora 1971); (3) from 1965 to 1979 encompasses the Growth Years, a time when Mexico-United States migration was growing rapidly; and (4) from 1980 to the present is the Modern Era. A residual fifth category contains retablos whose dates could not be firmly established.

The largest number of retablos (27%) come from the Bracero Era, followed in frequency by the Modern Era and the Growth Years (at about 19% each), and the least frequent period is the Early Years (around 9%). Roughly 26% of the retablos could not be dated with certainty. Given the limited number of retablos in our sample, we only examine temporal shifts in the main subject categories.

Issues surrounding Homecoming appear to be significant in all periods, with the exception of the Bracero Era, when Medical Problems dominate. The problem of Getting by in the United States is notably salient in the Early and Growth Years of U. S. migration. Although this category is also prevalent to some extent during the Bracero Era, it is underrepresented during the Modern Era. As

Table 11.3
Distribution of retablos through time.
(Percentage by subject and by supplicant's gender and destination, N=124)

| | Period of Migration | | | | |
	Early Years 1900-1939	Bracero Era 1940-1964	Growth Years 1965-1979	Modern Era 1980-1993	Undated Retablos
Subject Matter					
Making the trip	18.2%	20.6%	4.4%	16.7%	12.5%
Finding one's way	9.1	8.8	4.4	0.0	0.0
Legal problems	9.1	5.9	13.0	29.1	15.8
Medical problems	0.0	41.2	17.4	16.7	24.9
Getting by in U.S.	36.3	17.6	39.1	8.3	18.8
Homecoming	27.3	5.9	21.7	16.7	24.9
Unnamed miracles	0.0	0.0	0.0	12.5	3.0
Gender of Supplicant					
Male	50.0%	48.5%	47.8%	66.7%	52.0%
Female	50.0	51.5	52.2	33.3	48.0
U.S. Destination of Supplicant					
Border area	9.1%	20.6%	4.4%	12.5%	6.3%
California	0.0	26.5	26.1	16.7	15.6
Texas	18.2	14.7	21.7	12.5	9.4
Other	45.4	17.6	4.4	16.7	15.6
Unknown	27.3	20.6	43.4	41.6	53.1
Total retablos	11	34	23	24	32
Percentage	8.9%	27.4%	18.5%	19.4%	25.8%

transnational movement has become routine and institutionalized, therefore, issues relating to "Getting by" have receded into the background, since, unlike
their predecessors, migrants arriving after 1980 can count on a host of friends,
relatives, and compatriots, as well as a range of formal and informal contacts, to
facilitate their entry and employment within the United States (Massey et al. 1994).
Perhaps the most striking trend over time is the increasing salience of Legal Problems, in particular those related to documentation. From the Early Years
to the Modern Era, the percentage of retablos dealing with legal problems increases from 9% to 29%; and after 1980, issues related to the acquisition of
legal documents dominate all others. This trend reflects the fact that, since the
late 1970s, U. S. law has become increasingly restrictive with respect to Mexican immigration. In 1976, Mexico was placed under a quota of 20,000 immigrants for the first time, and in 1978 it was forced into a worldwide ceiling of
290,000 immigrants, which was subsequently reduced to 270,000 in 1980 (Jasso
and Rosenzweig 1990:28-29). These changes have made fewer immigrant visas
available to Mexican nationals, causing those who do manage to acquire papers
to be very grateful when they get them.

Retablos also provide important clues about the geographic origins and destinations of U. S. migrants, as well as their sex. It is common for supplicants to
end a votive text with their name, community, and state of origin, information
that can be used to discern the gender and geographic origins of migrants to the
United States. Votive texts also commonly relate where the miraculous event
occurred, and this information can be used to discern U. S. destination sites.
Table 11.4 shows the distribution of retablos in our sample broken down by
gender, Mexican origin, and U. S. destination of the supplicant. In most cases,
the gender of the supplicant could be established from the picture or the text. In
general, men and women are about equally represented among votaries. Among
the migrants who left paintings at the shrines we considered, 46% were men,
42% were women, and 12% were classed as gender unknown. Among those
whose gender could be established from information included on the retablo,
53% were men and 47% were women.

A large number of the votive texts and paintings contained no information
about geographic origins or destinations. Some 58% of the works provided no
state or community of origin in Mexico, and 38% gave no geographic data about
the destination in the United States. Frequently a U. S. destination was indicated only by the initials "E.U." ("Estados Unidos") or U.S.A., or by vague
references to *"el norte."* The large frequency of unknown places in Mexico
probably reflects an assumption by votaries that unless the state of origin is
named, it is implicitly understood to be that where the image is located. Since
roughly 60% of the retablos in our sample are dedicated to images in Jalisco, a
large share of the "unknown" retablos probably originate in that state, one that
is notably under-represented in the frequency distribution (only 2% of the retablos

Table 11.4
Distribution of retablos by gender, Mexican origin, and U.S. destination of supplicant
(Totals for geographic categories shown in bold, N=124)

Gender or Place	N	%	Gender or Place	N	%
Gender of Supplicant			*U.S. Destination*		
Male	57	46.0	Border Region	**14**	**11.3**
Female	52	41.9	California	**24**	**19.4**
Unknown	15	12.1	Los Angeles	10	8.1
			Other	14	11.3
Mexican Origin			Texas	**18**	**14.5**
Guanajuato	**36**	**29.0**	Other	**21**	**16.9**
San Luis Potosí	**6**	**4.8**	Arizona	2	1.6
Other	**10**	**8.1**	Colorado (Denver)	3	2.4
Aguascalientes	1	0.8	Florida	1	0.8
Baja California	1	0.8	Idaho	1	0.8
Durango	1	0.8	Illinois (Chicago)	6	4.8
Jalisco	2	1.6	Kansas	1	0.8
Michoacan	2	1.6	Michigan	1	0.8
Tamaulipas	1	0.8	Nebraska	1	0.8
Zacatecas	2	1.6	New Mexico	3	2.4
Unknown origin	**72**	**58.1**	Ohio	1	0.8
			Wisconsin	1	0.8
			Unknown destination	**47**	**37.9**

in the sample refer explicitly to Jalisco), especially given this state's prominence as a migrant-sending region. Even allowing for the under-representation of retablos from Jalisco, however, the number of votive paintings from the state of Guanajuato is remarkable, testifying to its importance as a cradle for this popular artistic tradition. Nearly 30% of all the retablos in our collection, and nearly 70% of those whose origins are known, were prepared or commissioned by someone from Guanajuato, despite the fact that around 80% of the offerings were made to shrines in Jalisco, San Luis Potosí, or Zacatecas (see table 11.1). A large number of supplicants must therefore have left Guanajuato to pay their respects to an image in another state, even though Guanajuato itself has several shrines with well-established votive traditions.

The state of Michoacan is notable for its absense in table 11.4. Despite being situated in the heart of the west-central region, and although it traditionally has been one of the most important migrant-sending states in Mexico, only two retablos in the sample give Michoacan as a place of origin. This relative absence probably reflects, at least in part, the Indian heritage of the state, the homeland of the Tarascans. As discussed earlier, votive painting took hold most strongly in mestizo areas that were not directly evangelized by colonial priests. The only hint of a votive tradition in Michoacan is that surrounding Nuestra Señora de la Salud, in Patzcuaro (Giffords 1974). Although this icon supported an active tradition of retablo painting before 1900 (see Montenegro 1950), it has now died out.

Apart from Guanajuato, San Luis Potosí, the home of El Señor del Saucito, is the only other state of origin mentioned with any frequency (about 5% of the retablos in our collection). Other states that receive mention are the western states of Aguascalientes and Zacatecas, and the northern states of Baja California, Durango, and Tamaulipas. The community names listed on the retablos typically refer to tiny rural hamlets, often with poetic names such as "Coesillo," "Rancho de la Palma," or "Rancho el Saucillo," suggesting the rural, campesino origins of many migrants to the United States.

The distribution of U. S. destinations mentioned in the retablos (see table 11.4) illustrates the uneven regional concentration of Mexican migrants to the United States (Bartel 1989; Jasso and Rosenzweig 1990). California and Texas together account for about 35% of the retablos in the sample, and 57% of those in which destinations could be ascertained. The most important single destination is Los Angeles (8% of the retablos in the sample), followed by Chicago (5%) and Denver (2%). Some 12% of the texts make a vague reference to some location along the border; and the remaining destinations are scattered throughout the Midwestern states of Illinois, Kansas, Nebraska, Ohio, Wisconsin, or among the Southwest states of Arizona, Colorado, and New Mexico. One person mentions a place name in Florida.

We can shed additional light on U. S. destinations when we examine them by period (see table 11.3). During the Early Years, migrant destinations were diverse and scattered, and California had not yet emerged as a significant area of attraction. A diversity of destinations is typical of migration flows during their early stages of development, before social networks and strong connections to employers arise to channel people to specific sites (Jones 1981; Massey et al. 1994).

The shift to California occurred during the Bracero Era, when the U. S. Department of Labor recruited large numbers of Mexicans for specialized work in that state's expanding agricultural economy. The dominance of California continued through the Growth Years as the relative importance of other states declined. Although destinations appear to have become more diverse again during the Modern Era, interpretation is clouded somewhat by the rather large number of retablos in the unknown category.

Trends in the gender composition of migrants across periods also are shown in table 11.3. In general, sex ratios are relatively even as one moves from the Early Years through the Growth Years of migration. It is only in the Modern Era, after 1980, that the sex composition becomes unbalanced, with a pronounced upward shift in the prevalence of men. The parallel increase in the frequency of legal problems suggests this shift may stem from the Immigration Reform and Control Act (IRCA) of 1986, which authorized a legalization program for undocumented agricultural workers, a group that is heavily male. By requiring migrants to prove that they had worked in U. S. agriculture during 1985 or 1986, the program put a premium on documentation and produced a bounty of retablos after in 1989 and 1990 from grateful men who had managed to qualify for legal status.

One last way to shed light on the nature of Mexico-United States migration is to cross-tabulate gender and destination by subject category, an exercise carried out in table 11.5. In general, men and women appear to be equally concerned with the problems of Making the Trip and Getting by in the United States. Within these categories, the sex composition of votaries is about even. Among retablos dealing with Legal Problems and Medical Problems, however, female votaries are somewhat more prevalent, comprising about 60% of the votives mentioning these themes. Except for the most recent period that included IRCA, therefore, women appear to face legal issues in migration more frequently than men.

Two categories were dominated by males, however. All of the votive paintings that dealt with Finding One's Way in the United States were prepared by males, and 58% of those who expressed gratitude for Homecoming were likewise men. When the latter category is broken into votives left by migrants and those left by family members, however, a pronounced gender disparity arises. All of the homecoming retablos left by migrants were commissioned or executed by men, but 62% of those offered by family members were left by women. To a considerable extent, it seems, men migrate while women remain behind and wait.

When destinations are classified by subject categories we find, not surprisingly, that retablos concerned with Making the Trip are dominated by refer-

Table 11.5
Distribution of retablo subjects by gender and U.S. destination of supplicant

	Subject of Retablo					
	Making the Trip	Finding One's Way	Legal Problems	Medical Problems	Getting By	Home-coming
Gender of Supplicant						
Male	50.0%	100.0%	40.0%	42.3%	45.8%	57.9%
Female	50.0	0.0	60.0	57.7	54.2	42.1
U.S. Destination of Supplicant						
Border Region	66.7%	20.0%	0.0%	0.0%	0.0%	4.4%
California	0.0	20.0	0.0	36.6	37.1	4.4
Texas	11.1	20.0	16.7	26.7	14.8	0.0
Other	0.0	20.0	16.7	26.7	18.5	13.0
Unknown	22.2	20.0	66.6	10.0	29.6	78.2
Number	18	5	18	30	27	22

ences to the Border Region (67% of all cases). In contrast, those focusing on Legal Problems refer to Texas or other states; and retablos dealing with life abroad generally mention Texas or California. Among votive works covering Medical Problems, for example, 38% are by migrants from California and 28% by migrants from Texas, together comprising roughly two-thirds of the sample. In the "Getting by" category, 37% are from California and 15% are from Texas (yielding a total of 52%). In the category "Finding One's Way," however, U. S. destinations are evenly distributed.

Remarkably, retablos that touch on the theme of Homecoming generally do *not* mention specific U. S. place names: 78% of these retablos were coded as destination unknown. This high figure reflects the isolation of migrants from their family members. A majority of the homecoming retablos were left by parents, sisters, or brothers, not the migrants themselves, and these people frequently do not know the exact whereabouts of their loved ones until they actually return, and then often only vaguely.

CONCLUSION

Many earlier studies have documented the remarkable degree to which U. S. migration has been incorporated into the social life of western Mexico (for a review see Durand and Massey 1992). This finding is hardly novel. Most prior works, however, have relied on the standard tools of social science: ethnographic fieldwork, statistical analyses, and case studies. These approaches lead to an abstract understanding that is divorced from the emotional reality of the underlying behavior. Retablos provide a more tangible and compelling view of the complex phenomenon of international migration, one that packs considerably more punch than mere statistics. Although we can reproduce only one of them here (see front cover), the 40 color plates contained in Durand and Massey (1995) give a hint of the emotional power of retablos as compelling works of popular art.

Retablos reveal unambiguously and unequivocally the degree to which U. S. migration has become a core part of the collective experience of the Mexican people. Working in the United States is now an institutionalized feature of that nation's culture and society. It has been interwoven into the rituals of daily religious life and has itself transformed those rituals. In western Mexico, seeing a retablo signed in Los Angeles, Dallas, or Chicago is as natural seeing one from Guadalajara, Morelia, or León.

At present, hundreds of thousands of families in western Mexico have a member on "the other side" and know firsthand about the joys, privations, sorrows, and devotions of migratory life. Migrants customarily maintain close ties with their relatives at home, and while working abroad, they dream of returning to build a house, open a store, buy land, or retire in luxury. And if these dreams remain elusive, at least they can look forward to making a visit to the local shrine to pay homage to a venerated image. Each year thousands make such a pilgrimage to appear before images of the Virgin located in Zapopan, Talpa, and San Juan, or to thank images of Christ in Mineral de Cata, San Luis Potosí, San Felipe, or Plateros. Retablos are important because they depict a side of migration usually not told in statistical reports or even in detailed interviews with migrants. Going to *el norte* has become a rite of passage for young men, synonymous with adventure, excitement, and personal esteem. It represents a source of pride and satisfaction for those who return with goods and money. Success in the United States is a frequent subject of boasts and exaggerated stories. In this atmosphere, those who have not fared well are apt to remain silent. They do not want people to think they were lazy or afraid. Only to a sacred image can they tell the truth and reveal their true stories of sadness, fear, and apprehension.

Retablos testify to the feelings and experiences of people who migrate back and forth to work in a strange land. In Diego Rivera's (1979:55) words, they are "the one true...pictorial expression of the Mexican people," and they get at the heart of the matter in a way that academic reports never can. After looking at the pictures presented here, and seeing how deeply migration has become rooted in the popular culture of western Mexico, one intuitively grasps why simply passing a new law or changing a bureaucratic regulation will not easily end the ongoing flow of people across the border. For better or for worse, international migration is pulling Mexico and the United States closer together and blending their peoples and cultures in new and exciting ways. The process of binational union is now far too advanced to be controlled easily by the political and economic actors who set it in motion. Whatever one's feelings about it, the cultural synthesis embodied in these retablos is probably the way of the future.

REFERENCES CITED

Alvarez, José Rogelio
    1987 *Enciclopedia de México, Tomo XII.* Secretaría de Educación Pública y
        Enciclopedia de México, Mexico City.
Bartel, Ann
    1989 Where do the New U. S. Immigrants Live. *Journal of Labor Economics* 7:371-91.
Carrillo Dueñas, Manuel
    1986 *Historia de Nuestra Señora del Rosario de Talpa.* Impresos Alfa, Mexico City.
Casillas, Luis Alberto
    1989 *Apuntes para la historia del Señor de la Misericordia.* Editorial Privado,
        Tepatitlán, Mexico.

Cornelius, Wayne A.
    1976   Outmigration from Rural Mexican Communities. *Interdisciplinary Communication Program Occasional Monograph Series* 5(2):1-39.
Cousin, Bernard
    1982   *Le Miracle et le Quotidien: Les Ex-votos Provençaux, Images d'une Societé.* Sociétés, Metalités, et Cultures, Paris.
Craig, Richard B.
    1971   *The Bracero Program: Interest Groups and Foreign Policy.* University of Texas Press, Austin.
Creux, René
    1979   *Les Ex-Voto Racontent.* Editions de Fontainnemore, Geneva.
Dagodag, W. Tim
    1975   Source Regions and Composition of Illegal Mexican Immigration to California. *International Migration Review* 9:499-511.
Decouflé, Pierre
    1964   La Notion d'Ex-Voto Anatomique chez les Etrusco-Romains. *Latomus, Revue d'Etudes Latines* 72:5-41.
de la Maza, Francisco
    1950   Los retablos dorados de Nueva España. *Enciclopedia Mexicana del Arte.* Ediciones Mexicanas, Mexico City.
Durand, Jorge, and Douglas S. Massey
    1992   Mexican Migration to the United States: A Critical Review. *Latin American Research Review* 27:3-42.
    1995   *Miracles on the Border: Retablos of Mexican Migrants to the United States.* University of Arizona Press, Tucson.
Egan, Martha
    1991   *Milagros: Votive Offerings from the Americas.* Museum of New Mexico Press, Santa Fe.
Espenshade, Thomas J.
    1990   Undocumented Migration to the United States: Evidence from a Repeated Trials Model. In *Undocumented Migration to the United States: IRCA and the Experience of the 1980s,* edited by Frank D. Bean, Barry Edmonston, and Jeffrey Passel, pp. 159-181. The Urban Institute, Washington D. C.
Fernandez, Celestino
    1983   The Mexican Immigration Experience and the Corrido Mexicano. *Journal of Studies in Latin American Popular Culture* 2:115-130.
Gamio, Manuel
    1930   *Mexican Immigration to the United States.* University of Chicago Press, Chicago.
    1931   *The Mexican Immigrant: His Life Story.* University of Chicago Press, Chicago.
Genaro Cuadriello, Jaime
    1989   *Maravilla Americana: Variantes de la Iconografía Guadalupana.* Patrimonio Cultural del Occidente, Guadalajara, Mexico.
Giffords, Gloria K.
    1974   *Mexican Folk Retablos: Masterpieces on Tin.* University of Arizona Press, Tuscan.
    1991   The Art of Private Devotion: Retablo Painting of Mexico. In *Catalogue to the Exhibit "The Art of Private Devotion: Retablo Painting of Mexico",* pp. 33-63. InterCultural Institute and the Meadows Museum, Dallas-Fort Worth.

Goldring, Luin P.
1995   Gendered Memory: Reconstructions of Rurality among Mexican Transnational Migrants. In *Creating the Countryside: The Politics of Rural and Environmental Discourse*, edited by E. Melanie DuPuis, and Peter Vandergeest, pp. 303-329. Temple University Press, Philadelphia.

Herrera, Hayden
1983   *Frida: A Biography of Frida Kahlo*. Harper and Row, New York.

Herrera-Sobek, María
1979   *The Bracero Experience: Elitelore vs. Folklore*. UCLA Latin American Center, Washington D. C.

Hondagneu-Sotelo, Pierette
1992   Overcoming Patriarchal Constraints: The Reconstruction of Gender Relations Among Mexican Immigrant Women and Men. *Gender and Society* 6:393-415.

Jasso, Guillermina, and Mark R. Rosenzweig
1990   *The New Chosen People: Immigrants in the United States*. Russell Sage, New York.

Jones, Richard D.
1981   Channelization of Undocumented Mexican Migrants to the United States. *Economic Geography* 58:156-176.

Juárez Frías, Fernando
1991   *Retablos Populares Mexicanos: Iconografía Religiosa del Siglo XIX*. Inversora Bursátil, Mexico City.

Kossoudji, Sherrie A.
1992   Playing Cat and Mouse at the U. S.-Mexican Border. *Demography* 29:159-180.

Lafaye, Jacques
1976   *Quetzalcóatl and Guadalupe: The Formation of Mexican National Consciousness, 1531-1813*. University of Chicago Press, Chicago.

López de Lara, J. Jesús
1992   *El Niño de Santa María de Atocha*. Fourth edition. Santuario de Platerios. Fresnillo, Zacatecas.

Massey, Douglas S., Luin P. Goldring, and Jorge Durand
1994   Continuities in Transnational Migration: An Analysis of 19 Mexican Communities. *American Journal of Sociology* 99:1492-1533.

Massey, Douglas S., Rafael Alarcón, Jorge Durand, and Humberto González
1987   *Return to Aztlán: The Social Process of International Migration from Western Mexico*. University of California Press, Berkeley.

Massey, Douglas S., and Audrey Singer
1995   New Estimates of Undocumented Mexican Migration and the Probability of Apprehension. *Demography* 32:203-213.

Montenegro, Roberto
1950   *Retablos de México/Mexican Votive Paintings*. Ediciones Mexicanas, Mexico City.

Moyssén, Xavier
1965   La pintura popular y costumbrista del Siglo XIX. *Artes de México* 61, Año XIII.

North, David S., and Marion F. Houstoun
1976   *The Characteristics and Role of Illegal Aliens in the U. S. Labor Market: An Exploratory Study*. Linton, Washington D. C.

Oblate Fathers
1991 *A Short History of the Virgin of San Juan del Valle Shrine.* Pamphlet. Oblate
Fathers, San Juan, Texas.

Olveda, Jaime
1980 La Feria de San Juan de los Lagos. *El Informador* 7 September. Guadalajara, Mexico.

Orendain, Leopoldo
1984 Exvotos. In *Cuarto Centenario de la Fundación del Obispado de Guadalajara,
1548-1948*, pp. 279-290. Artes Gráficas, Guadalajara, Mexico.

Ranney, Susan, and Sherrie Kossoudji
1983 Profiles of Temporary Mexican Labor Migrants to the United States. *Population and Development Review* 9:475-493.

Reichert, Joshua S.
1982 A Town Divided: Economic Stratification and Social Relations in a Mexican
Migrant Community. *Social Problems* 29:411-423.

Rivera, Diego
1979 *Arte y Política.* Editorial Grijalbo, Mexico City.

Sánchez Lara, Rosa María
1990 *Los retablos populares: exvotos pintados.* Universidad Nacional Autónoma
de México, Instituto de Investigaciones Estéticas, Mexico City.

Schroeder, Francisco Arturo
1968 Plateresco. *Retablos Mexicanos: Artes de México* 106, Año XV.

Siems, Larry (editor)
1992 *Between the Lines: Letters Between Undocumented Mexican and Central American Immigrants and their Families and Friends.* The Ecco Press, Hopewell, New Jersey.

Solís, Felipe
1991 *Tesoros Artísticos del Museo Nacional de Antropología.* Editorial Aguilar,
Mexico City.

Taylor, Paul S.
1933 A Spanish-Mexican Peasant Community: Arandas in Jalisco, Mexico. *Ibero-American*, vol 4. University of California Press, Berkeley.

Toor, Frances
1947 *A Treasury of Mexican Folkways.* Crown Publishers, New York.

Townsend, Richard F. (editor)
1992 *The Ancient Americas: Art from Sacred Landscapes.* Prestel Verlag, Munich.

U. S. Immigration and Naturalization Service
1992 *1991 Statistical Yearbook of the Immigration and Naturalization Service.* U. S.
Government Printing Office, Washington D. C.

U. S. Bureau of the Census
1991 The Hispanic Population of the United States: March 1991. *Current Population
Reports*, Series P-20, No. 455. U. S. Government Printing Office, Washington D. C.

Valle Arizpe, Artemio
1941 *Notas de Platería.* Editorial Polis, Mexico City.

Woodrow, Karen A., and Jeffrey S. Passel
1990 Post-IRCA Undocumented Immigration to the United States: An Assessment
Based on the June 1988 CPS. In *Undocumented Migration to the United States:
IRCA and the Experience of the 1980s*, edited by Frank D. Bean, Barry Edmonston,
and Jeffrey S. Passel, pp. 33-76. The Urban Institute, Washington D. C.

12

Puerto Rican Transnational Migration and Identity

Impact of English-Language Acquisition on Length of Stay in the United States

Azara L. Santiago-Rivera and Carlos E. Santiago

Our conception of transnational migration is of a process in which individuals and/or their families cross borders, leading to the emergence of significant communities of migrants (and return migrants) in the regions of origin and of destination. Upon reaching a threshold level of immigration, the process of migration and return to the country of origin takes on a unique dynamic that fosters continuous migratory movements that are independent of the original causes of migration. This interpretation is consistent with Massey et al.'s (1994) view of cumulative causation in migration.[1] Thus, transnational migration is fundamentally transformative, impacting the regions of origin and of destination as well as the migrants themselves.

At an aggregate level, transnational migrants serve as agents of societal change. There are two fundamentally important features. First, the process of transnational migration leads to the establishment of communities of emigrants and immigrants whose numbers have surpassed a threshold level such that they impact surrounding nonmigrant communities—in effect, moving beyond the enclave. Second, these communities are continually fed by new participants in this process of mobility, creating a back and forth syncretized transmission of ideas, attitudes, and cultural behaviors.

The nature of transnational migration implies an increase in the importance of the role of language acquisition and maintenance compared with the place-to-place immigration common to the United States during the early part of this century.[2] The implication is that the acquisition of the dominant language in the region of destination is crucial to social and economic mobility for immigrants. But, as the likelihood of return remains a real possibility, it is also important to retain and pass on the dominant language of the country of origin. Thus, bilingual skills become a prized commodity for the repeat or circular migrant in contrast to the nonmigrant or the migrant who engages in fewer moves.

In this paper, we examine the Puerto Rican experience with transnational migration. Some might argue that to talk about Puerto Rican-United States migration in a *transnational* context may be a misnomer inasmuch as Puerto Rico remains a territory of the United States and Puerto Ricans hold U. S. citizenship. But we argue that Puerto Rican migration represents a classic example of transnational migration given the two conditions listed above—the number of migrants have surpassed a threshold level, and circular and cumulative processes are now evident. Furthermore, linguistic and cultural differences between Puerto Rico and the United States are not trivial, leading some authors to conclude that Puerto Ricans residing in the U. S. constitute a 'deterritorialized nationality' (Hernández and Scheff 1996). Thus, the specific aspect of transnational migration examined herein is the changing role of language—particularly English-language acquisition and its potential impact on identity—on the part of the migrant and the return migrant.

Our work here also differs from earlier research in a number of important respects. First, we focus on a specific ethnic group—Puerto Ricans residing in the United States and in Puerto Rico. Second, we compare migrants by recency of migration within this group. Most comparative research in this area contrasts the experiences of various ethnic or racial groups or those between immigrant groups and the native population. Third, we examine the effect of English-language proficiency on the likelihood of migration. Again, research in this area generally estimates an earnings function rather than a migration function. Fourth, we determine the extent to which English-language proficiency impacts the length of a Puerto Rican migrant's stay in the United States before a return to the island. Finally, we compare the empirical findings for 1980 and 1990. Hence, the evidence highlights the relationship between English-language proficiency and migration as opposed to that between English-language proficiency and earnings.

TRANSNATIONAL NATURE OF PUERTO RICAN MIGRATION

Puerto Rican communities have existed in the United States prior to the large-scale emigration of the 1950s.[3] But, it is during the 1950s that the Puerto Rican population in the United States surpassed the threshold level that set the stage for significant numbers of migrants to return to Puerto Rico from the mainland. The return migration phenomenon among Puerto Ricans was documented early on in the seminal work of Hernández (1967). Using 1960 U. S. Census figures, Hernández (1967:6) concluded the following:

> Large-scale entry and dispersal, the formation of ethnic neighborhoods, adjustment and adaptation, the evolution of the second generation—these were the major aspects of Puerto Rican life on the mainland in the 1950s. By 1960, the movement of Puerto Ricans to the United States had dwindled to an annual total of about 15 to 20 thousand. During recent years, the outflow has remained approximately the same, but it is tending to decrease. Meanwhile, a steadily increasing number of migrants are returning to Puerto Rico, a reverse movement which cancels the net gain the population on the mainland by way of migration. Hence, the mainland community has ceased to be augmented in a significant manner by new arrivals, and the Puerto Rican migration northward appears to be nearing an end. Nor is a large-scale renewal of emigration likely in the immediate future.

Hernández underestimated the potential for a resurgence of net emigration from Puerto Rico. During the 1980s, net emigration from Puerto Rico increased, almost doubling levels of the previous decade (table 12.1).[4] However, it is also clear that the large-scale migratory movement of the 1950s has not been repeated. Moreover, Puerto Rican migration no longer serves as the "safety-valve" for population pressure that it once was. The increase in the Puerto Rican population is now primarily a function of birth and mortality rates.

Postwar migration has certainly left its mark on the geographic dispersion of the Puerto Rican population. Of the approximately six million individuals that self-identified as "Puerto Rican" in the United States and Puerto Rican

Table 12.1
Net Migration from Puerto Rico, 1970 - 1990

Type of Migration	1970 - 1980	Percentage of 1980 Population	1980 - 1990	Percentage of 1990 Population
In-migration	391,280	12.2	316,173	9.0
Out-migration	457,093	14.3	432,744	12.3
Net-migration	-65,813	2.1	-116,571	3.3

Sources: U.S.Bureau of the Census (1983 and 1993)

decennial census of 1990, forty-five percent resided in the continental United States.[5] Clearly Puerto Rican migration to the United States satisfies part of the first criterion and all of the second criterion for a transnational process.

The geographic distribution of Puerto Rican migration to the United States has also undergone significant transformation over the years. Whereas New York City was the primary area of destination of Puerto Rican migrants for many years, and still comprises the largest concentration of Puerto Ricans, Puerto

Ricans have been moving directly to other areas without first passing through New York City.[6] The fastest growing Puerto Rican communities in the United States today are those located in mid-size cities in the Northeast and in areas of the state of Florida. This process of dispersion, particularly throughout states of the Northeast that have been losing total population, has led to a dramatic increase in the presence of Puerto Ricans in mid-size communities. For example, by 1990 Puerto Ricans comprised over twenty percent of the total population of cities such as Hartford, Camden, Bridgeport, Lawrence, and Passaic (Rivera-Batiz and Santiago 1994). The simultaneous process of dispersal and concentration reflects the development of social networks and a complex process of dissemination of information about jobs and opportunities with a significant impact on Puerto Rican migration.

Another characteristic of present-day Puerto Rican migration that coincides with our notion of a transnational process is that the migrant's length of stay in the United States prior to returning to the island has been declining over time (this is shown in table 12.2). Of all return migrants in 1980, 36.2% stayed less than two years in the United States, while 38.6% had resided in the United States for more than ten years prior to their return. By 1990, the percentage of all return migrants who had stayed in the United States less than two years increased to 46.4, while that of those who returned after living in the United States for ten or more years decreased to 23.5. These figures illustrate clearly that a larger fraction of the return migrant pool is spending less and less time in the United States prior to returning to the island. Information on how frequently individual migrants make the move between Puerto Rico and the United States is not available, but the consensus among many scholars is that frequency has increased at the same time that duration of stay has decreased.

This characteristic of Puerto Rican migration—increased frequency of migration and reduced duration of stay—is representative of what many have termed the phenomenon of circular or commuter migration (Torre et al. 1994). The circularity of the migration stream is consistent with the conception of transnational migration presented in this paper. It is also fundamentally different from the place-to-place immigration that has characterized the United States for much of this century.

Table 12.2
Percentage distribution of migrants to the United States, by length of stay

Length of Last Stay in the U.S.	1980	1990
6 months to 1 year	19.9	24.3
1 to 2 years	16.3	22.1
3 to 4 years	10.7	15.3
5 to 9 years	14.5	14.8
10 or more years	38.6	23.5

Source: U.S. Bureau of the Census (1993). Authors' tabulations.

The economic determinants of Puerto Rican migration have been given most attention in the quantitative social science literature (Fleisher 1963; Friedlander 1965; Maldonado 1976). This has been particularly true within the context of place-to-place Puerto Rican migration, but it remains to be seen whether it holds for a more complex process such as circular migration. The rational economic agent model that underscores much of the empirical literature can be open to question in the context of circular migration in which repeated moves disrupt employment prospects, job stability, schooling of one's children, and even individual and family adjustment. While the human capital model of migration has proved quite successful at explaining place-to-place migration, it is hard pressed to explain circular migration. Some have even argued that the lower socioeconomic status of Puerto Ricans residing in the United States compared to other ethnic and racial groups can be partly attributed to the frequency with which Puerto Ricans move between the island and the United States.[7]

Public policy's role in the process of migration is often relegated to a position of less importance than market forces. In the Puerto Rican context, however, public policy towards migration has been a crucial determinant of the magnitude and direction of the flow of labor between the island and the United States. The large outflow of labor during the 1950s was clearly encouraged by the island government because it could reduce population pressure, and hence, increase income per capita. Subsidized transportation costs and relocation assistance were just part of the incentives provided to encourage people to migrate to the United States.

The use of public policy to influence migration between Puerto Rico and the United States has not been limited to the decade of the 1950s. During the mid-1970s, revisions were made to the manner in which federal minimum wage statutes were applied to the island. In particular, the system of exemptions to the federal statutory minimum wage was dismantled bringing parity to minimum wage levels between Puerto Rico and the United States by the end of the decade. At the same time, the social safety net on the island was extended to include food stamps and other federal transfers. These policies had the effect of slowing migration to the United States at a time when the primary destination of Puerto Ricans, New York City, was in the throws of a severe financial crisis (Santiago 1991).

To demonstrate that economic factors are currently less of a determinant of Puerto Rican migration than they once were, a time series model estimates Puerto Rican in- and out-migration on a monthly basis from 1970 to 1987. The purpose is to determine the extent to which economic variables explain rates of in- and out-migration compared to past values of migration.[8] Table 12.3 presents the percentage contribution to the variance of forecasts in a nine variable time series (vector autoregressive) process. The primary variables of interest are the rates of in- and out-migration and the model includes wages and unemployment rates in Puerto Rico and New York City as well as wage, unemployment, and expected wage differentials between Puerto Rico and New York City. In column (1)

Table 12.3
Percentage variance decompositions, twelve months ahead, in nine variable vector autoregressive system, 1970:1 - 1987:6

Innovation Variable	(1) In-migration	(2) Out-migration	(3) Wage (PR)	(4) Unemployment Rate (PR)	(5) Wage (NY)	(6) Unemployment Rate (NY)	(7) Unemployment Differential	(8) Wage Differential	(9) Expected Wage Differential
In-migration	51.54	37.37	1.64	5.26	1.17	4.99	5.39	4.53	5.29
Out-migration	16.12	29.49	2.87	1.34	16.58	2.62	2.10	14.56	7.32
Wage (PR)	3.13	3.81	89.89	3.07	20.62	7.55	7.64	23.31	13.45
Unemployment rate (PR)	16.20	16.38	0.20	77.82	0.73	32.57	6.74	1.38	31.63
Wage (NY)	4.57	3.64	3.21	3.42	57.51	1.72	0.64	31.32	10.80
Unemployment rate (NY)	2.37	2.08	0.16	7.38	1.12	46.69	65.70	0.86	11.08
Unemployment differential	1.44	1.75	0.09	0.36	1.61	0.48	5.22	2.82	1.06
Wage differential	1.48	1.79	1.57	0.28	0.32	0.37	0.48	20.46	17.10
Expected wage differential	3.16	3.70	0.40	1.06	0.34	3.02	6.10	0.77	2.27

Source: Santiago and Basu (1996)

Note: PR = Puerto Rico; NY = New York City

it is noted that 51.54% of the forecast variance of in-migration (to Puerto Rico) is explained by past in-migration itself while 16.12% is explained by out-migration. Of the economic variables, only the unemployment rate in Puerto Rico explains a relatively large fraction (16.2%) of the forecast variance of in-migration. A similar pattern is noted with out-migration—a greater fraction of its forecast variance is explained by past values of out- and in-migration than some of the economic variables. Again, the exception is the rate of unemployment in Puerto Rico, which explains 16.38% of the forecast variance of out-migration.

These results do not negate the effect of relative labor market variables on in- and out-migration, but they do suggest that other factors may better explain present-day Puerto Rican migratory movements. We use this evidence to suggest that the influence of relative wages and unemployment, so important during the early stages of mass migration, have given way to other forces. Thus, this result is consistent with our notion of transnational migration and cumulative causation.

Evidence has been provided to argue that the Puerto Rican migratory experience should be studied in a transnational context. Clearly, the sheer number of migrants is indicative of its impact on communities in the areas of origin and destination. That there is further evidence of repeat or circular migratory processes also suggests that information on conditions in both geographic areas is being widely disseminated.

MIGRATION, LENGTH OF STAY, AND ENGLISH-LANGUAGE ACQUISITION

Language acquisition is an important factor in the ability of immigrants to make social and economic gains. To the extent that the immigrant's native language differs from that of the country of destination, the immigrant will need to engage in a language-learning process to expand his or her options in the labor market. Portes and Rumbaut (1996:196) describe the manner in which this process operates intergenerationally:

> Those in the first generation learned as much English as they needed to get by but continued to speak their mother tongue at home. The second generation grew up speaking the mother tongue at home but English away from home—perforce in the public schools and then in the wider society, given the institutional pressure for anglicization and the socioeconomic benefits of native fluency in English. The home language of their children, and hence the mother tongue of the third generation, was mostly English.

English-language acquisition is obviously an important factor in the His-panic immigrant's adaptation to the United States labor market although there is disagreement concerning its quantitative impact. Some studies (Borjas 1984; Reimers 1983, 1985) report that the quantitative impact of English-language proficiency on Hispanic earnings is small, while others (Grenier 1984; Kossoudji 1988; McManus et al. 1983; Rivera-Batiz 1988, 1990, 1991, 1992; Tainer 1988) have found that earnings of Hispanics in the labor market are significantly affected by English-language proficiency.

English-language proficiency among Puerto Ricans born on the island varies considerably by migrant status and length of last stay in the United States, as illustrated in table 12.4. The island nonmigrant population is not bilingual by any stretch of the imagination. Only 20% of the population stated that they were proficient in English (i.e., they spoke it 'easily'). This figure increased only slightly to 22% of the population between 1980 and 1990. Fifty percent of the island nonmigrant population stated that they did not speak English at all in 1980 and 1990. Nonetheless, it is also the case that English-language proficiency has improved among Puerto Ricans residing on the island and in the United States, both migrant and nonmigrant alike. As previously mentioned, this can be attributed to increases in educational attainment on the island, movements of people with better English-language skills, and a population of Puerto Ricans increasingly educated in English in the United States.

We developed an empirical model to test the relationship between English-language proficiency and migration.[9] The model specifies a linear relationship between a response variable, y^*, defined by the following expression:

$$y_i^* = b'x_i + u_i$$

where x_i represents a list of independent regressors, and u_i is a stochastic error term. The parameters to be estimated are b'. Although y_i^* is unobservable, we do observe the following:

$$y = 1 \text{ if } y_i^* > 0$$
$$y = 0 \text{ otherwise}$$

Let us assume that y_i^* reflects the decision to migrate and that all we truly observe is if someone has migrated or not, captured by the value of y. To estimate the parameters β', a maximum likelihood procedure is required and we posit a functional form for the cumulative distribution of u_i as the logistic function.

Thus, the first part of our exercise involves the estimation of a logit model. The estimates appear in table 12.5. The dependent variable of columns (1) - (4) distinguishes between the Puerto Rican-born, ages 20 - 54, who migrated and those who did not. Columns (1) and (2) present the results for those Puerto Ricans residing on the island in 1980 and 1990, and columns (3) and (4) provide results for Puerto Ricans residing in the United States in 1980 and 1990. The main independent regressor of interest is the measure of English-language proficiency that appears in the census. The control variables include gender, age, marital status, industry, and occupation. Variables are defined in table 12.6.

Table 12.4
English-language proficiency among Puerto Rican nonmigrants and return migrants
1980 and 1990, in percentage of group (ages 20-54)

Group	English-language Proficiency 1980			English-language Proficiency 1990		
	(1) Easily	(2) With Difficulty	(3) Not at All	(4) Easily	(5) With Difficulty	(6) Not at All
Nonmigrant resident of Puerto Rico	20.0	27.0	52.8	22.2	27.0	50.8
Return migrant to Puerto Rico	46.3	30.7	23.0	50.3	27.7	21.9
Puerto Rican-born, residing in the U.S.	72.2	21.0	6.8	79.9	15.9	4.2
Puerto Rican-born, residing in the U.S., but living in Puerto Rico 5 years earlier	54.3	28.5	17.2	60.6	26.4	13.0
By Length of Last Stay in U.S.						
6 months to 1 year	27.1	30.9	41.9	32.4	31.0	36.6
1 to 2 years	35.3	34.7	29.9	44.3	31.4	24.3
3 to 4 years	40.6	36.3	23.1	54.3	27.0	18.7
4 to 5 years	41.6	34.2	24.2	58.7	25.4	15.9
6 to 9 years	43.8	33.2	22.9	55.6	27.5	16.8
10 or more years	64.9	25.8	9.4	67.8	22.0	10.2

Sources: U.S. Bureau of the Census (1983, 1993)

The results show considerable correspondence between 1980 and 1990, both in terms of the likelihood of migration and in the length of stay in the United States prior to returning to the island. Compared with Puerto Rican nonmigrants, return migrants tended to be older in age and had higher levels of educational attainment, but they also were apt to be less proficient in the use of the English language. When we compared more recent Puerto Rican migrants in the United States with earlier Puerto Rican migrants, we found that the former were older in age and had less educational attainment, but greater English-language proficiency. This suggests that for the successful migrant—characterized as one who stays in the United States for a longer period of time—lower educational attainment can be compensated for by English-language proficiency. In other words, English-language proficiency is a better predictor of migrant success than is educational attainment.[10]

The results concerning the length of last stay in the United States prior to returning to the island reinforce the previous findings. Again, the results are consistent over time. Those Puerto Rican migrants who returned to Puerto Rico after a relatively short stay in the United States tended to be single males, of

Table 12.5
Standardized estimates of the relative importance of Puerto Rican migrant's English-language proficiency (persons ages 20-54)

| | Dependent Variables | | | | | |
| | Likelihood of Migration (Logistic Function) | | | | Duration of Last Stay (Linear Regression) | |
Regressors	(1) 1980 Census of Puerto Rico	(2) 1990 Census of Puerto Rico	(3) 1980 U.S. Census of Puerto Ricans	(4) 1990 U.S. Census of Puerto Ricans	(5) 1980 Census of Puerto Rico	(6) 1990 Census of Puerto Rico
Sex	-0.010	0.002	0.072*	0.013	0.538**	0.373**
Age	0.174*	0.157*	0.325*	0.406*	0.062**	0.046**
Marital status	0.070*	0.020	0.003	0.070*	-0.044**	-0.020**
Education	0.398*	0.326*	-0.252*	-0.326*	-0.089**	-0.091**
English-language proficiency	-0.618*	-0.561*	0.356*	0.431*	1.022**	0.839**
Industry	0.077*	0.075*	0.023	0.014	-0.0002**	-0.0002**
Occupation	-0.181*	0.127*	0.046	-0.0001	0.0001	0.0001
Number of observations	62,414	72,867	30,665	28,963	9,632	9,237
-2 Log likelihood	46,683.32	48,841.53	13,253.51	18,829.74		
F-Statistic					473.17**	322.05**
Adjusted R-Square					0.255	0.196

Notes:

The dependent variable of equations (1) and (2) takes the value of 1 if the person resided in the U.S. in the previous ten years and 0 otherwise. The dependent variable of equations (3) and (4) takes the value of 1 if the person migrated from Puerto Rico in the last five years and 0 otherwise. The dependent variable of equations (5) and (6) is the length of time a migrant spent in the U.S. prior to returning to Puerto Rico. Parameter estimates for equations (5) and (6) are non-standardized regression coefficients.

*Statistically significant value at the .0001 level of significance.

**Statistically significant t-statistic at the 0.0001 level of significance.

Table 12.6
Definition of independent regressors

Variable	Definition
Sex	Gender: 1 = female, 0 = male
Age	Age of individual in years
Marital	Marital status:
	0 = Currently married, not separated 1 = Widowed 2 = Divorced 3 = Separated 4 = Single
Education	Educational attainment in years
English	Ability to speak English:
	Scale of 1 to 3 (in 1990); 1 to 4 (1980), where 1 = Not at All and 3 (1990) or 4 (1980) = Very Well.
Industry	Classification of industry of employment
Occupation	Classification of occupation of employment

Sources: U.S. Bureau of the Census (1983, 1993)

relatively young age, with little English-language proficiency. But, the findings also indicate that those Puerto Rican migrants with greater educational attainment tended to return to the island after a relatively short stay in the United States.

The results present a complex picture of transnational migration. On the one hand, it appears that there is a conduit of young male migrants, with relatively few labor market skills, who migrate frequently between Puerto Rico and the United States, spending short periods of time in the U. S. On the other hand, there are some migrants with relatively high educational attainment, but limited English-language skills, who are facing a difficult time adjusting to the United States, which may be reflected in their low labor market participation. It is likely that these disillusioned migrants with higher educational attainment on the island are finding that their skills are not fully valued in the U. S. labor market because of their relative lack of English-language proficiency.

One might argue that short-term circular migrants are responding not only to relative economic conditions in Puerto Rico and the United States but also to potential discrimination owing to their limited English-language proficiency. This may, in turn, constitute a revolving labor pool. Specifically, the migration of more educated individuals may be attributed to aspects of relative deprivation in which the migrant attempts to improve his or her socioeconomic standing by leaving the island. Once in the United States, the migrant's lack of English-language proficiency proves a serious drawback to sustained socioeconomic mobility. At this stage of the analysis, these explanations are simply conjecture, but they do point to multiple causal factors in Puerto Rican migration.

IMPLICATIONS FOR PUERTO RICAN ADAPTATION AND IDENTITY

A number of studies have shown that English-language acquisition contributes to occupational achievements (Bean and Tienda 1987; Stolzenberg 1990) and successful adaptation to the dominant U. S. culture (Berry 1980; Gushue and Sciarra 1995) among relatively recent immigrants. Meléndez, Carre, and Holvino (1995) have argued that the lack of English-language proficiency is serving as a barrier to obtaining employment commensurate with experience and educational attainment among Latinos in the United States. They also emphasized that the negative stereotypic images of Latinos, as portrayed in the media, may be contributing to biases present in employment practices. Meléndez and colleagues (1995:105) persuasively point out "At the same time that stereotypes influence our perceptions about members of other social groups, they also influence perceptions about one's group and one's self-concept." Thus, if one is judged as less qualified because of limited vocabulary skills in English, regardless of previous work experience and educational attainment, compounded by negative images (i.e., Latinos portrayed as lazy and emotional), the perception will have a profound impact on an individual's identity as a contributing member of society and his or her ability to be socioeconomically mobile. In fact, Estrada (1993) speculated that for some Latino groups a shift from one economic status to another may be associated with changes in what ethnic label they choose to self-identify (i.e., White, American Indian, or Hispanic-origin identifiers).

Through a series of interviews, Oboler (1995) exemplified the relationship between English-language proficiency and its impact on identity. For instance, many of her interviewees stated that their struggle to adjust to a new way of life in the United States centered on dealing with the prejudice and racism experienced because of their limited English-language speaking skills. Oboler pointed out that these negative experiences affected their sense of self. As such, Puerto Ricans who leave the island and come to the United States in search of better opportunities may find themselves struggling with not only the language barrier but also the attitudes and behaviors of others, which may limit their access. Thus, these experiences may serve as the impetus to spend a shorter time in the United States.

Although such studies have increased our understanding of the potential barriers that may be contributing to limited socioeconomic mobility, as a measure of adjustment to U. S. society, and its relationship to identity, most of these studies have examined the Hispanic population as a whole. It is well recognized that the various subgroups that compose the Hispanic population differ in such aspects as the historical relationship with the United States and, in particular, migration patterns. As such, the distinctness of the Puerto Rican transnational migration experience as circular in nature must be taken into consideration when examining such factors as English-language acquisition, participation in the U. S. labor market, and identity. The finding that limited English-language skills affect length of stay in the United States may partially explain this migration pattern.

CONCLUSIONS

We have attempted to demonstrate the importance of English-language acquisition and proficiency in the process of Puerto Rican transnational migration. Whereas in the past, relative economic forces predominated in the determination of place-to-place migration, today, it is language proficiency and educational attainment that are increasingly important in the context of transnational migration. Both English-language proficiency and educational attainment influence decisions regarding the frequency of migration and a migrant's length of stay in complex ways. It appears that educational attainment alone is not sufficient to assure a Puerto Rican migrant's success in the U. S. labor market if the person's English-language skills are inadequate. While English-language proficiency may compensate for low educational attainment among Puerto Rican migrants, one cannot say that the reverse is true. Likewise, the links among identity development, English-language acquisition and proficiency, and migration status need to receive much more attention than they have in the literature to date. We believe that these findings are important to better understand the complexities of transnational migration.

NOTES

1. Among the characteristics of cumulative causation cited by Massey and his colleagues are self-perpetuation, importance of networks, relative deprivation via remittances, land inequality, and transnational culture. The threshold level of immigration is difficult to quantify but certainly occurs after a community has been established and can be clearly identified and where there is some evidence of back and forth migration.
2. The distinctions between place-to-place, return, and circular migration can be illustrated by the following: Place-to-place migration occurs when an individual moves from point A to point B. Return migration occurs when an individual moves from point A to point B and then back to A. Circular migration is illustrated by a move from point A to B to A and then back to B.
3. For an excellent account of the establishment of Puerto Rican communities in the United States, see Sánchez-Korrol (1994).
4. As table 12.1 clearly shows, net emigration increased during the 1970s compared with the 1980s but total out-migration and total in-migration continue to decline.
5. See Rivera-Batiz and Santiago (1994) for information on the demographics of the Puerto Rican population resident in the United States. Prior to 1950, the Census

Bureau allowed identification of Puerto Ricans only by birthplace and excluded those residents of the continental United States who had some Puerto Rican parentage or ancestry. From 1950 on, the census data allowed Puerto Ricans to be identified by birthplace and parentage. The 1970 Census of Population classified Puerto Ricans as (1) those who were born in Puerto Rico, (2) those with both parents born in Puerto Rico, (3) those with one parent born in Puerto Rico and the other parent born in the United States, and (4) those whose father was born in Puerto Rico and mother was born in an outlying area. Only the 1980 and 1990 censuses allowed for self-identification.

6.   For a comprehensive examination of the socioeconomic status of Puerto Ricans in the United States, see Rivera-Batiz and Santiago (1994).

7.   Tienda and Díaz (1987:A-27) put it in the following terms when they argue that circular migration "separates them [Puerto Ricans] from other inner-city minority groups...[and] severely disrupts families and schooling, leading inevitably to a loss of income." A similar conclusion is reached by Borjas (1990:251) when he states that "the work of Oscar Lewis, however, suggests that back-and-forth migration between Puerto Rico and New York City is an important factor in explaining the relatively poor labor market performance of Puerto Ricans in the United States" (see *La Vida* published in 1965 by Random House, New York). Although Borjas' argument may be valid, it is widely recognized that Lewis's research on Puerto Ricans is seriously flawed. There may be other factors that contribute to the circular migration phenomenon. One such factor is citizenship status. Given that Puerto Ricans are U. S. citizens and have easier access to air transportation, Rivera-Batiz and Santiago (1996) argue that these factors may facilitate back and forth migration behavior.

8.   The model is described more fully in Carlos E. Santiago and Kisalaya Basu (1996).

9.   See Maddala (1986) for a complete description of the empirical model and its attributes.

10.   The correlation coefficient between educational attainment and English-language proficiency is positive and its value is approximately 31 percent.

REFERENCES CITED

Bean, Frank D., and Marta Tienda
1987   *The Hispanic Population in the United States.* Russell Sage Foundation, New York.
Berry, John
1980   Acculturation as Varieties of Adaptation. In *Acculturation: Theory, Models and Some New Findings,* edited by Amado M. Padilla, pp. 9-25. Westview Press, Boulder.
Borjas, George
1984   The Economic Status of Male Hispanic Migrants and Natives in the United States. In *Research in Labor Economics,* edited by Ronald Ehrenberg, pp. 65-122. JAI Press, New York.
1990   *Friends or Strangers: The Impact of Immigrants on the U. S. Economy.* Basic Books, New York.
Estrada, Leobardo F.
1993   Family Influences on Demographic Trends in Hispanic Ethnic Identification and Labeling. In *Ethnic Identity: Formation and Transformation among Hispanics and other Minorities,* edited by Martha E. Bernal, and George P. Knight, pp. 161-

179. State University of New York Press, Albany.

Fleisher, Belton
1963 Some Economic Aspects of Puerto Rican Migration to the United States. *Review of Economics and Statistics* 45:245-253.

Friedlander, Stanley
1965 *Labor Migration and Economic Growth.* MIT Press, Cambridge.

Grenier, Guillermo
1984 The Effects of Language Characteristics on the Wages of Hispanic-American Males. *Journal of Human Resources* 19:35-52.

Gushue, George V., and Daniel T. Sciarra
1995 Culture and Families. In *Handbook of Multicultural Counseling*, edited by Joseph G. Ponterotto, J. Manuel Casas, Lisa A. Suzuki, and Charlene M. Alexander, pp. 586-606. Sage Publications, Thousand Oaks, California.

Hernández, David, and Janet L. Scheff
1997 Puerto Rican Geographic Mobility: The Making of a Deterritorialized Nationality. *Latino Review of Books* 2(3):2-8.

Hernández Alvarez, Jose
1967 *Return Migration to Puerto Rico.* Greenwood Press, Westport, Connecticut.

Kossoudji, Sherrie A.
1988 English Language Ability and the Labor Market Opportunities of Hispanic and East Asian Immigrant Men. *Journal of Labor Economics* 6:205-228.

Maddala, G. S.
1983 *Limited-Dependent and Qualitative Variables in Econometrics.* Cambridge University Press, New York.

Maldonado, Rita
1976 Why Puerto Ricans Migrated to the United States, 1947-73. *Monthly Labor Review* 99(9):7-18.

Massey, Douglas S., Joaquín Arango, Graeme Hugo, Ali Konaonci, Adela Pellegrino, and J. Edward Taylor
1994 An Evaluation of International Migration Theory: The North American Case. *Population and Development Review* 20:699-751.

McManus, Walter, William Gould, and Finis Welch
1983 Earnings of Hispanic Men: The Role of English Language Proficiency. *Journal of Labor Economics* 1:101-130.

Meléndez, Edgardo, F. Carre, and Evangelina Holvino
1995 Latinos Need Not Apply: The Effects of Industrial Change and Workplace Discrimination on Latino Employment. *New England Journal of Public Policy, Special Issue: Latino in a Changing Society, Part I* 11:87-115.

Oboler, Suzanne
1995 *Ethnic Labels, Latino Lives: Identity and the Politics of (Re)presentation in the United States.* University of Minnesota Press, Minneapolis.

Portes, Alejandro, and Rubén G. Rumbaut
1996 *Immigrant America: A Portrait.* University of California Press, Berkeley.

Reimers, Cordelia
1983 Labor Market Discrimination Against Hispanic and Black Men. *Review of Economics and Statistics.* 65:570-579.
1985 A Comparative Analysis of the Wages of Hispanics, Blacks, and Non-Hispanic

Whites. In *Hispanics in the U. S. Economy*, edited by George Borjas, and Marta Tienda, pp. 27-75. Academic Press, Orlando.

Rivera-Batiz, Francisco L.
1988 *English Language Proficiency and the Economic Progress of Immigrants.* U. S. Department of Labor, Washington D. C.
1990 Literacy Skills and the Wages of Young Black and White Males in the U. S. *Economic Letters* 32:377-382.
1991 The Effects of Literacy on the Earnings of Hispanics in the United States. In *Hispanics in the Labor Force*, edited by Edwin Meléndez, Clara Rodríguez, and Janis Barry, pp. 53-75. Plenum Publishers, Cambridge.
1992 Quantitative Literacy and the Likelihood of Employment Among Young Adults. *Journal of Human Resources* 27:313-328.

Rivera-Batiz, Francisco, and Carlos E. Santiago
1994 *Puerto Ricans in the United States: A Changing Reality.* National Puerto Rican Coalition, Washington D. C.
1996 *Island Paradox: Puerto Rico in the 1990's.* Russell Sage Foundation, New York.

Rodríguez, Clara E.
1988 Circulating Migration. *Journal of Hispanic Policy* 3:5-9.

Sánchez-Korrol, Virginia
1994 *From Colonia to Community: The History of Puerto Ricans in New York City.* University of California Press, Berkeley.

Santiago, Carlos E.
1991 Wage Policies, Employment, and Puerto Rican Migration. In *Hispanics in the Labor Force*, edited by Edwin Meléndez, Clara Rodríguez, and Janis Barry, pp. 225-246. Plenum Publishers, Cambridge.

Santiago, Carlos E., and Kisalaya Basu
1996 Circular Migration and Labor Market Dynamics. Manuscript on file at the Department of Economics, State University of New York, Albany.

Stolzenberg, Ross M.
1990 Ethnicity, Geography and Occupational Achievement of Hispanic Men in the United States. *American Sociological Review* 55:143-154.

Tainer, Evelina M.
1988 English Language Proficiency and the Determination of Earnings Among Foreign Born Men. *Journal of Human Resources* 23:108-122.

Tienda, Marta, and William Díaz
1987 Puerto Rican Circular Migration. *The New York Times,* 28 August.

Torre, Carlos A., Hugo Rodríguez Vecchini, and Wilfredo Burgos
1994 *The Commuter Nation: Perspectives on Puerto Rican Migration.* University of Puerto Rico Press, Rio Piedras.

U. S. Bureau of the Census
1970 *Census of Population: Puerto Rico.* U. S. Government Printing Office, Washington D. C.
1983 *Census of Population and Housing, 1980: Public Use Microdata Samples, Puerto Rico* [machine-readable data files]. Bureau of the Census, Washington D. C.
1993 *Census of Population and Housing, 1990: Public Use Microdata Samples, Puerto Rico* [machine-readable data files]. Bureau of the Census, Washington D. C.

Epilogue

In First Person

13

Lost in Translation

Ilan Stavans

My heart is in the East and I am at the edge of the West. Then how can I taste what I eat, how can I enjoy it? How can I fulfill my vows and pledges while Zion is in the domain of Edom, and I am in the bonds of Arabia?

—Judah Halevi

Work of good prose has three steps: a musical stage when it is composed, an architectonic one when it is built, and a textile one when it is woven.

—Walter Benjamin

I was born in Mexico City, 7 April 1961, on a cloudy day without major historical events. I am a descendant of Jews from Russia and Poland, businessmen and rabbis, that arrived by sheer chance in Veracruz, on the Atlantic coast next to the Yucatán peninsula. I am a sum of parts and thus lack purity of blood (what proud renaissance Iberians called *la pureza de sangre*): white Caucasian with Mediterranean twist, much like the Enlightenment philosopher Moses Mendelssohn and only marginally like the Aztec poet Ollin Yollistli. My idols, not surprisingly, are Spinoza and Kafka, two exiles in their own land who chose universal languages (Portuguese and Hebrew to Latin, Czech to German) in order to elevate themselves to a higher order, and who, relentlessly, investigated their own spiritually beyond the reach of orthodox religion and routine. Ralph Waldo Emerson, in *Essays: Second Series* (1844), says that the reason we feel one man's presence and not another's is as simple as gravity. I have traveled from Spanish into Yiddish, Hebrew, and English; from my native home south of the Rio Grande far and away—to Europe, the Middle East, the United States, the Bahamas, and South America—always in search of the ultimate clue to the mysteries of my divided identity. What I found is doubt.

I grew up in an intellectually sophisticated middle-class, in a secure, self-imposed Jewish ghetto (a treasure island) where gentiles hardly existed. Money and comfort, books, theater and art. Since early on I was sent to a Yiddish day school, Colegio Israelita de México in Colonia Narvarete, where the heroes were Sholom Aleichem and Theodor Herzl while people like José Joaquín Fernández de Lizardi, Agustín Yáñez, Juan Rulfo, and Octavio Paz were almost unknown; that is, we lived in an oasis completely uninvolved with things Mexican. In fact, when it came to knowledge of the outside world, students were far better off talking about U. S. products (Hollywood, TV, junk food, technology) than about matters native—an artificial capsule, our ghetto, much like the magical sphere imagined by Blaise Pascal: its diameter everywhere and its center nowhere.

Mother tongue: the expression crashed into my mind at age twenty, perhaps a bit later. The father tongue, I assumed, was the adopted alternative and illegitimate language (Henry James preferred the term "wife tongue"), whereas the mother tongue is genuine and authentic—a uterus: the original source. I was educated in (into) four idioms: Spanish, Yiddish, Hebrew, and English. Spanish was the public venue; Hebrew was a channel toward Zionism and not toward the sacredness of the synagogue; Yiddish symbolized the Holocaust and past struggles of the Eastern European labor movement; and English was the entrance door to redemption: the United States. Abba Eban said it better: Jews are like everybody else except a little bit more. A polyglot, of course, has as many loyalties as homes. Spanish is my right eye, English my left; Yiddish my background and Hebrew my conscience. Or better, each of the four represents a different set of spectacles (near-sight, bifocal, light-reading, etc.) through which the universe is seen.

THE ABUNDANCE OF SELF

This multifarious (is there such a word) upbringing often brought me difficulties. Around the neighborhood, I was always *el güerito* and *el ruso*. Annoyingly, my complete name is Ilan Stavchansky Slomianski. Nobody, except for Yiddish teachers, knew how to pronounce it. (I get mail addressed to Ivan Starlominsky, Isvan Estafchansky, and Allen Stevens.) After graduating from high school, most of my friends, members of richer families, were sent abroad to the United States or Israel to study. Those that remained, including me, were forced to go to college at home to face Mexico *téte a téte*. The shock was tremendous. Suddenly, I (we) recognized the artificiality of our oasis. What to do? I, for one, rejected my background. I felt Judaism made me a pariah. I wanted to be an authentic Mexican and thus foolishly joined the Communist cause but the result wasn't pleasing. Among the *camaradas*, I was also "the blondy" and "the Jew." No hope, no escape. So I decided to investigate my ethnic and religious past obsessively and made it my duty to really understand guys like Maimonides, Arthur Koestler, Mendelssohn, Judah Halevi, Hasdai Crescas, Spinoza, Walter Benjamin, Gershom Scholem, Martin Buber, Franz Rosenzweig, Abraham Joshua Heschel. It helped, at least temporarily—nothing lasts forever.

Years later, while teaching medieval philosophy at Universidad Iberoamericana, a Jesuit college in downtown Mexico City, during the 1982 Lebanon invasion, a group of Palestinian sympathizers threw rotten tomatoes at me and my students (99 percent gentiles). Eager to manifest their anger, and protest, they had to find an easy target and I was the closest link to Israel around. The whole thing reminded me of a scene that took place at age fourteen, while sitting in Yiddish class at Colegio Israelita. Mr. Locker, the teacher, was reading from I. J. Singer's *The Family Carnovsky*—a story of three generations in a German-Jewish family enchanted with the nineteenth-century Enlightenment, slowly but surely becoming assimilated into German society until the tragic rise of Nazism brought unthinkable consequences. The monotonous rhythm of the recitations was boring and nobody was paying much attention. Suddenly, a segment of the story truly captivated me: the moment when Jegor, eldest son of Dr. David Carnovsky's mixed marriage to Teresa Holbeck, is ridiculed in class by Professor Kirchenmeier, a newly appointed principal it the Goethe Gymnasium in Berlin. Singer describes the event meticulously: Nazism is on the rise; the aristocracy, and more specifically the Jews, are anxious to know the overall outcome of the violent acts taking place daily on the city street; racial theories are being discussed and Aryans glorified. Feverishly anti-Jewish, Kirchenmeier, while delivering a lecture, calls Jegor to the front to use him as a guinea pig in illustrating his theories. With a compass and calipers, he measures the length and width of the boy's skull, writing the figures on the board. He then measures the distance from ear to ear, from the top of the head to the chin, and the length of the nose. A packed auditorium is silently watching. Jegor is then asked to undress. He is terrified and hesitates, of course; he is ashamed and feels conspicuous because of his circumcision. Eventually other students, persuaded by Kirchenmeier, help undress the Jew, and the teacher proceeds to show in the "inferior" Jewish strain the marks of the rib structure. He finishes by calling attention to Jegor' genitals whose premature development shows "the degenerate sexuality of the Semitic race."

Astonishment. What troubled me most was Jegor's inaction, I suppose it was natural to be petrified in such a situation, but I refused to justify his immobility. So I interrupted Mr. Locker to ask why didn't the boy escape. A deadly silence invaded the classroom. It was clear I had disturbed the other students' sleep and the teacher's rhythm. "Because he couldn't, he simply couldn't," was the answer I got. "Because that's the way lives are written" I don't know or care what happened next. As years went by I came to understand the concept of the almighty Author of Authors as intriguing, and the scene in Yiddish class as an allegory of myself and Mexican Jews as an easy and palatable target of animosity. At the Jesuit college almost a decade later, I was the marionette holder's Jegor Carnovsky—God's joy and toy: the Jew.

KALEIDOSCOPE

Bizarre combination—Mexican Jews: some 60,000 frontier dwellers and hyphen people like Dr. Jekyll and Mr. Hyde, a sum of sums of parts, a multiplicity of multiplicities. Although settlers from Germany began to arrive in "Aztec Country" around 1830, the very first synagogue was not built in the nation's capital until some fifty-five years later. From then on, waves of Jewish immigrants came from Russia and Central and Eastern Europe—Ashkenazim whose goal was to make it big in New York (the Golden Land) but since an immigration quota was imposed in the United States in 1924, a little detour places them in Cuba, Puerto Rico, or the Gulf of Mexico (the Rotten Land). Most were Yiddish-speaking Bundists: hard-working peasants, businessmen, and teachers, non-religious and entrepreneurial, escaping Church-sponsored pogroms and government persecution whose primary dream was never Palestine. Hardly anything physical or ideological differentiated them from the relatives that did make it north to Chicago, Detroit, Pittsburgh, and the Lower East Side—except, of course, the fact that they, disoriented immigrants, couldn't settle where they pleased. And this sense of displacement colored our future.

Migration and its discontent. I have often imagined the culture shock, surely not too drastic, my forefathers experienced at their arrival: from *mujik* to *campesino*, similar types in a different milieu. Mexico was packed with colonial monasteries where fanatical nuns prayed day and night. Around 1910 Emiliano Zapata and Pancho Villa were making their Socialist Revolution, and an anti-Church feeling (known in Mexico as *La Cristiada* and masterfully examined in Graham Greene's *The Power and the Glory*) was rampant. Aztecs, the legend claimed, once sacrificed daughters to their idols in sky high pyramids, and perhaps were cannibals. Undoubtedly this was to be a transitory stop—it had to. It was humid and at least in the nation's capital, nature remained an eternal autumn. I must confess never to have learned to love Mexico. I was taught to retain a sense of foreignness—as a tourist without a home. The best literature I know about Mexico is by European and American writers: Italo Calvino, André Breton, Jack Kerouac, Graham Greene, Joseph Brodsky, Antonin Artaud, Katherine Anne Porter, Malcolm Lowry, Harriet Doerr...I only love my country when I am far and away. Elsewhere—that's where I belong: the vast diaspora. Nowhere and everywhere. (Am I a name dropper? Me, whose name no one can pronounce?)

OUT OF THE BASEMENT

When the Mexican edition of *Talia in Heaven* (1989) came out, my publisher, Fernando Valdés, at a reception, talked about the merits of this, my first (and so far only) novel. He applauded this and that ingredient, spoke highly of the innovative style, and congratulated the author for his precocious artistic maturity. Memory has deleted most of his comments. I no longer remember what he liked and why. The only sentence that still ticks in my mind, the one capable of overcoming the passing of time, came at the end of his speech, when he said: "For many centuries, Latin America has had Jews living in the basement, great writers creating out of the shadow. And Ilan Stavans is the one I kept hidden until now." A frightening metaphor.

In the past five hundred years, Jews in the Hispanic world have been forced to convert to Christianity or somehow to mask or feel ashamed of their ancestral faith. Their intellectual contribution, notwithstanding, has been enormous. Spanish letters cannot he understood without Fray Luis de León and Ludovicus Vives, without Fernando de Roja's *La Celestina* and the anti-Semitic poetry of Francisco de Quevedo, author of the infamous sonnet "A man stuck to a nose." *Erase un hombre a una nariz pegado, érase una nariz superlativa, érase una alquitara medio viva, érase un peje espada mal barbado.* In the Americas, a safe haven for refugees from the Inquisition and later on for Eastern Europeans running away from the Nazis, Jewish writers have been active since 1910, when Alberto Gerchunoff, a Russian immigrant, published in Spanish his collection of interrelated vignettes, *The Jewish Gauchos of the Pampa*, to commemorate Argentina's independence. He switched from one language to another to seek individual freedom, to validate his democratic spirit, to embrace a dream of plurality and progress. Yiddish, the tongue of Mendel Mokher Sforim and Sholem Aleichem, was left behind; Spanish, Cervantes' vehicle of communication—Gerchunoff was an admirer of *Don Quixote*—became the new tool, the channel to entertain, educate, and redeem the masses. Like Spinoza, Kafka, Nabokov, and Joseph Brodsky, he was the ultimate translator: a bridge between idiosyncrasies. The abyss and the bridge. Many decades later, some fifty astonishing writers from Buenos Aires and Mexico to Lima and Guatemala, including Moacyr Scliar, Clarice Lispector, and Mario Szichman, continue to carry on Gerchunoff's torch, but the world knows little about them. The narrative boom that catapulted Gabriel García Márquez, Carlos Fuentes, and others from south of the Rio Grande to international stardom in the sixties managed to sell a monolithic, suffocatingly uniform image of the entire continent as a Banana Republic crowded with clairvoyant prostitutes and forgotten generals, never a multicultural society. To such a degree were ethnic voices left in the margin that readers today know much more about Brazilians and Argentines thanks to Borges' short stories "Emma Zunz" and "The Secret Miracle," and Vargas Llosa's novel *The Storyteller*, than to anything written by Gerchunoff and his followers. Sadly and in spite of his anti-Semitic tone, my Mexican publisher was right: in the baroque architecture of Latin American letters, Jews inhabit the basement. And yet, *la pureza de sangre* in the Hispanic world is but an abstraction: native Indians, Jews, Arabs, Africans, Christians...the collective identity is always in need of a hyphen. In spite of the "official" image stubbornly promoted by governments from time immemorial, Octavio Paz and Julio Cortázar have convincingly used the salamander, the *axolotl*, as a symbol to describe Latin America's popular soul, always ambiguous and in mutation.

AMERICA, AMERICA

I honestly never imagined I could one day pick up my suitcases to leave home once and for all. And yet, at twenty-five I moved to New York, I was awarded a scholarship to study for a master's at the Jewish Theological Seminary and, afterwards, perhaps a doctorate at Columbia University or elsewhere. I fled Mexico (and Spanish) mainly because as a secular Jew—what Freud would have called "a psychological Jew"—I felt marginalized, a stereotype, (little did I know!) a true chameleon, a bit parochial and near-sighted, a nonconformist with big dreams and few possibilities. Like my globe-trotting Hebraic ancestors, I had been raised to build an ivory tower, an individual ghetto. By choosing to leave, I turned my past into remembrance: I left the basement and ceased to he a pariah. *Talia in Heaven* exemplifies that existential dilemma. Its message simultaneously encourages Jews to integrate and openly invites them to escape; it alternates between life and memory. Paraphrasing Lionel Trilling, its cast of characters, victims of an obsessive God (much like the Bible's) who enjoys ridiculing them, are at the bloody crossroad where politics, theology, and literature meet. To be or not to be. The moment I crossed the border, I became somebody else: a new person. In *Chromos: A Parody of Truth*, Felipe Alfau says: The moment one learns English, complications set in. "Try as one may, one cannot elude this conclusion, one must inevitably, come back to it." While hoping to master the English language during sleepless nights, I understood James Baldwin, who, already exiled in Paris and quoting Henry James, claimed it is a complex fate to be an American. "America's history," the black author of *Nobody Knows My Name* wrote, "her aspirations, her peculiar triumphs, her even more peculiar defeats, and her position in the world—yesterday and today—are all so profoundly and stubbornly unique that the very word "America" remains a new, almost completely undefined, and extremely controversial proper noun. No one in the world seems to know exactly what it describes." To be honest, the rise of multiculturalism, which perceives the melting pots, a soup of diverse and at times incompatible backgrounds, has made the word "America" even more troublesome, more evasive and abstract. Is America a compact whole, a unit? Is it a sum of ethnic groups unified by a single language and a handful of patriotic symbols? Is it a Quixotic dream where total assimilation is impossible, where multiculturalism is to lead to disintegration? And Baldwin's statement acquires a totally different connotation when one goes one step beyond, realizing that "America" is not only, a nation (a state of mind) but also a vast continent. From Alaska to the Argentine pampa, from Rio de Janeiro to East Los Angeles, the geography Christopher Columbus mistakenly encountered in 1492 and Amerigo Vespucci baptized a few years later is also a linguistic and cultural addition: America the nation and America the continent. America, America: I wanted to find a room of my own in the two; or two rooms, perhaps?

ON BEING A WHITE HISPANIC AND MORE

Once sealed, I suddenly began to be perceived as Hispanic (i.e., Latino)— an identity totally, alien to me before. (My knowledge of spoken Latin is minimal.) To make matters worse, my name (once again?), accent, and skin color were exceptions to what gringos had as the "Hispanic prototype." In other words, in Mexico I was perceived as Jewish; and now across the border, I was Mexican. Funny, isn't it? (My face, according to official papers I qualify as a white Hispanic, an unpleasant term if there was ever one.) Once again, an impostor, an echo. (An impostor, says Ambrose Bierce in *The Devil's Dictionary*, is a rival aspirant to public honors.)

Themselves, myself, Hispanics in the United States—some 22,254,159 according to the 1990 census: white, black, yellow, green, blue, red...twice Americans, once in spite of themselves. They have been in the territories north of the Rio Grande even before the Pilgrims of the Mayflower. And with the Guadalupe Hidalgo Treaty signed in 1848, in which Generalísimo Antonio López de Santa Ana gave away and subsequently sold half of Mexico to the White House (why only half?), many of them unexpectedly even unwillingly, became a part of an Anglo-Saxon, English-speaking reality. Today after decades of neglect and silence, decades of anonymity and ignorance, Latinos are finally receiving the attention they deserve. The second fastest growing ethnic group after the Asians, their diversity of roots—Caribbean, Mexican, Central and South American, Iberian, and so on—makes them a difficult collectivity to describe. Are the Cuban migrations from Holguín, Matanzas, and Havana similar in their idiosyncratic attitude to that of Managua, San Salvador, and Santo Domingo? Is the Spanish they speak their true *lingua franca*, the only unifying factor? Is their immigrant experience in any way different from that of previous minorities—Irish, Italian, Jewish, what have you? How do they understand and assimilate the complexities of what it means to be American? And where do I, a white Hispanic, fit in?

Nowhere and everywhere. In 1985, I was assigned by a Spanish magazine to interview Isaac Goldemberg, a famous Jewish-Peruvian novelist who wrote *The Fragmented Life of Don Jacobo Lerner*. When we met at the Hungarian Pastry Shop at Amsterdam Avenue and 110th Street, he told me, among many things, he had been living in New York for over two decades without mastering the English language because he didn't want his Spanish to suffer and ultimately evaporate. Borges says in his short story "The Life of Tadeo Isidoro Cruz (1829-1874)": "Any life, no matter how long or complex it may be, is made up essentially of a single moment—the moment in which a man finds out, once and for all, who he is." That summer day I understood my linguistic future lay in the opposite direction from Goldemberg's. I would perfect my English and thus become a New York Jew, an intellectual animal in the proud tradition celebrated by Alfred Kazin and I did. In just a single moment I understood who I could be.

THE DOUBLE

To write is to make sense of conditions in and around. Didn't somebody already say this? Jean Genet, John Updike? I am a copy, an instant replay, a shadow, an impostor. Everything is an echo. To live is to plagiarize, to imitate, to steal.

I have always had the feeling of living somebody else's life. When I first read Felipe Alfau's *Locos: A Comedy of Gestures*, I was possessed by the idea that, had I been born in 1902 in Barcelona, as had its author, I would have written his book. The exact same sensation was repeated when discovering Pinhas "Der Nister" Kahanovitch's *The Family Mashber*, a masterpiece of Soviet Jewish fiction by a writer who died in a Russian hospital in 1950 as a result of Stalin's purges. And my mother keeps a yellowish school photograph I once gave her. It was taken when I was eight or nine: although smiling, I really don't look happy. In the back it has a brief line written: "With love from a non-existent twin brother." Furthermore, I am often sure I am being observed by an omniscient Creature (with capital "C"), who enjoys inflicting pain and laughs at the sorrow of His creatures. I cannot but equate the act of writing to God's impact on Nature. He is simultaneously absent and present in His creation, granting birth and death—the Absolute Novelist, a marionette holder with a vivid imagination and a bad sense of humor (even if I-He laughs).

"TOTAL FORGETERY"

Acting was my father's trade. As I was growing up, I remember feeling amazed by his incredible talent. I adored him. Watching his performances, I would be pushed to what Sören Kierkegard regarded as "an existential vacuum—a mystery." Was he really the man I knew or, instead, a mask-carrier? I was particularly fond of him taking me along on Sunday afternoons. We would leave home alone after lunch. While driving an old Rambler, he would ask me about school and friends, about ideas and books, masturbation and a girl's sexuality. He was a hero, a man of integrity like few others, the only guy I knew who was actually happy, very happy, a few minutes every day: on stage. Then, as my father would park the car, I would begin noticing a slow change of attitude, a metamorphosis, as if a veil, an abyss was now setting us apart. Another self would graciously descend to possess him, to take the man I knew and loved away from me. A few minutes later, I would witness how, without shame, he would undress in front of a mirror, put on a bathrobe, and begin to hide his face in cosmetics. He was becoming somebody else, a stranger, a ghost: today a hotel owner, next season a boxer, a cancer patient, a Jewish prisoner in Germany. His breathtaking masks were infallible: they always hid my dad's true self, deformed it. As a result of that transformation, I felt totally alone.

Alone and lonely. The whole phenomenon inspired in me mixed feelings: I was astonished by the magic and frightened at the same time; I hated the whole thing and yet would literally do anything to return tomorrow and witness it anew. My father would then ask a handyman to seat me behind the stage, next to a curtain, in order for me to watch the show. And that, oh God, was his and my greatest moment on earth, the one we awaited even more eagerly than the facial and physical change he underwent to become a character. With a difference: In front of an audience, he was happy; I, on the other hand, was scared to death—invaded by the kind of fear that simultaneously generates joy and sorrow. What did others think of his "new" self? Could they recognize the true face behind the mask? Was he an impostor?

Alone and lonely and full of envy, I would feel an overwhelming sense of envy—profound and disturbing jealousy toward the audience. They received all of his attention, which, in normal circumstances, I would keep for my own, or at most, share with my brother and sister. They would be manipulated, seduced by his talents. Why was he so eager to become other people and take a rest from himself? And hide behind a mask? Even more suspiciously, why did the viewers pay to have him taken away from me? How could people pay for my father to cease being himself? The Author of Authors, the Impostor of Impostors: God as playwright. In my eyes the entire universe was a vast and mysterious theater in which he (Yahweh, Adonai, Elohim, the Holy Spirit, the Father of Fathers) would capriciously establish what people, the actors are to do, to say, to think, to hope. My dad's actual stage was a microcosmos that inspired me to philosophize about religion and eschatology, about freedom and determinism. I wondered: while acting, was my father free to refuse pronouncing a certain line of the script? Could he talk to me at least once during the performance (through his real and unimported self)? I also wondered if I, Ilan Stavans (a.k.a. Ilan Stavchansky Slomianski), was free to stop being his son? Could I also become other people—like Shakespeare, be one and many? To answer these questions, I became a novelist. To write is to make sense of confusion in and around. (It was me who said that.)

To write, perchance to dream. (Or vice versa?) Not long ago an interviewer asked me why I didn't follow his footsteps and enter the stage. My response was short and somewhat condescending. Deep inside, I dislike actors. I find their vulnerability, their trendiness and exhibitionism disturbing. I would rather live in the shadow than in the spotlight. I love the theater of the mind and have a terrible fear of dying. It might sound absurd but I see literature as brother to memory and theater as symbol of the ephemeral present. I write in order to remember and be remembered. Death is the absence of recollection—what Luis G. Rodríguez calls "total forgetery." Theater, on the other hand, is *performance art,* a transitory game. It is only alive during a night show, afterwards it's gone...forever. Nothing remains, nothing. Except perhaps a handful of yellowish photos and (luck permitting) an award or two. And if the theater is like a vanishing photograph, writing is signing one's name on concrete: a proof of existence ("I was here..."). But incorporating past and present images, a narrative plays with Time (with a capital "T") in an astonishing fashion: it makes reality eternal. Marcel's desire for his mother's goodnight kiss in Proust's *Remembrance of Things Past* is not a pre-World War I scene alone but, unquestionably an image for the ages. When death turns me into a ghost, at least something, one ingenious thought or a breath of life, will remain on a written page like those of Virgil, Dante, and Cervantes. Perhaps and perhaps not. The only certainty is that a library is a triumph over nothingness. And yet, the warm, warm human contact my dad encounters while performing is always reinvigorating. Literature, on the other hand, is a secluded activity. Isolation, silence, detachment, escape. You hope someone will read you someday, although nothing (not even the timing of God's laughter) is certain. Thus, decades away of those Sunday afternoons when my father would take me along to his show, I still confess I feel envy. He can be happy, I cannot. I honestly wish I could at times take vacations from myself—like him, have another self. It must be refreshing. Isolation, silence.

Before death and after. Literature, I'm perfectly sure, is no palliative to cure spirit's suffering. The day I die, people will not interrupt their routines, and why should they? They will make love, eat, defecate, smoke, and read. They will smile and cry and kiss and hate. It will matter to no one (not even my dearest ones, really) that my life has ceased to be and all is over. The show will go on. Grief—a strange and dishonest feeling. When Calvino and Danilos Kiš, two mentors, died, did I cry? (Albert Camus' protagonist in *The Stranger* is incarcerated for not crying during his mother's funeral.) I did pray for their souls and after that...nothing. Only through literature, I feel, can I transcend myself. To write is to overcome the imperfections of nature. I do it every day, every day, every day, every...otherwise, I sense that a day's 86,400 seconds are meaningless and in vain.

THINGS TO COME

A future encyclopedia, to be published in Brussels in 2087, states that at age thirty-one I wrote a book, *Imagining Columbus*, about the Genoese admiral's fifth and final voyage of discovery, one not across the Atlantic but through the human imagination. That I was the author of a controversial reflection on the identity of Hispanics in the United States, and a volume of early short stories, collectively called in English, *The One-Handed Pianist*. It mentions the fact that somewhere after 1995, I published a novel about a Belgian actor of Jewish descent, who has trouble distinguishing where reality ends and begins (poor Konstantin Stanislavsky! Or is it Konstantin Stavchansky?)—inspired, obviously, by his dad's trade—translated into numerous languages, the volume was enthusiastically received by critics and readers. Afterwards, I wrote another novel, this one in the style of Vargas Llosa, about the exiled family of a Latin American dictator, after which I won numerous grants and prizes, was internationally applauded and commemorated.

It discusses my multilingualism. After a literary beginning as a Yiddish playwright and short fiction writer, I moved first into Spanish and then into English, translating and reinventing myself. (Although I wrote English with case and distinction, I spoke like a tourist.) If, as Nabokov once claimed, our existence is but a brief crack of light between two eternities of darkness, why not take advantage and be two writers at once? The entry also states that I left an echo, an echo, an echo. Critics praised my oeuvre comparing it to precursors and successors like Kafka, Spinoza, and Borges. Because of my dual identity, in Mexico, I was considered a "bad citizen." My themes always dealt with God as manipulator of human conscience and my existential journey could be reduced to a verse by the Nicaraguan *modernista* poet Rubén Darío: "To be and not to know." My style is very precise and direct, akin to religious insights. Cyril Connolly says in *Unquiet Grave* "The more books we read, the sooner we perceive that the only function of a writer is to produce a masterpiece. No other task is of any consequence." The encyclopedia claims that toward the end of life, I wrote extraordinarily lasting short stories, as if everything that preceded them was a prophecy. Finally, it states that I died on 18 August 2033, with some twenty-two original books to my credit. After a consuming sickness, I contemplated suicide but a sudden attack impeded me from arriving at a nearby New York hospital and nothingness took over. That was also a rainy day without major historical events. God witnessed my death and pretended to suffer, although His was of course an actor's gesture. In fact, He laughed: I was (am) his joy and toy.

Contributors

EDNA ACOSTA-BELÉN is Distinguished Service Professor of Latin American and Caribbean Studies, and Women's Studies, and Director of the Center for Latino, Latin American, and Caribbean Studies (CELAC) at the University at Albany, State University of New York. Her publications include *The Puerto Rican Woman: Perspectives on Culture, History, and Society; Teaching Puerto Rican Women's History* (with B. Sjostrom); *Researching Women in Latin America and the Caribbean* (with C. Bose); *Women in the Latin American Development Process* (with C. Bose); and *The Hispanic Experience in the United States* (with B. Sjostrom).

ALLAN F. BURNS is Professor and Chair of the Department of Anthropology at the University of Florida in Gainesville. He has worked in the Yucatan of Mexico on issues of Mayan language and culture as well as in Chiapas and Guatemala. Burns is the director of the student Yucatan Exchange program at Florida. In addition to his books and articles on Maya culture, he has produced several professional videos on the Guatemalan Maya diaspora to Florida and has developed video training workshops for indigenous people in Chiapas, the United States and the South Pacific.

JORGE DURAND is Research Professor in the Department for the Study of Social Movements at the University of Guadalajara, Mexico. He is the author of *Más Allá de la Línea: Patrones Migratorios entre Mexico y Estados Unidos* (Beyond the Border: Migration Patterns Between Mexico and the United States), published in 1994 by Mexico's National Council on Culture and the Arts and *El Norte es Como el Mar: Entrevistas a Trabajadores Migrantes en Estados Unidos* (The North is Like the Sea: Interviews with Migrants Workers in the United States) published in 1996 by the University of Guadalajara Press. Durand and Massey have collaborated in research on Mexico-U.S. migration for fifteen years, and are co-authors of *Return to Aztlán: The Social Process of International Migration from Western Mexico* (University of California Press 1987) as well as *Miracles on the Border: Retablos of Mexican Migrants to the United States* (University of Arizona Press, 1995), which won a Southwestern Book Award.

DUNCAN EARLE is Associate Professor of Anthropology at the University of Texas in El Paso. He has dedicated much of his career to integrated community development and has published widely on those issues. Since 1977 he has worked with low-income Spanish-speaking populations in Guatemala, Mexico and the United States, in issues of health, housing, education, micro-lending and other related issues. He worked with Save The Children, designing, implementing and evaluating a development program for over one hundred communities of the Highlands of Guatemala. More recently he has carried out research on low-income communities along the Texas border with Mexico. A former Melon Fellow, and recipient of Fulbright and Ford Foundation grants, he has served as editor for the *Journal of Borderlands Studies* and as Executive Secretary of the Association for Borderlands Studies.

JUAN FLORES is Professor of Sociology and Cultural Studies at the City University of New York Graduate School and a member of the Department of Black and Puerto Rican Studies at Hunter College. In recent years he has been a visiting professor in Latino Studies at Rutgers, Princeton and Columbia universities, and in the Spring semester 1998 was Visiting Professor of Ethnic Studies at Harvard. His books include *Divided Borders: Essays on Puerto Rican Identity*, the *Memoirs of Bernardo Vega; Divided Arrivals: Narratives of the Puerto Rican Migration 1920-1950;* and *On Edge: The Crisis of Latin American Culture.* He has published in many journals, including *Daedalus, Modern Language Quarterly, Diacritics,* and the *Journal of Ethnic Studies.*

NINA GLICK SCHILLER is Associate Professor of Anthropology and Co-coordinator of the Race, Culture, and Power Minor at the University of New Hampshire. Beginning in 1987, Glick Schiller began to examine the transnational practices of immigrants settled in the United States. With Linda Basch and Cristina Szanton Blanc, she edited *Towards A Transnational Perspective On Migration: Race, Class, Ethnicity, and Nationalism Reconsidered* and co-authored the book *Nations Unbound: Transnational Projects, Postcolonial Predicaments, and Deterritorialized Nation-States.* Glick Schiller also published a series of articles exploring in more depth the Haitian experience of migration and the development of Haiti as a transnational nation-state. Glick Schiller is the founding editor of the journal *Identities: Global Studies in Culture and Power.* Recent special issues include *Race and Place* (vol. 3, no. 4), *The Politics of Culture* (vol. 4, no. 1), *Transnational Processes; Situated Identities* (vol. 4, no. 2), and *Regimes of Truth* (vol. 4, no. 3/4).

LILIANA R. GOLDIN is Associate Professor of Anthropology and Latin American and Caribbean Studies at the University at Albany, State University of New York. She has published widely in such journals as *Human Organization,*

Journal of Quantitative Anthropology, Ethnology, Mesoamerica, Comparative Studies in Society and History, and *Economic Development and Cultural Change.* She has written on issues of economic restructuring in rural Latin America, economic strategies of Mayas and non-Mayas in Guatemala, and the processes of economic and cultural change. She is currently working on a monograph entitled *Ideology in Production: Making Perspectives in Rural Guatemala.*

MICHAEL KEARNEY is Professor of Anthropology at the University of California, Riverside. His main areal focus is Mexico and the United States as they are situated within global society and economy. He is currently engaged in fieldwork with Mixtec, Zapotec, and other indigenous communities in Oaxaca and with migrants from these communities in the greater border area of California and beyond. He works closely with several indigenous organizations in Mexico and the United States. He is also concerned with how changing global contexts influence the sociology, theory, and practice of anthropology. His most recent book is *Reconceptualizing the Peasantry: Anthropology in Global Perspective,* Westview Press, 1996.

DOUGLAS S. MASSEY is the Dorothy Swaine Thomas Professor of Sociology at the University of Pennsylvania and Chair of the university's Department of Sociology. He is the co-author of *American Apartheid: Segregation and the Making of the Underclass* (Harvard University Press, 1993) and most recently of *Worlds in Motion: Understanding International Migration at Century's End* (Oxford University Press, 1998).

VICTOR D. MONTEJO is a Jakaltek Maya and an anthropologist from Guatemala. He did his graduate studies in the United States. (M.A., University at Albany, State University of New York; Ph.D., University of Connecticut). He has lectured in the United States, Central America and Europe. He is the author of several books, including *Testimony: Death of a Guatemalan Village* (1987); *The Bird Who Cleans the World and Other Mayan Fables* (1991); *El Q'anil: The Man of Lightning* (1984); *Sculpted Stones* (1996); and *Las Aventuras de Mister Puttison entre los Mayas* (1998). Montejo has taught at Bucknell University, Pennsylvania, and at the University of Montana. Currently, he is Associate Professor of Native American Studies at the University of California, Davis.

SUZANNE OBOLER is Associate Professor of Latino Studies and American Studies at Brown University. She is the author of *Ethnic Labels, Latino Lives: Identity and the Politics of (Re)Presentation in the United States,* (University of Minnesota Press, 1995). Her current research focuses on racial ideologies and citizenship in the Americas.

CARLOS SANTIAGO is Professor of Latin American and Caribbean Studies and Economics at the University at Albany, State University of New York, and currently serves as Associate Vice President for Academic Affairs. He is a founding co-editor (with E. Acosta-Belén) of the *Latino Review of Books*. In addition to numerous articles, he is the author of three books: *Island Paradox: Puerto Rico in the 1990s* (with F. Rivera-Batiz, 1996); *Puerto Ricans in the United States: A Changing Reality* (with F. Rivera-Batiz, 1994); *Labor in the Puerto Rican Economy: Postwar Development and Stagnation* (1992) and co-editor of *Recovery or Relapse in the Global Economy: Comparative Perspectives on Restructuring in Central America*, (with J. Melmed-Sanjak and A. Magid, 1993). His research interests include labor market issues, structural adjustment and debt, and labor migration to the United States.

AZARA L. SANTIAGO-RIVERA is Assistant Professor in the Departments of Latin American and Caribbean Studies and Counseling Psychology at the University at Albany, State University of New York. She obtained a Ph.D. in counseling from Wayne State University in 1991. Her research areas include multicultural counseling issues and Latino ethnic identity. She has published in such journals as the *Journal of Counseling and Development*, *Professional Psychology: Research and Practice*, and *The New England Journal of Public Policy*. She is on the editorial boards of the *Journal of Counseling and Development* and the *Latino Review of Books*.

ILAN STAVANS teaches at Amherst College. His many books include *The Hispanic Condition* (Harper Collins), *Art and Anger* (University of New Mexico Press), *The Oxford Book of Latin American Essays* (Oxford University Press), *A Cartoon History of Latinos in the United States* (Avon), and *The One-Handed Pianist and Other Stories* (University of New Mexico Press). He has been a Guggenheim Fellow, a National Book Critics Circle Award nominee, and the winner of the Latino Literature Prize.

Index

A